MERCHANTS OF HOPE

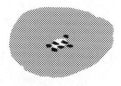

THE LEGACY OF THE GREAT WAR
A series sponsored by the Historial de la grande guerre Péronne-Somme

General Editor
JAY WINTER

Other titles in the series

Antoine Prost
IN THE WAKE OF WAR
'Les Anciens Combattants' and French Society

Patrick Fridenson
THE FRENCH HOME FRONT 1914–1918

Stéphane Audoin-Rouzeau
MEN AT WAR 1914–1918

Gerald D. Feldman
ARMY, INDUSTRY, AND LABOR IN GERMANY 1914–1918

MERCHANTS OF HOPE

British Middlebrow Writers and the First World War, 1919–1939

ROSA MARIA BRACCO

BERG

PROVIDENCE/OXFORD

First published in 1993 by
Berg Publishers Limited
Editorial offices:
221 Waterman Street, Providence, RI 02906, USA
150 Cowley Road, Oxford, OX4 1JJ, UK

© Rosa Maria Bracco 1993

Library of Congress Cataloging-in-Publication Data
Merchants of hope : British middlebrow writers and the First World War,
1919–1939 / Rosa Maria Bracco.
p.   cm. — (Legacy of the Great War)
Includes bibliographical references and index.
ISBN 0–85496–706–0
1. English literature—20th century—History and criticism.   2. Sherriff, R. C.
(Robert Cedric), 1896–1975. Journey's end.   3. World War, 1914–1918—
Literature and the war.   4. War stories. English—History and criticism.   I. Title.
II. Series.
PR478.W65B73   1992
820.9'358—dc20   92–12330
                                                                      CIP

A CIP catalogue record for this book is available from the British Library.

Printed in the United States by Edwards Brothers, Ann Arbor, MI.

To my parents, Carlo and Rita Bracco

Contents

Acknowledgements

I am very grateful to Dr Ian Britain and Dr Jay Winter for their intellectual guidance; Janice Fairholm helped me a great deal with her expert librarian's skills. I would also like to thank the archivists of the Kingston Records Office for their kind assistance. In the writing of this book I have benefitted enormously from the delightful company of my friends in England and in Guinea, and from long-distance support from Australia and Italy.

Introduction

The war had many facets: Bruce Bairnsfather saw Old Bill, and laughed and drew him, and laughed again. Siegfried Sassoon saw only poor ignorant boys sobbing out their last breath for a cause which they knew nothing about. Most of us saw these extremes of Comedy and Tragedy, and the means between them.

(Alfred McLelland *Burrage, War is War*)

For the wars we fight today are not like other wars, and the warders of them are not like other warders. If we do not see in them the saga and the epic, how shall we tell of them?

(J. B. Morton, *The Barber of Putney*)

1 Irony, Modernism and Tradition: Modes of Interpretation

1 Irony and Modern Memory

The Great War bequeathed to the twentieth century a literature revealing the futility of war: this is the history lesson which every student learns at school, together with the war poems which depict so incisively the slow massacring in the trenches of the old notions of heroism in battle. The works of Owen and Sassoon, Ford and Graves, however, were accompanied by a host of minor literature which attempted to rescue war from futility not through the defunct rhetoric of glory and honour, but by describing for its readers the link between the suffering and the lessons of the war, and an uninterrupted pattern of historical, and in particular English, significance. This study presents an account of the English memory of the Great War in the fiction of the 1920s and 1930s which did not have the literary quality to survive the test of time, but whose ascription of sustaining and irreducible meaning to history, legitimized by parochial strands of traditional and national value, has left its conspicuous imprint in what John Dunn has so aptly called 'superannuated structures of belief.'[1]

Notes to the Introduction can be found on page 19

1

In *The Great War and Modern Memory* Paul Fussell describes what he sees as a literary hiatus engendered by the experience of war. He locates in war writings the key elements of the ironic mode. Fussell's central conclusion is this: 'I am saying that there seems to be one dominating form of modern understanding; that it is *essentially ironic*; and that it originates largely in the application of mind and memory to the events of the Great War.'[2]

Fussell makes reference to Northrop Frye's *Anatomy of Criticism* (1957), where fiction is classified according to the literary distinctions in Aristotle's *Poetics*. Frye defines modes of fiction according to the protagonists' power of action, which can be greater than that of the reader, the same, or less. The mode is 'high-mimetic' when the hero's power of action is perceived as greater than ours; 'low-mimetic' when the hero's experience is similar to that of the reader; and 'ironic' when his power of action is less. He relates these modes to the history of literature and makes them coincide, respectively, with epic and tragedy, the bourgeois novel of the eighteenth and nineteenth centuries, and modern literature.[3]

Fussell's contention is that the war gave rise to a body of writing which is ironic not only because of its 'dynamics of hope abridged',[4] but also because of its protagonists' limited scope of action. In Frye's words:

> If inferior in power or intelligence to ourselves, so that we have the sense of looking down on a scene of bondage, frustration, or absurdity, the hero belongs to the ironic mode. This is still true when the reader feels that he is or might be in the same situation, as the situation is being judged by the norms of a greater freedom.[5]

Fussell does refer to the 'transitional' nature of war writings, which contain also a low-mimetic emphasis and often employ a traditional literary style which contrasts with the great modernist works of T. S. Eliot, Virginia Woolf and James Joyce:[6] but the essential point is about irony.

The Great War and Modern Memory depicts responses to the horror of modern warfare through both the shedding of older models of literary representation provided by the military experience of the past and the creation of new myths generated by the war. Fussell describes the mythopeic faculty of the soldiers as actively at work in the war years. He presents the troglodyte world of trench warfare, described in 'very un-modern' rumours, sacrificial themes, legends and superstitions.[7] Bernard Bergonzi in *Heroes' Twilight* asserts that the dominant movement in the literature of the Great War was 'from a myth-dominated to a demythologized world.'[8] 'No' – counters Fussell – 'almost the opposite. In one sense the movement was towards myth, towards a revival of the cultic, the mystical, the sacrificial, the prophetic, the sacramental, and the universally significant. In short, towards fiction.'[9] Fussell interprets the mythopeic quality of war literature in terms of Frye's ironic category, which in its last phase develops the demonic and apocalyptic imagery of frustration and bondage.[10]

Fussell's handling of the question of a modern mode of literary representation is flawed by a too precise dichotomy between old and new ways of addressing the question of war, between traditional perceptions and modern ones. The word 'modern' can become a comprehensive analytical term which excludes too easily links with traditional assumptions and legacies. If soldier-writers did need to develop an ironic mode in order to describe the new, terrible nature of trench warfare, their writings were still concerned with 'an ancient set of questions related to the aftermath of war'[11]: the literature of war deals with the age-old issues of tragic death, violent change, and survival.

This book will maintain that the presentation of the memory of war in minor fiction – which George Dangerfield called the 'Baedeker of the soul'[12] – relies on a spiritual rather than demonic imagery, and on the derivation of the rational and the moral out of the irrational. It is 'essentially low-mimetic': 'If superior neither to other men nor to his environment, the hero is one of us: we respond to a sense of common humanity, and demand from the poet the same canons of probability that we find in our own experience.'[13] I argue that the popular literature of the Great War reveals the reality and the strength of the resistance against an ironic interpretation of the war.

This contention about a low-mimetic cultural understanding relates also to much criticism of war literature. In the 1920s, Cyril Falls and Douglas Jerrold offered their well-known protests against novels which, in their opinion, debased the soldier's experience by emphasizing its horror, and dwelling on exaggerated accounts of the drunkenness and debauchery of the men at war. Falls's annotated bibliography of war books, and its foreword, presented a strident denunciation of the demeaning of patriotic virtues.[14] Jerrold's article, published at the height of the war-novel boom, decried the emotional attitudes which reduced a condemnation of war to the exposure of its more squalid manifestations. He considered it dangerous to 'deny the dignity of tragic drama to the war,' and advocated a depiction of war which was 'unadorned by the marvellous, the epic or the obscene.'[15]

Fifty years later Andrew Rutherford and Michael Howard have both condemned an exclusively ironic interpretation of the literature of the First World War for stripping the military experience of its inspiringly human values. In *The Literature of War, Five Studies in Heroic Virtue* Rutherford maintains that the modern anti-heroic bias rests on moral, aesthetic and historical assumptions which have influenced to a dangerous degree the judgment of readers, who read of heroic examples as an experience which goes against their expectations of literature and life.[16] He deplores the modern incapacity to understand the value of heroism: 'The assumption that heroism, like saintliness, is obsolete as an ideal, and that the literature of heroism belongs to the childhood of the individual or of the race, seems typical of current intellectual opinion. Fortitude is out of fashion as a virtue.'[17] In his opinion the ironical mood represents a simplification of the 'complex nature of adult experience' in the Great War.[18] To illustrate this he cites several examples of human values, of individual and group expressions of deep courage, of companionship, and of the profound involvement of the soldiers with their military experience at the front. He quotes Sassoon's remark about being inspired in his 1917 protest by 'a comprehensive memory of war especially in its intense and essential humanity.'[19] Rutherford shifts the emphasis from ironic to low-mimetic, with the protagonist – a hero in spite of his unglamorous experience – involved in an inhuman war which does *not* dehumanize him.

Michael Howard makes the same point when he observes that the British soldier maintained his 'self-respect' in the face of horrible conditions.[20] In his review of Fussell's book, Howard objects to the comparison of First World War language to the works of Norman Mailer and Thomas Pynchon because of the sexual explicitness employed by the latter to expose the obscenity of war. His argument is clear: 'If obscenity was, literally, kept off the scene by the Western literary tradition, it was from a sound instinct that it added little to our understanding of the world and subtracted much.' In such a tradition, war was viewed as 'high tragedy':

> To the tradition dating back to Homer and the Old Testament, a tradition nurtured on generations of such tragedies, the tradition so well understood by David Jones and not ignobly expressed by the literary Edwardians, the four-letter words of Mailer and his colleagues cannot really add very much.[21]

Howard concludes his survey of war literature by agreeing with Fussell's assertion that the European literary tradition 'is a narcotic, masking the essential obscenity of war', but adds this important qualification:

> Yet one does not have to make a value judgment about war itself to accept that the whole corpus of European literature suggests that military experience, by deepening men's understanding and widening their knowledge of themselves and one another; by enhancing their perceptions both of torment and of ecstasy; by confronting them with novel impressions, terrifying, sickening, tedious, occasionally delightful; by creating for them new relationships and new challenges; has, when it has been properly understood and interpreted, immeasurably enriched that understanding of mankind, of its powers and its limitations, of its

splendours and its miseries, and not least of its relationship to God, which must lie at the root of all societies that lay any claim to civilization.[22]

'...*when it has been properly understood and interpreted*': the human values of the war hinge on the subsequent attribution of meaning by the survivors, on their recapturing of control, emotional and cognitive, over their ordeal. This recovery of meaning does not merely involve a deeper understanding of crucial facets of human psychology. It is infused with the divine, through the access it affords to religious revelation; and it is a source of inestimable social value, as a 'relationship to God' is at the basis of *all* societies. The reference to God, all societies, and civilization suggests a coherent totality of meaning as the possible outcome of the war experience, and indirectly as the goal of literary investigation.

2 Tradition Triumphant: Echoes of the Past in War Literature

In a consideration of the role of traditional cultural references in war literature, the comments of historians and literary critics about a work as steeped in myth as David Jones's *In Parenthesis* are particularly interesting. Fussell finds that this fiction/epic poem ultimately fails in its portrayal of war: 'The war will not be understood in traditional terms: the machine gun alone makes it so special and unexampled that it simply can't be talked about as if it were one of the conventional wars of history. Or worse, of literary history.'[23] Bergonzi's discussion of Jones's work seems more accurate. Although he disregards the myths created during the war, he refers to the myths developed in post-war literature 'as a means of restoring contact with the past', and points out that David Jones 'resembles his contemporaries in seeing the actualities of the war against a background of traditional values'.[24]

M. S. Greicus concludes his brief survey of English literature on the First World War with a consideration of David Jones's work. He writes that *In Parenthesis* emphasizes the major note in war novels by stressing, through the exploration of the myth of battle, 'the underlying sameness of experience that is visible in the war literature of the past.'[25] The war novelists, Greicus adds, all shared an adventure as old as time itself which provided a common cultural background.[26]

J. D. Enright suggests that Jones's work may be seen as an attempt to offer that consolation of which Owen wrote in a preface to a future work of poetry found among his papers after his death:

> My subject is War, and the pity of War.
> The Poetry is in the pity.
> Yet these elegies are to this generation in no sense consolatory. They may be to the next. All a poet can do today is warn. That is why the true Poets must be truthful...[27]

The consolation provided by the sense of continuity in experience is one of the refuges to which people seek most frequent psychological access. Whether the idea of meaningful links in time is illusion or reality, it acts as a powerful cultural agent and cannot be dismissed as an irrelevant accretion of modern perception.

In investigating war literature it is necessary to adopt a flexible approach which takes into account different influences, distinguishes between style and content,[28] and traces the connections between the new style and the influence of past literary modes and experience. Diane de Bell, for example, links the markedly private nature of much war writing to the literary movement of Romanticism, and relates this individualism to the 'political failure' of English intellectuals.[29]

Irony itself has an ancient literary history. In her article on the *Iliad*,[30] Simone Weil has observed that might – which, when wielded over men, makes things of them, and when unleashed at its full extent turns them into corpses – is the subject and hero of war. The utter powerlessness of the hero whose body is dragged by a chariot after a death 'alleviated by no comforting fiction, no consoling immortality, no faint halo of patriotic glory' is very similar to the condition of 'bondage, frustration, or absurdity' which characterizes the protagonists of Northrop Frye's ironic mode;[31] yet it is 'high-mimetic' and two literary stages removed from modern irony.

In the introduction to his 1930 compilation of war slang and songs, the novelist John Brophy attacked the notion of irony as specific to the Great War.

> Plain-speaking about war, the cold eye and the literal tongue turned upon what lies beyond the flag-waving and speech-making, the deliberate lowering of exalted spirits – this sort of realism is often supposed to be the discovery of the 1914–18 soldier.[32]

Against this notion of newness of response, he argued that the 'disillusionment, the bitterness, the grousing of soldiers of the past' was only concealed from contemporary knowledge by the romantic representations of the time. 'Even a Great War does not utterly transform national character', he stressed at the conclusion of his forceful argument of continuity. Irony, past and present, was to be understood as the humour of soldiers, a 'method of outwitting misfortune.'[33]

An uncompromisingly ironic, modern tone does characterize much war poetry, which also often condemns the social and political conditions which made war possible. These poets, however, were not looking back to the war years from the context of a different social reality, but were writing while psychologically and physically enclosed within the horror of war. J. D. Enright argues that the negative poetry of Sassoon had specific propagandistic motives,[34] whereas within the medium of fiction, through which he depicted a more complete picture, Sassoon's work tended to become 'sentimental in a conventional way.'[35] Fiction has a more detached and a more comprehensive perspective.[36] As Klein comments, prose narrative 'taking over in part the tradition of the great epics, is especially suited to the full re-creation of historical events and states of society.'[37]

Irony denotes a disassembling of meaning; in the literary ironic mode meaning is dissolved and lost in the morass of loss of control over one's situation. The opposite emerges again and again in post-war recollections and reconstructions: the retrospective fashioning and presentation of a coherent significance. Robert Graves in the early 1970s received a letter from a young American accusing him of not being politically radical. In his withering reply Graves, in a mode very different from that of his *Goodbye to All That*, reminded him of his participation in the First World War, and referred to it as an authentic social struggle.

> You have not fought in a real war. None of your generation has... 'Police action' with mass murder of civilians, defoliants, poisoning of the earth...are not wars but obscene outrages...and in the original Latin sense of obscenus ('unlucky', 'inauspicious', because of breaking human and divine law.) This implies divine punishment.
>
> The First World War was started by the German invasion of Belgium, without excuse; we fought to rescue Belgium & our French allies, and we fought honourably throughout....Maxima debetur senibus reverentia![38]

The memory here is no longer ironic.[39]

3 Modernists Versus Traditionalists

A consideration of the discussion surrounding the ironic mode draws our attention to a debate which is concerned not merely with the choice of critical tools to apply to literature, but with the very question of perception and definition of modern culture. The twentieth-century compulsive habit of contrasting the modern and the traditional in cultural artifacts is the heritage of a real conflict of views; yet its contemporary description is often surprisingly simplistic. In the *Dictionary of Literary Biography* the British writers of 1900-29 are listed in two volumes: 'Traditionalists' and 'Modernists'.[40] Among the modernists are included Michael Arlen and Sheila Kaye-Smith, middlebrow writers in the very same mould as James Hilton, Frank Swinnerton and Compton Mackenzie, who are all three ranked as traditionalists. R. H. Mottram is listed as a modernist. The labelling of Storm Jameson as a modernist, while Ford Madox Ford is relegated to the company of the traditionalist Mary Webb, indicates the arbitrary criteria of selection for either category. Assessments of the divide between modernists and traditionalists of the inter-war years rest uneasily with such judgments.

In a series of speeches delivered at the City Literary Institute in London in 1929, tradition and experiment in literature were discussed by prominent contemporary figures.[41] Interestingly, both speakers for tradition in the novel and in poetry, Mottram and Blunden, were famous war writers; their analysis of the contemporary break with the literary past contained no ironic element. Mottram pointed to the romantic and the didactic as vital ingredients of the English novel. His rhetoric was nostalgic,[42] but the language he used to describe the development of the nineteenth-century novel was an evident, if perhaps unconscious, projection of the crises of Mottram's own times. This parallelling of historical turning-points establishes a strict nexus of meaning between the heyday of the low-mimetic novel and the more divided literary climate of the post-war age. Mottram argued that Dickens, whom he acclaimed as the creator of the great nineteenth-century novel, found that he could not remain anchored to romance and Jane Austen's comfortable world, and consequently weighed the literary scales in favour of the didactic element, which together with the romantic forms the English novel.

> Although employing the romantic faculty to the verge of the fantastic, Dickens could not prevent from sticking through it the bones and sores of starved ill-treated bodies that formed the cannon – or rather factory-fodder of that phase of the industrial era, let loose by his post-war period. With all his romantic vitality, his humour, his pathos, his subject-matter conscripted him into the ranks of the satirists. He was, for all his extravagances, a great confirmer of the tradition of the English novel.[43]

This capacity to balance change and tradition was accomplished so memorably by 'a member of that poor suburban clerkdom which we know to be numerically more characteristic of British life than the dominant upper middle classes.'[44] 'Post-war', 'cannon-fodder', the social vision of a writer of the same lower-middle class extraction as himself: these images mirror Mottram's own experience and set it in a precise English tradition.

Mottram commends the 'moral, social, in some cases, almost political propaganda' of Arnold Bennett's and John Galsworthy's work: not for them the 'vapid' pursuit of art for art's sake. For these two writers the role of English literature is to relate the meaning of the particular to the whole, of the present to the universal, in an engagement with values which transcends the human limitation of death.

> They are human beings, treading our British earth and deeply concerned with its destinies. For this purpose they yoke their satire...to the aspiration towards perfection, so that it arises from the natural irony of existence. Both frequently employ the mere passage of time as a means of accumulating that modifying stream of incident that wears down the most solid-looking human structures and slowly

and logically moves on the mortal drama...Then life passes on, and in giving their turn to others, unconsciously relates us in our true value to the whole...You know the line of Amiel; 'Que vivre est difficile, O mon coeur fatigué!' Our English novelists have a vision saner and more robust.[45]

Mottram takes leave of his audience with 'a nineteen-eighteen feeling': 'Do you remember the headline of a newspaper of that date? "All is quiet on the Western Front, but the situation is not without danger. The morale of the troops is excellent" '. His audience is the troops; it is up to them not to let cheap imitations of the novels he has been discussing swamp and kill the tradition which is in their trust.[46]

Blunden, in his defence of tradition in poetry, declared that the 'question before the house of bards is not what to concoct, but what to recapture out of the prodigious word-experience of the Englishman.'[47] He described the contemporary withdrawal from this stock of literary riches as a moment of crisis, a faltering in the wide historical movement of the tradition of English language and literature.

> It is when tradition herself fails, through some commotion or malady, that we lose sight of the economy of human achievement. When she, by the bad effects of industrial greed and European war, or by half-education, is not sure of herself, we suffer for it.[48]

Moving away from tradition, which is the 'edifice of experience, the constitution of our society, and the test of the future',[49] can only prefigure grave cultural danger. A denial of the way in which the work of today's artist, musician and writer is inextricably bound with the past leads to the hysteria of uprootedness. The indispensable foundation of lasting literary achievement is tradition.

> . . .the past can assure us that in all that is destined to survive there will be found no hysterical, miraculous, demon-begotten departure from the past. The leap forward will have been made possible by a steady and accurately judged jumping-off place. In its preparation there needs be no feverish anxiety or palaver about the future style of civilization. On this ground many modern talents come to grief; the terror of seeming five minutes behind next Friday distracts and exhausts. Those with things to say spend their enthusiasm in distorting the ways of saying them.[50]

The impact of the argument is made stronger by the running together of old and new social images. Tradition, which is now personified and given the female gender, may at first be 'astonished and aggrieved when a steam-engine advances, leaving the driver of the Norwich stage-coach snapping his whip at the posturing smoke' or when the radio fills the old evening quiet. But upon reflection she realizes that she cannot be too worried by these phenomena: '...she only has to look at the poster on the Underground, setting forth the Londoner's means of transit through the ages, to feel at home in 1929 as in 1829; she may see even her stage-coach, disguised as new necessity demands, gliding out from Paddington.'[51] When the past can feel so cozily familiar with the present, the need for irony, or for radically new literary forms, is redundant. Fussell describes Blunden's 'Arcadian Recourses' in *Undertones of War* as an expression of his ultimately total opposition to war, as a process of selection 'from the armory of the past weapons against it which seem to have the greatest chance of withstanding time.'[52] But reliance on tradition cannot be simplified to a mere literary strategy; as Blunden's protest against the 'demon-begotten departure from the past' makes clear, it involves a social perception which precludes any ironic analysis.

2 The Middlebrow Novel

The genre examined in this book is middlebrow fiction. This term, now in virtual disuse, was coined in the 1920s to designate those novels and plays which made no attempt to go beyond or, as the writers themselves would have put it, to deviate from comfortably familiar presentations. In a brief earlier work I delineated the history of this mediocre literary group, distinguished only by big sales figures, and argued its claim to a prominent place in the history of culture as a carrier of contemporary values.[53] The inter-war bestsellers I examined – that rare commercial phenomenon which could ensure the survival of publishing houses and make magazine-celebrities of its writers – were at the forefront of a mass of more modestly-performing novels and plays from which I have drawn for this study.

The Education Act of 1870 created a generation of people equipped perhaps not with an education, but with the capacity to read and write. This caused an explosion of popular fiction at the same time that a generation of writers was isolating itself from an increasingly philistine literary environment. By the 1920s the Yellow Press had absorbed much quack writing, and the fiction market was divided into novels written according to a formula (lowbrow), the innovative, modernist narratives (highbrow), and, chronologically the last in this trio of literary phrenology, middlebrow fiction. The term 'middlebrow' is a product of the inter-war years (the Oxford English Dictionary traces the first appearance of the word to 1925[54]) and reflects a literary phenomenon which is well delimited within the two world wars. The Penguin paperbacks started a new era in the production of fiction and, more ominously, the bombarding of the London publishing premises during the Second World War marked the end of the literary heyday of the middlebrow novel.

Middlebrow novels laid claim to respectable status but rarely pretended to any lasting literary value. They ranged widely in quality, from the well-constructed novels of J. B. Priestley to the barely grammatical sentimentality of A. S. M. Hutchinson,[55] but most of them have fallen deservedly by the wayside. George Orwell – borrowing a term from G. K. Chesterton – called this fiction 'Good Bad Books', whose writers 'it is quite impossible to call "good" by any strictly literary standard, but who are natural novelists and who seem to attain sincerity partly because they are not inhibited by good taste'. He argued that there is a place for such novels, as they remind us that 'art is not the same thing as cerebration'; often unashamedly autobiographical, they have an authenticity which holds strong appeal.[56] Orwell's judgment differs sharply from Virginia Woolf's pithily swift dismissal of this 'betwixt and between' literature.[57]

These novels were the staple of the circulating libraries; they adorned bookshop windows, filled review columns and, most importantly, made up the bestseller lists. Middlebrow fiction was the mainstay of the book industry. To peruse the pages of the *Bookseller*, the book trade periodical, is to trace the history of this inter-war literary phenomenon: the defence of their success as the indispensable financial backbone of the industry; the role of the circulating libraries in propagating this fiction; the emergence of the multifarious Book Clubs, compasses of middlebrow taste; the booksellers' monthly lists of bestsellers. Not many people knew about E. M. Forster, but few would be unfamiliar with the names of Frankau, Deeping, and Priestley, who from a commercial point of view were the most successful and prominent literary figures of their time. The term 'middlebrow' is also indispensable for describing the British theatre of the inter-war years, commercially monopolized by the works of such playwrights as John Van Druten, J. M. Barrie and Noel Coward. West End theatres thrived on such productions. As will be shown later, the success of *Journey's End* was on a scale which made it the theatrical event of the inter-war years, launched the careers of several theatre figures, and established Gollancz's publishing house on a sound financial basis.

Writing her 'anthropological' study of the reading public in 1932, Q. D. Leavis could not have done without the new literary label. She pointed out that the choices of the Selection Committee of the Book Society (which could hail the publication of Galsworthy's *A Modern Comedy* as 'a real event in the story of modern English literature') ensured that 'a middlebrow standard of values has been set up' and 'that middlebrow taste has thus been organised.'[58] Book-promoting organizations of this kind played constantly on the dichotomy of the familiar and the pretentiously clever. One of the Book Guild's chief aims was 'to avoid indulging in the deplorable affectation of recommending as a work of 'genius' the sort of thing which is dubbed clever simply because it is mainly unintelligible and written in an obscure manner, or boosting some foreign work simply because it is foreign, and the author's name difficult to pronounce.'[59]

The term 'middlebrow' represented a symbol for the centre in more than one sense. It stood in the vast space between lowbrow fiction, designed merely to entertain, and highbrow works, increasingly alienated from a common reference of values. Its authors were from the middle classes and addressed a middle-class audience; they mediated between conflicts and extremes, and balance was their alleged trademark.

One role of middlebrow literature in the inter-war years was to keep the canon of nineteenth-century fiction, as it understood it, alive and functioning by safeguarding it against modernism. While it acknowledged and described disorientation and loss of religious belief in the face of social change, it ultimately reaffirmed historical continuity and the coherence of faith. Modernism – a term which reflects more accurately attitudes towards its writers and poets than the nature of the literary movement – represented for the great majority of the reading public a shocking break with the tradition of nineteenth-century narratives. Middlebrow novels were clearly modelled on nineteenth-century fiction, and enthusiastic reviewers established numerous comparisons with writers like Dickens and Trollope. This commitment to the literature of the past century appears a paradox when set against the famous arguments of I. A. Richards and the Leavises,[60] who deplored the explosion of lowbrow and, especially, of middlebrow fiction as a corruption of the great tradition of English literature. Middlebrow fiction, however, attempted to establish continuity not with great literature but with the past: they employed the nineteenth-century structure of well-rounded narratives, with clearly structured plots and definite endings, and they assumed the presence of an audience bound by a community of values. They viewed English language and the English novel as the expression of unalterable, shared values and tradition; they defied cultural obsolescence and transitoriness. Even when they recognised aesthetic brilliance, they viewed the work of modernists as a degradation of such encoded values. The literary tradition within which they placed themselves was not examined aesthetically but upheld as a source of moral literary value, the natural outcome of the history of English literature. Historically, of course, the nineteenth-century novel is the quintessential middle-class novel, the product of the industrial revolution, with its corollary concepts of development, progress, and moral perfectibility.

Middlebrow war novels depict the period which represented for many the watershed between the reliable past and the confusing present, the tragic break between old and new. They attempt not to camouflage the horror of war but to soften the impact of the break it represented by reasserting links with the past; even when lamenting the disruptive consequences of the war they still imply the possibility of readjusting the various parts and making them whole and functional again. In middlebrow novels there is not a dynamic representation of the way in which, to use Yeats's expression, the centre of society could not hold any more, but instead a stress on man's individualistic determination as the pivot of a society in which, for all its modern attributes, one could clearly discern the age-old pattern of choice and solution. If literary critics cried that standards were degenerating, the middlebrow writers were hard at work making sure that social and personal values did not.

This effort of moral reinforcement involved an attack on 'modern' culture which has not yet died out. Frank Swinnerton, prolific middlebrow literary commentator and novelist of the inter-war years, in 1977, at the age of 92, wrote a review of Holger Klein's *The First World War in Fiction*. He did not like this collection of essays, which to him represented the modern tendency to 'reduce the great map of individual effort to order', to analyze and categorize literature as if it were a scientific specimen. He backed his argument, typically, with a reference to the nineteenth century: modern literary critics 'bring to the contemplation of any imaginative work a whole armoury of sociological, biological and psycho-analytical values (because the name of Freud must be added to those of Marx and Darwin) which were never considered by Fielding, Jane Austen or Walter Scott, nor even by such seminal critics as Coleridge and Hazlitt.'[61]

1 The Baedeker of the Memory of War

The terms of inclusion into this bibliography of war fiction have been extremely open, and have aimed at presenting a complete presentation of the memory of war in minor English novels; the extraordinary success of the play *Journey's End*, one of the cultural events of the inter-war years in England, has dictated its inclusion. Autobiographical memoirs thinly disguised as fictional accounts; civilians' stories of the home front they knew, or their description of the ordeal in the trenches they never even saw; novels where the soldiers' experience is the centre of the narrative, and novels where the war years occupy a limited segment within a wide chronological span; all have been considered in order to obtain a broad overview of the themes and perceptions making up the official memory of war presented by literature. This investigation has taken into consideration all novels regardless of their sales figures. Some did not even get a review; several were not the product of professional writers, but first novels – in some cases followed by no others – written under the compulsion to communicate the memory of the war. The style of these novels is firmly set within the confines of traditional structures. The only, and very limited, literary attempt at a different construction is John Brophy's *The World Went Mad* (1934), where, following a device which the author claimed was suggested to him by the cinema, each separate story is linked to the next by an image or a turn of phrase. Interestingly, this single 'experiment' is exclusively concerned with unity and continuity of narrative.

The inter-war periodization of the discussion of the memory of war can hardly be more precise: these years were dominated by the memory of a war which separated the new world from the old with a violent rupture, and by the spectre of the possibility and consequences of a sequel. The chronology of these works shows the same pattern of publication as that of the better known war novels, although on a different scale. After a spate of novels in 1919[62] there was a sharp decrease in numbers during the following years (from thirty-nine in 1919 to seven in 1925), which reflected popular unwillingness to address such a recent trauma. Still, between 1920 and 1928 several novels of great interest appeared, including three bestsellers: *The Way of Revelation* (1921), *Simon Called Peter* (1921) and *Tell England* (1922). The hopelessly melodramatic *The Woman of Knockaloe* (1923) by Hall Caine, the Grand Old Man of Romance, made the first direct, and very successful, appeal in popular fiction for friendship between the English and Germans. J.B. Priestley praised Patrick Miller's *The Natural Man* for revealing at last the 'Truth' about war by striking a balance between extreme representations. Priestley's remarks show how in 1924 there already existed a debate about war literature.

> The first war stories were a mixture of crude adventure tales and patriotic rant: war...was a glorious adventure; the Allied soldiers were all brave fellows, the enemy troops were all cowardly dogs; there was no life like a soldier's...Then came disillusion. We were promptly shown sensitive young men dragged from their charming studios, their editions-de-luxe and sets of Japanese prints, and plunged into mud and blood; and the army in actual combat was shown to be nothing but obscenity and slaughter, and out of it nothing but a stupid farce. As rewards for heroes, Victoria Crosses went out of fashion and courts-martial came in.[63]

1929 marked the beginning of the great boom of war literature. In 1929 and 1930 thirty-two middlebrow novels were published that discussed the war on different levels: this was a higher number than was produced throughout the 1930s.

This book is structured in three parts: a sociological analysis, a thematic section, and a final case study. The first chapter examines the question of intention in war literature through a collective biographical study of its authors. It will show the homogeneity of their class origin, and the extent of their involvement in social issues of their time. These creators of literary signposts of history were contemporary mediators and communicators in a variety of roles beside authorship; among them were journalists, teachers, publishers, and editors. As well as novels, they produced a wealth of non-fictional works. The most enthusiastic example of identification with the readers' experience was Edward John Thompson's *You Have Lived Through All This: An Anatomy of the Age* (1939), a history of his times told throughout in the second person singular.

These writers represented one of the last bodies of literary opinion in England to view their function as a public and social one. The authors' theses preceded and overwhelmed their narratives, revealing openly their ideological bias. From the point of view of orthodox history, politics, or sociology, theirs are undoubtedly second-rate works of analysis; but they represent fascinating examples of a vigorously active, committed effort to offer an exegesis of change in modern society. It is the social consciousness of the writers, their inserting themselves into a wider dialogue of shared social knowledge and assumptions, that reveals them as important agents of cultural communication, as sources of explanations and meanings, even in the simple role of narrators of common experience. This first chapter examines no fiction. The concerns of these authors' activities and the syntheses of judgment expressed in their non-fictional works (and often in autobiographies) prefigure the themes of their novels.

The second section, of three chapters, analyzes the novels. It starts with a study of the overt attributions of meaning to the war, from the shrill anti-German invectives and the celebration of patriotic sacrifice of the 1919 novels to the message of brotherhood and condemnation of the waste of war of the 1929–30 war-novel boom. The following chapter investigates the way in which the war was shown to modify identity. Many novels attempted to convey the elusive, exclusive world of the soldiers – the intimacy with fear which narrowed down existence to the present terror or the impending one, and the companionship of those who shared in this continuous gamble with life – through a spiritual language which alone could derive meaning out of brutalization and death. Also, in many novels one finds an extensive portrayal of the ambiguity of the common experience, with on one side the soldiers's ordeal in the trenches, and on the other the varied responses of civilians, women, and conscientious objectors behind the lines and at home. The final chapter of this section shows how popular fiction often established parallels between the experience of First World War soldiers and military and historical tradition, in the effort to absorb a terrible experience within the fabric of the common cultural heritage. Had the readers of these popular novels read *In Parenthesis*, they would have understood perfectly the numerous references to past military experience.

The description of the middlebrow literary climate of the inter-war years, and the survey of the themes of the war novels produced in these years, provide the analytical background necessary to understand the phenomenon of Sherriff's *Journey's End,* the play which has continued to provide the archetypal image of the English experience in the trenches. The last section looks at the impact of this work and at its endurance as a symbol of the memory of the Great War by examining in detail both the history of the author's experience in France in 1916-17 and of his later fictional creation.

This book touches diffidently on the history of perception. Historical reality is shaped by the way in which people understand it and remember it. War fiction is invested with all the emotion of a lived experience, and with all the polemical fervour of the involvement with an issue which has been at the centre of a nation's experience and reality and is determining its present and future. The discussion of social changes affecting middle-class attitudes in the 1920s and 1930s necessarily referred back to the war. The main body of evidence in this book consists of moral data, values, myths and traditions which made up people's perceptions of themselves and their society. This study does not attempt to establish all the 'real' correspondences between the fiction and the experience of the writers, nor to offer its own re-creation of the war years through the evidence presented by the novels. Its historical territory is the inter-war years; its sources the imagery that popular writers presented in their work; its aim to seek patterns of value and meaning in such images. This reading is predicated upon the notion that the fictional structure of the memory of war is an important source of social and cultural history. Eric Leed posits an interesting analogy between reading a text and reading war:

> Just as the meaning of text may not lie in the purposes of an author...but in its impact upon those who imaginatively enter it, the meaning of the war was commonly felt to lie in the self-awareness, consciousness, fears, and fantasies that it engendered in those who were forced to inhabit a world of violence they had not created.[64]

In this study I attempt to read, in addition, the 'self-awareness, consciousness, fears, and fantasies' of those writers who lived on the edge of or quite outside the violent world of the front: all kinds of survivors contribute their memory of the war.

In the preface to the three-volume series on patriotism published in 1989,[65] its editor, Raphael Samuel, explains that the project grew out of 'anger at the Falklands War.'

> For the first time since Passchendaele...the authentic accents of 'Vitai Lampada' – 'play up and play the game' – could be intoned without embarrassment by a British Prime Minister; even – as it turned out – endorsed by the electorate.[66]

This book shares the aim of this recent work of exploring the understanding of patriotism and national identity of a certain period. Another common point is the wavering between the adjectives 'British' or 'English' as the most apt reference to perception of identity; in the end I also opted in the title for the former term, more 'formal, abstract and remote', as it avoids the assumption of a 'common culture.'[67] At the same time, precisely because such a presupposition was common, the term 'English' was used even by non-English novelists to define a familiar notion of identity, so often related to English literature and the countryside of England. It is in reflection of such perceptions that it is employed in this study.

2 Mapping out the Terrain of the Inter-war Years

After the Great War cartographers had to redraw their atlases. *The Times Survey Atlas*, which came out in 1923 and was arguably the best atlas to date, was the culmination of the work of three generations of the Bartholomew family at the Edinburgh Geographical Institute. After the war the changes were entrusted to a new editor, John I. Bartholomew, who succeeded his father in 1920. He had enlisted in 1914, and served in France, where he was wounded, received the MC, and served on Haig's staff.[68] This process of redrawing the borders of reality, of completing a job disrupted by the upheaval of war – with the final stages the responsibility of a young survivor of the war – epitomizes the common predicament of the post-war years.

Fussell has pointed out the changed nature of perception of reality due to the reshaping of Europe after the war:

> Fragmenting and dividing anew and parcelling-out and shifting around and repositioning – these are the actions implicit in the redrafting of frontiers. All these actions betray a concern with current space instead of time or tradition. All imply an awareness of reality as disjointed, dissociated, fractured.[69]

He argues a connection between this perceptual change and the juxtaposition of quotations and disjunction of narratives in works such as *The Wasteland*, the *Cantos* and *Ulysses*: 'In modern writing the expectations attaching to the old, readily understandable order of reasonable narrative sequence...are defeated.'[70] The modernist literature of the post-war years reflected in style and content the real sense of deprivation of the old security and disorientation within the new fragmented reality.[71]

Samuel Hynes, in his recent *A War Imagined*, has stressed the feeling of 'radical discontinuity'[72] bequeathed by the War to English culture. He describes how great Modernists like Eliot and Pound, Virginia Woolf and Lawrence, whose literary representations and imaginings of war were all negative, presented 'recent history as discontinuous and fragmented, civilization as ruined, the past as lost.' Hynes maintains that such themes and perception of history 'turn up everywhere in the popular literature of the Twenties', appealing to all levels of readers.[73] He points, for example, to the lengthy references in A. S. M. Hutchinson's bestseller *If Winter Comes* to the bitter, divisive legacy of the war. Hynes finds these all the more remarkable in view of Hutchinson's patriotic attitude and of the final assertion in the novel that with the war over England is now 'at peace, victorious; those dark years done. England her own again.'[74] The description of post-war greed and class hatred, however, cannot be split up analytically from the novel's resolution of hope, with the former a reflection of dominant mythology and the latter the facile outcome of a conventional mind. Rather, the discussion of contemporary problems is a deliberate outlining of a state of affairs for which a solution is worked out by patterning meaning out of the material of disaster.

If the title *The Wasteland*, and Yeats's line 'Things fall apart; the centre cannot hold',[75] are by now literary icons of a period of discontinuity and fragmentation, a whole body of work, 7s 6d novels which formed the staple of publishers' lists, needs to be reopened to reveal a set of evidence concerned not with describing the alienated role of the writer, nor with presenting a reality of irreconcilable fragments, but rather with offering an analysis of their society which would serve as a blueprint for reconstituting the fragments into a familiar picture.

Gilbert Adair, in discussing Bernard Levin's *Enthusiasms* ('robustly Georgian title')[76] calls his language 'bereft of ideas.'

> Whatever meanings it may once have been capable of generating, there is absolutely nothing remaining to be said in an idiom which can refer without irony to 'the wonders and the mysteries of the human soul' or to works of art as pointing the way 'to our human understanding of our human duty, the duty to be transformed, to rise from darkness into light, to pursue the will-o'-the-wisp of integration and completeness until it turns out to be no will-o'-the-wisp but the shining sea of eternal truth.'[77]

In the post-war age of the modernists Eliot and Woolf, and of Spender and Auden, such references of value were used again and again by popular writers who invoked it not merely as a kind of social incantation from the past to counteract the modern rift in the social fabric, but also as a contemporary moral model, tested and modified in dynamic relation to modern realities. That period is not so remote, nor its tensions about modernity so neatly resolved, that this language of meaning should be glibly pronounced defunct.

These writers were the social cartographers of the new reality, engaged in a task as real as that of the people involved in the redrawing of the maps of

Europe. One novelist, Cecil Roberts, a former war correspondent, wrote the 'literary supplement' of the People's Atlas. This was no perfunctory introduction, but a guide to the new world, a didactic exercise of direction into new territory. The advice, though couched in rhetoric, was grounded in reality, and included the following practical aids: the Peace Treaty in full, the Labour treaty drawn at the Versailles Conference, and statements about the way to peace in the new world by various speakers, including the English and French Prime Ministers and Philip Gibbs, prolific novelist and former war correspondent.

The history of middlebrow writers' reflections on the 1914-18 war involves us not only with the study of the memory of war, but also with the efforts of a community of writers to use the tools of the past to redraw the outlines of Englishness.

Notes to Introduction

1. John Dunn, 'Politics without Greed or Envy', *Times Higher Education Supplement*, 2 March 1990, p. 13. Hereafter, for all books the place of publication is London unless otherwise stated.

2. Paul Fussell, *The Great War and Modern Memory*, 1977 (first published 1975), p. 35 (my italics)

3. Northrop Frye, *Anatomy of Criticism*, Princeton, 1957, pp. 33 ff.

4. Fussell, *The Great War and Modern Memory*, p. 35.

5. Frye, *Anatomy of Criticism*, p. 34.

6. Fussell, *The Great War and Modern Memory*, p. 312.

7. *Ibid.*, p. 115.

8. Bernard Bergonzi, *Heroes' Twilight, A Study of the Literature of the Great War*, 1965, p. 198.

9. Fussell, *The Great War and Modern Memory*, p. 131.

10. *Ibid.*, pp. 312–13. Daniel Bell, similarly, describes the 'demonic' as the reflection of life devoid of meaning, that is, beyond the traditional solutions of the irrational provided by religion. Daniel Bell, 'The return of the sacred? The argument on the future of religion.' (*British Journal of Sociology*, Vol. 28, no. 4, December 1977, p. 428.)

11. Jay Winter, *The Great War and the British People*, 1985, p. 304.

12. George Dangerfield, *The Strange Death of Liberal England*, 1983 (first published 1935), p. 381. Dangerfield describes the difference between enduring fiction and minor literature in terms of the specificity of its historical moment: the former, in his opinion, encapsulates the 'soul of man, undated', while minor literature is 'the Baedeker of the soul, and will guide you through the curious relics, the tumbledown buildings, the flimsy palaces, the false pagodas, the distorted and fantastical and faery vistas which have cluttered the imagination of mankind at this or that brief period of its history.'

13. Frye, *The Anatomy of Criticism*, p. 34.

14. Cyril Falls, *War Books*, 1929.

15. Douglas Jerrold, *The Lie About the War*, 1930, pp. 10, 48.

16. Andrew Rutherford, *The Literature of War, Five Studies in Heroic Virtue*, 1978, pp. 6 ff.

17. *Ibid.*, p. 1.

18. *Ibid.*, p. 65.

19. *Ibid.*, pp. 69–70. The humanity Sassoon is referring to is the presence he feels of his dead companions of the Battles of the Somme and Arras. He sees their faces, hears their voices: 'These were the dead, to whom life had been desirable'. (Cited in *Ibid.*) This essential humanity of war

was described in haunting terms by Frederic Manning in *Her Privates We*: 'A man might rave against the war; but war, from among its myriad faces, could always turn towards him one, which was his own. There was no man of them unaware of the mystery which encompassed him, for he was a part of it; he could neither separate himself entirely from it, nor identify himself with it completely.' (Cited in Bergonzi, *Heroes' Twilight*, pp. 191–2.)

20. Michael Howard, 'Military Experience in Literature', *Essays by Divers Hands: Being the Transactions of the Royal Society of Literature*, (New Series), Vol. 41, 1980, p. 39.

21. *Times Literary Supplement*, 5 December 1975, p. 1435.

22. Howard, 'Military Experience in Literature', p. 39.

23. Fussell, *The Great War and Modern Memory*, p. 153.

24. Bergonzi, *Heroes' Twilight*, pp. 198–200, 211.z

25. M.S.Greicus, *Prose Writers of World War I*, (Writers and Their Work, no. 231), 1973, p. 42

26. *Ibid.*

27. J. D. Enright, 'The Literature of the First World War', *The New Pelican Guide to English Literature*, Vol. 7, Harmondsworth, 1983, pp. 211, 208.

28. Winter, *The Great War and the British People*, p. 304.

29. Diane de Bell, 'Strategies of Survival: Robert Graves, *Goodbye to All That*, and David Jones, *In Parenthesis*', in Holger Klein (ed.), *The First World War in Fiction, 1976, p. 162.*

30. Simone Weil, 'The *Iliad* or the Poem of Force', in *Simone Weil: An Anthology*, (edited by Siân Miles), 1986, p. 183. This article was written in 1939–40 and was first published in the *Cahiers du Sud* (December 1940-January 1941).

31. Fussell, *The Great War and Modern Memory*, pp. 311–12.

32. John Brophy, *Songs and Slang of the British Soldier: 1914–1918* (edited with Eric Partridge), 1930, p. 7.

33. *Ibid.*, p. 8.

34. Robert Graves remarked that 'Modernism in Mr. Sassoon is an intelligent, satiric reaction to contemporary political and social Bluffs; it is not a literary policy.' ('Modernist Poetry and Civilization', *A Survey of Modernist Poetry*, 1927, cited in Enright, 'The Literature of the First World War', p. 204.)

35. Enright, 'The Literature of the First World War', p. 204.

36. Fussell holds that what are often considered memoirs, like Sassoon's and Graves's works, are in fact a form of fiction, as they were written at a temporal distance which allowed the authors to structure their narratives in a way which highlighted what they saw as the 'significances of their memories.' (Fussell, *The Great War and Modern Memory*, pp. 310-311.)

37. Klein, *The First World War in Fiction*, p. 4.

38. Cited in Martin Seymour Smith, *Robert Graves: His Life and Work*, 1982, p. 564. The Latin sentence was a deliberate distortion of *Maxima debetur puero reverentia* (Juvenal, xiv, 47), thus shifting the prescription of respect for the boy to that for elders.

39. But it is still tormented. As a very old man Graves would often say that he had murdered many men. When someone once objected 'That's hardly murder', he reasserted firmly: 'It is, you know'. (*Ibid.*, p. 566.)

40. *Dictionary of Literary Biography, British Novelists 1890–1929: Vol. 34 (Traditionalists)*, Vol. 36 *(Modernists)*, Detroit, 1985.

41. *Tradition and Experiment in Present-Day Literature*, 1929. The speakers for tradition were: R.H. Mottram for the novel, Edmund Blunden for Poetry, Ashley Dukes for Drama, A.J.A. Symonds for Biography, Rebecca West for Criticism. For experiment were J.D.Beresford for the novel, Edith Sitwell for poetry, C.K. Munro for drama, Osbert Burdett for biography, T.S. Eliot for criticism.

42. *Ibid.*, p. 10. Mottram judged the upper middle-class life portrayed by Jane Austen as 'still the most civilized and desirable in the world.'

43. R.H. Mottram, 'Tradition in the Novel', in *Ibid.*, p. 11.

44. *Ibid.*

45. *Ibid.*, pp. 20–21.

46. *Ibid.*, pp. 21–22.

47. Edmund Blunden, 'Tradition in Poetry', in *Tradition and Experiment,* p. 63.
48. *Ibid.*
49. *Ibid.,* p. 68.
50. *Ibid.,* pp. 68–9.
51. *Ibid.*
52. Fussell, *The Great War and Modern Memory,* p. 269.
53. Rosa Maria Bracco, *'Betwixt and Between',* Melbourne, 1990.
54. 'The B.B.C. claim to have discovered a new type, the "middlebrow". It consists of people who are hoping that one day they will get used to the stuff they ought to like.' Punch, 23 December 1925, p. 673. And three years later: 'The standard of "middle-brow" music and plays is always rather low.' Observer, 17 June 1928, p. 26. *(Oxford English Dictionary.)*
55. Most memorably J.B. Priestley's *The Good Companions* (1929) and *Angel Pavement* (1937) and A.S.M. Hutchinson's *If Winter Comes* (1921).
56. George Orwell, *Tribune,* 2 November 1945, in *The Collected Essays, Journalism and Letters of George Orwell,* Vol. 4: *In Front of Your Nose, 1945–1950,* Harmondsworth, 1970, pp. 37–41.
57. Virginia Woolf, 'Middlebrow', *The Death of the Moth,* 1942, p. 115.
58. Q.D.Leavis, *Fiction and the Reading Public,* 1932, pp. 22–4.
59. Ibid., p. 25. Leavis was citing Ethel Mannin in *The Bookworm's Turn,* published by the Book Guild.
60. See I.A. Richards, *Principles of Literary Criticism,* London, 1924; F.R. Leavis, *Mass Civilization and Minority Culture,* Cambridge, 1930; F.R.Leavis and Denys Thompson, *Culture and Environment: The Training of Critical Awareness,* 1934; Q.D.Leavis, *Fiction and the Reading Public,* 1932.
61. Frank Swinnerton, 'All Pinned Down', *Books and Bookmen,* March 1977, pp. 54, 55.
62. Included in the discussion also is Frederick Sleath's Sniper Jackson, published in November 1918.
63. *London Mercury,* September 1924, p. 539.
64. Eric J. Leed, *No Man's Land: Combat and Identity in World War I,* 1979, p. 36.
65. Raphael Samuel (ed.), *Patriotism: The Making and Unmaking of British National Identity,* Vol. 1: *History and Politics,* Vol. 2: *Minorities and Outsiders,* Vol. 3: *National Fictions,* 1989.
66. *Ibid.,* Vol. 1: *History and Politics,* p. x.
67. *Ibid.,* pp. xii–xiii.
68. Leslie Gardiner, *Bartholomew: 150 years,* 1976, pp. 62–3.
69. Paul Fussell, *Abroad: British Literary Traveling Between the Wars,* Oxford, 1980, p. 36.
70. *Ibid.*
71. Modernism was not, of course, a product of the war. Yet writers like Eliot, Woolf, and Joyce, the most 'modern' and 'difficult' to read, and therefore the writers deemed to have made the strongest break with past literary modes, made their greatest impact in the 1920s.
72. Samuel Hynes, *A War Imagined: the First World War and English Culture,* 1990, p. ix.
73. *Ibid.,* pp. 348–9.
74. Cited in *Ibid.,* p. 349.
75. Yeats's poem 'The Second Coming', a powerful statement on contemporary civilization, was composed in January 1919 and was first published in November 1920. (A.Norman Jeffares, *Poems of W.B. Yeats's: A New Selection,* 1984, p. 246.)
76. Gilbert Adair, *Myths and Memories,* London, 1986, p. 28.
77. Cited in *Ibid.,* pp. 30–31.

Cholmondeley's niece. Oliver Madox Hueffer was the grandson of the painter Ford Madox Brown and the brother of Ford Madox Ford. Political parents were even fewer: Herbert Asquith was the Prime Minister's son, Stephen McKenna was Reginald McKenna's nephew, Justin Huntly MacCarthy's father had been a Nationalist MP.

Their education was predictably privileged. Of the sixty writers whose education could be traced, thirty-six attended private schools, only one of them a Catholic institution (Anthony Bertram at Douai Abbey), four were privately educated, and the other eighteen went to grammar school or similar institutions, like Sherriff's proto-public Kingston Grammar School. Twenty-nine went to Oxford and Cambridge (respectively nineteen and ten); of these, twenty had been to public schools. England was the focus geographically as well as ideologically. Sixty-four writers came from England, of whom fourteen were from the North; six from Ireland, eleven from Scotland, one from Wales. Lyons was born in South Africa and Baxter in Canada, but both settled in London; most of the other 'outsiders' also settled in the south of England.

Forty-five of these writers had seen active service or had been abroad as members of the army chaplain's service or in the Royal Army Medical Corps;[5] others had worked close to the fighting. John Buchan, H. F. P. Battersby, Cecil Roberts and Philip Gibbs worked as war correspondents, John Galsworthy spent five months in France as a masseur, Jerome Klapka Jerome volunteered as an ambulance driver in France, and Arnold Bennett travelled to France as propagandist for the government. Several writers were involved at various levels on the home front.[6] There was only one conscientious objector, Gilbert Cannan, and three avowed pacifists, Mary Agnes Hamilton, Henrietta Leslie and Herbert Tremaine. Of the twenty-eight women writers, Cicely Mary Hamilton worked in the Scottish Women's Hospital, Berta Ruck worked as a Land Army girl, May Sinclair spent a short time with the Field Ambulance Corps in Belgium, Carmel Haden Guest organized infant welfare centres in villages behind the Allied lines in Flanders, and Irene Rathbone worked as a nurse in France.

In a study concerned with the explorations of the meaning of war in the post-war years, it is of particular interest to examine these writers' inter-war occupations. Here was no Bloomsbury scenario of writers devoted exclusively to their art. Middlebrow writers concentrated their attention on ordinary human beings because they considered themselves ordinary and regarded their work as a reflection of the concerns and aspirations of a wide public. In the course of a conversation between Mary Agnes Hamilton and Virginia Woolf, the latter wondered what made one write. She was puzzled by Hamilton's reply that her motivation was a great interest in people, and countered that she was so not much interested in people as in 'the feel of life was assistant editor of the *London Mercury* from 1919 to 1922 and chief leader-writer of the *Evening Standard* from 1928 to 1935; George Blake was acting editor of *John O'London's Weekly* from 1924 to 1928 and of the *Strand Magazine* from 1928 to 1930. Graham Seton opened a news service office in the City in 1922, and became director of the London Press Exchange Limited. In the north, James Lansdale Hodson was News Editor of the northern edition of the *Daily Mail* from 1924 to 1929 (later special writer with the *News Chronicle*, *Sunday Times* and Allied Newspapers). Others exerted considerable cultural authority through their role as newspaper commentators. J. B. Morton began his long career as professional challenger of modern culture in the *Daily Express* in 1922 (with Arthur Beverley Baxter as his boss); Arnold Bennett was Great Britain's most important book reviewer in the *Evening Standard*, his sceptre of influence, at his death, passing to Howard Spring, who made an easy transition in the 1930s from middlebrow reviewing to middlebrow bestsellerdom; Charles Morgan joined the editorial staff of the London *Times* in 1921 as assistant to A.B.Walkley, dramatic critic, whom he succeeded when the latter died in 1926.[10]

The *Gramophone*, the name of the magazine Christopher Stone founded in 1923 with his brother-in-law Compton Mackenzie, could serve as an emblem of the broadcasting social role of these popular writers. The new medium of the radio also received important contributions from them. Stone acquired popularity as England's first 'disc jockey', with his own music programme. Vernon Bartlett was an extremely popular radio broadcaster on international affairs from 1927 to 1933; Gordon Stowell joined the Staff of BBC Radio Times in 1932, became Deputy Director in 1933 and was Editor from 1941 to 1944; Mary Agnes Hamilton was a governor of the BBC from 1933 to 1937.

Some of these educators in social values were also professional teachers. Gordon Stowell was Principal of Weston-super-Mare School of Science and Art from 1923 to 1926; Ronald Gurner taught all his life[11] and wrote about his idiosyncratic educational theories; F.O. Mann was an Inspector of Schools; W. F. Morris worked as an assistant lecturer at University College, Reading and then as headmaster of St John's School, Reading. Anthony Bertram was a lecturer in art history, V.W.W.S. Purcell in Far Eastern history; Edward Shanks lectured in poetry in Liverpool in 1926. Political activity attracted a smattering of interest. Arthur Beverley Baxter was Conservative MP for Wood Green for the period 1935–45 (and 1945–1950); Vernon Bartlett was Independent Progressive MP for Bridgwater (1938–50); A. P. Herbert was Independent Member for Oxford University (1935–50); Mary Agnes Hamilton was Labour MP for Blackburn from 1929 to 1931. Harold Spender contested Bath as a Liberal candidate in

1922; Graham Seton was Liberal candidate for the Uxbridge Division in 1923 and first Chairman of the Old Contemptibles Association; Cecil Roberts stood as Liberal Parliamentary candidate in 1922 for the East Division of Nottingham. Beyond party politics, Ingram was Vice-Chairman of the National Peace Council in 1929.[12]

2 The Intimate World of Publishing

Publishing and the book trade were an obvious occupational area for these writers. Hugh Walpole set up the Society of Bookmen in 1920; W.B. Maxwell was Chairman of the Society of Authors and of the National Book Council; Storm Jameson managed the British branch of Alfred Knopf in the mid-1920s and was President of the British section of PEN (1938–1945); Ernest Raymond became President of the Young PEN in 1933; Roland Pertwee served on the executive committee of the British branch of PEN;[13] George Blake was director of Faber and Faber from 1930 to 1932; and John Buchan acted for many years as advisory editor to Nelson.

The context of this world, the publishing trade of the inter-war years, accounts to some extent for the closeness within the literary environment. Publishing had developed little beyond that of Victorian days; the Net Book Agreement, with its agreement on fixed prices, protected the market, and one of its effects, as John Feather has pointed out, was 'to allow the trade to continue in familiar ways.' The book trade relied for its success on a 'move to the middle, the appeal to the popular taste of the educated middle class and its upper and lower borderlands.'[14] The middlebrow world of the inter-war years confirms Alan Swingewood's analysis of the myth of mass culture, whose origin in the nineteenth century he sees as a product not of the working class but of the success of middle-class commercial culture. Also, the antagonism between middlebrow and highbrow writers in these years supports his argument that the 'threat to high art', where it exists, derives from the classes who 'through voting habits, styles of life and ideological assumptions share uncritically in the values of capitalism.'[15]

Publishing was centred in London in the area around St Paul's and Bedford Square. Publishers' and readers' memories of those years evoke a bygone world of letters. The novelist H. E. Bates remembered the period when his first novel was accepted by Cape, in 1925, as 'good times for authors'. He lamented the disappearance of the fifteen to twenty periodicals, with different followings, edited by people like T. S. Eliot, Desmond MacCarthy, Alan Monkhouse, Middleton Murry, Leonard Woolf and J.C. Squire, which provided generous space for young authors to print their stories or poetry.[16] Novels could be printed more cheaply. The novelist suffered greatly from the change of economic climate following the Second World War, when the proportion of novels to the total number of books declined from almost a third in the 1930s to little more than a sixth. Rising publishing costs meant that a publisher needed to print at least 3,000 copies to cover his costs, whereas the figure for 1939 had been 1,500. Increasing costs also contributed to the gradual disappearance of the commercial library, the backbone of the novelist's trade.[17] Findlater calculates that whereas in 1938 a young writer with no family would need four pounds a week – which he could earn 'on the fringe of the literary world' – to rent a furnished bedsitter in London and live decently, by 1952 he would need nine pounds, by 1962 twelve pounds, and this for a much more frugal lifestyle.[18]

The 'character' of the publishing houses denotes a very different publishing environment from that which followed the Penguin paperback revolution and amalgamation in the industry. Conservative individualism characterized much of inter-war publishing, and found expression through the imprint of personalities. Edward Garnett, Cape's reader, enjoyed a 'completely free hand in his discoveries and choices',[19] thus leaving clearly his personal signature on the book list of the house. Michael S. Howard, son of one of the founding partners of Cape, also observed that the character of the small firm was 'imbued with the personalities of the founding partners...'[20] The most aggressive exponent of individualism was Ernest Benn, under whom Gollancz served his unlikely apprenticeship. He was the patron of the Individualist Bookshop, set up in 1927, which was 'pledged to the value of the individual...and consecrated to the purpose of combating by word and mouth the Socialist propaganda of collective management.'[21]

A belief in the idealistic, educational nature of the publishers' profession underlined pronouncements about the role of publishing. In May 1922 the bookseller G. B. Bowes, who had served in the war and retired as a major, gave a lecture to the Society of Bookmen on 'The Business of Bookselling' at Essex Hall in the Strand; W. B. Maxwell took the chair. Speaking of education, Bowes related it to the values learnt during the war: '...education is not all dry learning; it enlarges one's interests and sympathies and leads to a greater adaptability and comradeship, as was provoked by the war...'[22]

Business and idealism were determinedly not perceived as being at odds. W. G. Taylor, President of the Publishers Association and the managing director of Dent, asserted that the publishers' keen business sense was moderated by 'a *public spirited* attitude to their work', which allowed the publication of books that could not recoup their cost.[23] Charles Morgan reiterated this view with greater strength when, writing the history of the House of Macmillan in 1943, he painted a romantic picture of the business as one which combined idealism and commercial interests without violating either element. Morgan presented the firm as a splendid example of the social effect of personal effort: '...a publishing house is deeply and inescapably personal; only the devotion and the individuality of its chiefs can make or preserve it.' He spoke of the ideals of the founding brothers, Alexander and Daniel, as a 'tradition or, more truly a marked character' which bound the firm together and defined what 'a Macmillan book' was.[24]

Morgan's assertion that in publishing there are 'two principal aspects of publishing, the idealistic and the commercial, and the character of a firm must largely depend on its reconciliation of them',[25] was quoted by the publisher Stanley Unwin in his *Publishing in Peace and War*.[26] Unwin also quoted the editor of the *Spectator*, who had remarked that 'romance is a word inevitably and rightly associated with a great publishing-house. Publishing is business, of course, but is romance through and through.' The editor mentioned as a source of this romance the connection with 'great personalities' of the past, and Unwin added the feeling of 'building with permanent materials'. This perception of the past and of tradition as romantic and inherent to the business of letters, and the dependence of this romance on idealism, are, as we shall see, constant features of middlebrow novels. The term 'romance', so often employed by these writers, is best described by exclusion, as a view of the world which is not dogmatic, not intellectually self-conscious. It assumes the underlying glory and beauty of the ordinary. Ernest Raymond discussed his literary understanding of 'romance' in a treatise whose title, *Through Literature to Life*, emphasized the direct line between fiction and reality. His basic lesson was that literature is an author's vision of '*obvious* beauties'; realism and romance are indistinguishable, because romance lies behind 'everything in the world.'[27]

Bestsellers were not a predictable phenomenon, and in assessing their success it is important to remember that they could not be manufactured according to a commercial master plan. A. S. M. Hutchinson's *If Winter Comes* (1921) had a first printing of 5,000, but within a year over 100,000 copies were sold.[28] Figures of sale are not available, but some indication of the novels' success can be drawn from advertisements and editions. Desmond Flower in 1934 compiled a list of the major bestsellers from 1830 to 1930, based on the criterion of those novels which, surpassing the 100,000 mark within a short time of publication, 'took the country by storm'; only one novel per author was included.[29] The list includes Frankau's *Peter Jackson*, Hutchinson's *If Winter Comes*, Keable's *Simon Called Peter*, and Deeping's *Sorrell and Son*. These novels enjoyed extraordinary success; a much more limited sale still constituted a bestseller. Two thousand copies was considered good for a first novel. Cecil Roberts's first novel *Scissors* sold 12,000 copies in twelve months, earning £500, plus £400 on American editions and £300 on five translations; once the cost of British and American tax, two agents' fees and the typing bill were deducted (£400), he was left with a net profit of £800.[30]

The great number of first novels – twenty-six, of which eight were followed by no others [31] – underlines the need of these writers to communicate their interpretation of the war through the medium which could best convey the emotional, private level of memory. *The Way of Revelation* and *Tell England*, two of the greatest bestsellers among war novels, were the authors' first works; by 1939 *Tell England* had sold 300,000 copies.[32]

The importance of middlebrow fiction within the publishing industry can be judged by Gollancz's list. The publisher remembered for the Left Book Club built his firm on such bestselling authors as Dorothy Sayers, Daphne du Maurier, A. J. Cronin, and Eleanor Smith. This did not imply just an attentive eye to financial considerations. Gollancz's first great success was *Journey's End*, a play by an unknown clerk which he published and helped to produce against all commercial odds, motivated by his enthusiasm for the spirit of the play. His 'war list' also included Hodson's *Grey Dawn – Red Night* and Gordon Stowell's *The History of Button Hill*, two of the most remarkable war novels of the late 1920s; Pamela Hinkson's *The Ladies' Road* was another bestseller.[33] Commercial and moral intent were inseparable elements of this fiction, and in the inter-war years literary sale and instruction contracted an easy and fruitful alliance.

3 The Testimony of the 'Old Guard'

The average age of these writers in 1914, out of the ninety available, was just under 33. But if we take into consideration the writers of 1919 and those of 1929–1930, the average age shows a generational divergence. For the writers whose age could be determined,[34] the average was just under 38 in 1919, and just over 23 in 1929–1930. This difference reflects the proportion of writers who had served in the war: six for the first period, twenty-one for the second. Apart from Escott Lynn's rather juvenile stories,[35] all the narratives focusing on the ordeal of the soldier at the front were written by men who had undergone the same experience, and for many of them it took years to be able to handle closely such a traumatic memory. Frederick Sleath, A. P. Herbert and J .B. Morton, all young men, were notable exceptions; all three published novels in the first year after the end of the war describing life in the trenches.

A great number of older men started offering their assessments of the war as soon as it was over. Much as been written about the generational conflict of the post-war world. Yet it is also important to acknowledge the process of understanding of the younger generation's ordeal which is reflected in the 'middle-aged' fiction of the first few years after the Armistice. At the age of 48, Harold Begbie, whose obituary in the *Times* was headed 'A Social and Political Enthusiast',[36] presented in 1919 the first sympathetic account of a pacifist's choice. In the same year, John Buchan produced the successful thriller *Mr. Standfast*, while Jerome Klapka Jerome, Robert Hichens and Galsworthy, and John Locke at the beginning of 1920, all established 'old men' of the world of letters, offered their fictional interpretations of the experience of war.

William Babington Maxwell was the only older novelist with first-hand experience of the trenches, having gone to France at the age of 49 as a subaltern in the 10th Royal Fusiliers. At the end of 1916 he became General Barnes's aide-de-camp.[37] His war experience gave him a new lease on youth and made him profoundly appreciative of the role assumed by young men. This Victorian man from a wealthy family became the intimate protagonist of a twentieth-century tragedy, and emerged a champion of youth, bitterly condemning the old, idle class to which he had belonged, and which he forfeited through the war: 'I, too, dread the stupid old men. I dread the middle-aged men who are merely politicians and statesmen. I dread all men who had not personal experience of the last war.'[38]

War had been traumatic for the older generation, who witnessed powerlessly the death of the young on a massive scale. Buchan believed that middle-aged men in the war were those who suffered most grievously, partly because of the terrible physical strain, but above all because 'they saw the shattering of the house of life they had made for themselves, and despaired of building another.' Two short wartime holidays reassured him. One in the Cotswolds convinced him that 'the essential England could not perish. This field had sent bowmen to Agincourt; down that hill Rupert's men, swaying in their saddles, had fled after Naseby; this village had given Wellington a general; and from another parson's son had helped to turn the tide in the Indian Mutiny.' During the second trip, in his Tweedside hills, he engaged in conversation with a shepherd's wife who had sent four sons to the war.

> I felt that Jock and Jamie and Tom and Davie would return and would take up their shepherd's trade as dutifully as their father. Samothrace and Murmansk and Palestine would be absorbed, as Otterburn and Flodden had been, into the ageless world of the pastoral.
>
> It was our freedom from melodrama, our national gift of meiosis, our steady nerves which convinced me that we could build up the world anew and embody in it the best of the old. And something more – our power of domesticating the strange and terrible and making portents homely.[39]

This preoccupation with rebuilding is crucial to understanding the history of the memory of war. The vivid concern of middle-aged writers caused them to formulate solutions which set a pattern for later novels: the ever-stabilizing process of tradition, the land of England (and this from a Scottish writer) as the locus of unchanging meaning, and profound trust in the English character.

The senior member of the 'Old Guard', Thomas Henry Hall Caine, in 1923 wrote a parable of tragic love between an English woman and a German man. Such a statement from Caine was something of an event and received a vivid editorial encomium from Newman Flower. The latter praised the perceptual balance which is characteristic of so many middlebrow novels: the capacity for belief within the waste and cruelty of war:

> That the Great War has been in vain, that so much sacrifice, so much heroism, so many brave young lives have been thrown away, he would not for one moment say, being sure that in the long review of a mysterious Providence all these must have their place.

As a writer Caine could convey this essence, no matter how unpopular. A public re-presentation of the relationship between the English and the Germans, so soon after the War, implied a serious commitment from the elderly author. Flower commended Caine for staking himself 'on so bold a protestation on behalf of the things which are unseen...'[40]

Jerome Klapka Jerome and William Locke, known for their purely entertaining novels, were prompted by the war to write serious novels about the experience: *All Roads Lead to Calvary* (1919) and *The House of Baltazar* (1920) sounded a startlingly dissonant note in their literary careers. One reviewer of *Mountebank* judged Locke as one of 'that small band of authors who have gained more than they have lost from the experience of the war...he seems to have acquired a truer sense of values...'[41]

A striking example of the intervention by 'outsiders' into the dialogue about war was Philip Gibbs's introduction to his brother's *The Grey Wave* (1920), a non-fictional account of the subaltern's life and a denunciation of the narrow-minded leadership in war. In the same year he published his own war account, *Realities of War*, which Graham Seton, in his review of war literature, called 'a book which, though equalled, has not been excelled.'[42]

The tentacular process of information about the experience of the soldier is reflected in women's novels that attempted to fill the gap between the feminine and masculine memory of war. As we shall see, Phyllis Bottome's *A Servant of Reality* (1919) was a perceptive account of the soldier's ordeal as an encounter with a deeper kind of reality. In her autobiography *The Goal*, she gave an example of her own education about the men's war. While seeing her husband off to France at the Folkestone docks, she witnessed the hysterical fear of an officer who had to be led away in a pitiful state of convulsive collapse. The reaction of the small group watching the scene was initially hostile, with one woman crying out her disgust, but when Bottome pointed out that he would have to come back and that it would be all the harder for him the crowd suddenly fell silent.

It was as if those agonizing sobs and cries had created a new and more terrible knowledge of what our men were facing, a knowledge in which we could take no part except our sorrow.

Presently the broken officer came back. No one made a sound as he passed through the gates, his head bowed, his face red with shame; but after he had gone through there was a curious sigh that seemed to come from all of us together. It was as if his shame had been taken from him: and had become ours.[43]

This was a powerful moment of understanding, as it ventured briefly into the territory of fear, that most traumatic area of the soldier's identity.

4 Fiction as History

In *Gallipoli Memories*, Compton Mackenzie recalls a conversation he had with Patrick Shaw-Stewart, also from Oxford, one night soon after the failure of the Suvla landing. Mackenzie told his friend that he had been up to Oxford at the end of July 1914 to check a reference, and had walked in the 'emptiness of the Long Vacation, presage of a longer emptiness which would never again be filled in quite the same old way...' Cyril Bailey, a Fellow-Tutor of Balliol, had later confirmed this feeling by writing to him that *Sinister Street*, Mackenzie's very successful novel published in two volumes in 1913 and 1914, 'marked the end of an epoch and that Oxford could never be the same again.' 'But if six nights ago things had gone differently at Suvla,' Mackenzie said to his friend, 'the continuity might not have been broken. But now it must be, for the whole spirit of the war will change as it goes on...' Shaw-Stewart agreed with him. Mackenzie follows this poignant memory with a bitter denunciation of modern literary attitudes to war: 'And I have lived to hear Rupert Brooke sneered at for a romantic by the prematurely weaned young suckling-pigs of the next generation.' He commends the pages written by another 'RND survivor', Douglas Jerrold, at the end of his *The Hawke Battalion*, to the people who are 'as much nauseated as I am by the Teutonic hysteria which is the intellectual vogue of 1929.'[44]

What is most striking about this passage is the process of reconstruction of memory, in which literary artifacts act as historical landmarks, their significance indistinguishable from that of the events and attitudes they portray. Written at the time of the war novel boom, Mackenzie's passage looks back at a reflective, evaluative moment within the author's war experience, at the emotional turning point when he recognized the inevitability of a lengthy conflict which would cause a profound break with the past. The 'continuity' was gone. The world of 1914 was separated from the future by a chasm of violence and horror, and the rent was marked at both ends by an Oxford novel and the war literature of 1929.

Dangerfield found *Sinister Street* a text revealing of its time,[45] a judgment that Christopher Stone extended to all of Mackenzie's works:

> I firmly believe than when the history of the times comes to be written by literary historians, they will find the picture of the last thirty years more faithfully and brilliantly recorded in the writings of Compton Mackenzie than in those of any other contemporary author...[46]

Fiction about the war inevitably led to wider historical considerations. Kunitz describes Sylvia Thompson as a writer who laid no claims to being any more than a good escape novelist, whose characters had little interest in issues outside the confines of their private world.[47] Yet one cannot find a more eloquent example of the close interaction between fiction and history, between creative activity and social intent, than the foreword Thompson wrote to her very successful novel *Hounds of Spring*. She admitted that her aim of dealing with the 'essential tendencies' of the 1914–24 decade, when it was still so close, was perhaps 'presumptuous', as was her belief that her characters were 'in their infinitesimal way the human atoms which fused by Events, go to make that subtle mass of stuff that solidifies into History.' The author invoked the authority of the Regius Professor of History at Cambridge, Sir John Seeley, to justify the appearance of her romantic narrative.

> Modern History is a subject to which neither beginning nor end can be assigned. No beginning because the dense web of the fortunes of man is woven without a void; because in society as in nature the structure is continuous and we can trace things back uninterruptedly...No end because...history made and history making are scientifically inseparable and separately unmeaning.[48]

Sometimes the blurring of fiction and history was intentional. Terence Mahon's *Cold Feet* was published as a soldier's confession *edited*, not composed, by Mahon; in Bennet Copplestone's *The Last of the Grenvilles* the author himself, referred to as Copplestone, tells the story of his friend Dickie Grenville. Arnold Bennett's protagonist of *Lord Raingo* was based on D.A. Thomas, Lord Rhondda. It contained unmistakable portraits of Lloyd George and Winston Churchill, and caused much debate in the papers about the right of an author to depict so blatantly actual political figures.[49] Bernard Newman's *Spy* (1935) was a study of the nervous collapse of Ludendorff in September 1918. It indicated that a British officer, Newman himself, had made his way into Ludendorff's staff and had endeavoured to depress him psychologically. Newman cited in the book a previous maxim of his – 'the mind of the enemy commander is the basic target in war' – which prompted many enquiries as to whether the story was fictional or not.[50] Basil Liddell Hart was so impressed with Newman's account of a quicker outcome of war under more imaginative command in the novel *The Cavalry Went Through* (1930) that he included it for years in the reading he prescribed for his military students.[51] *Not So Quiet on the Western Front* (1930) and *Women of the Aftermath* (1933) by Helen Zenna Smith (whose real name was Evadne Price) created a deliberate ambiguity by giving the protagonist the same name as the author, although the latter had never been an ambulance driver in France.

A few writers could pinpoint the source or the time of their moment of imaginative revelation. According to Oliver Madox Hueffer, the 'germ' of his novel *"Cousins German"* was born while he listened to soldiers' talk in the trenches of Bois Grenier, near Armentières, in the summer of 1916. They were speaking of spying in high quarters. One or two months later, in the rest billets at Puchevilliers (behind the Somme line and known as Pushville), this notion matured into an idea for a novel.[52] Edward John Thompson's moving elegy *In Araby Orion* was inspired by the ordeal of a 'comrade' of his hit in the spine on 30 April 1918 in Jordan and having to be left to die;[53] the idea of Wilfrid Ewart's *The Way of Revelation* originated from discussions about Stephen McKenna's *Sonia*, which Stephen Graham 'found lying in the mud' at the front.[54] A. P. Herbert's *The Secret Battle* was based on the court-martial and execution of a sub-lieutenant in the Nelson Battalion (Royal Naval Division) after the attack on Beaucourt in November 1916.[55] Graham Seton's *W Plan*, his first novel, was conceived during 'a period of sub-consciousness' (following a gas attack) after the battle of Meteren on the 14th April, 1918,[56] when the realization of the German success impressed itself on his imagination and was reproduced later in the novel.[57] Comparing in his autobiography this experience and its fictional offspring, Seton mused:

> It is said that truth is stranger than fiction. What is truth? What is fiction? How much hallucination and mere make-believe? Who in telling the truth does not cloak it under the guise of fiction, or in telling the tale will not dress the story in all the trappings of truth?[58]

Purcell stated in the preface to his novel *The Further Side of No Man's Land* that he had chosen fiction to narrate his own war experience because he 'had found that a narrative, pure and simple, progressing carefully step by step, was liable to be stilted and unreal.'[59]

The portrayal of the pacifist who is the protagonist of Begbie's *Mr. Sterling Sticks It Out* was based on Stephen Hobhouse (1881–1961), who went to prison after refusing to accept alternative military work in the Friends Ambulance Unit. The imprisonment of this absolutist conscientious objector, a Quaker who on his religious conversion had renounced his inheritance in order to work in the slums of London's East End, had great public repercussions.[60] As Begbie explained in the preface to his novel, he was prompted to write this work in the winter of 1917 by the outrage he felt at the treatment of Quakers and Tolstoyans. The Press Bureau vetoed the publication of the book until after the end of the war. Sir Frank Swettenham, together with E. T. Cook in charge of vetting anti-patriotic propaganda, explained to the publisher that even though many pamphlets had been issued about the treatment of conscientious objectors, there was greater cause of concern about the work of a popular writer.[61]

On one occasion fiction turned out to be almost history by the trick of a posthumous coincidence. Cecil Roberts wrote *Spears Against Us* at the end of 1931. Shortly after publication, a British officer who had fought on the Austrian front sent him a letter containing photographs he had found scattered around the corpse of a young Austrian officer. In those photographs Roberts 'saw' his entirely imaginary hero Karl Edelstein, on the terrace of his castle, surrounded by his mother and two sisters, just as in the novel; the other photographs could also have served as illustrations for his fictional narrative. This officer had died only a few miles from Monte Tofana, where Karl met his death, within seven days of his fictional *alter ego*; the address on a postcard was only a few miles from the valley Roberts had chosen for his *Schloss* Edelstein. The novel had been inspired by a visit to Austria in 1928 during which Roberts had seen the terrible consequences of defeat and the degradation of the Austrian aristocracy. Just beyond the Italian frontier, in Cortina, he had visited a military cemetery where all the names were Austrian; men who had died young now resting forever in a foreign land. Later he wondered whether that moment of intense empathy with the dead had been the cause of the coincidence revealed several years later: 'Did I imagine my story, or in the intensity of concentration is there evoked a higher intelligence that uses one as a receptive instrument?'[62]

For Warwick Deeping, who before the war had written historical romances set in the Middle Ages, the war was the creative catalyst which made of him a very successful narrator of contemporary life. In a prefatory Author's Note to his *No Hero – This* he states that in a 'human record' in which fiction and reality were meshed together 'an author must feel profoundly responsible for the memories of others.'[63] Such a responsibility towards their audiences was expressed by these writers through a social and moral exegesis of the reality they fictionalized.

5 Writing with a Purpose

In *The English Novel of To-Day* Gerald Gould began his discussion of the war novel with McKenna's *Sonia* and described it as 'the outstanding example of a type, a species within the genus of the contemporary biographic. The species is sociological; it seeks to catch the time-spirit on the wing.'[64] Another reviewer spelled out the historical function performed by Stephen MacKenna's novels:

> The future historian, when he sets himself to describe the social features and characteristics of the present generation, will find his best and most realistic material in the notable fiction of our own time. It will tell him a good deal more than the dry facts and base statistics which he will find in the more orthodox sources of information. All this is particularly true of the Great War and the years following.[65]

Middlebrow novelists did not set out to exploit the tastes of the reading public, but they often succeeded in satisfying them. It is worth listening to Leonard Woolf's sympathetic and perceptive description of a bestseller:

> ...most contemporary best-sellers are written by second-class writers whose psychological brew contains a touch of naivety, a touch of sentimentality, the story-telling gift, and a mysterious sympathy with the day-dreams of ordinary people.[66]

War novels were informed by a didactic dialogue with their readers. 'This is a novel with a purpose', wrote the *Athenaeum* reviewer of A. M. N. Jenkin's *The End of a Dream*,[67] in a familiar form of announcement for these novels. Blatant topicality could be a cause of complaint: 'we are weary of novels with a purpose'[68] was a frequent cry, but it did not stop their flow. The expression 'novel with a purpose' was popularized by the Irish novelist and statesman Justin McCarthy (father of Justin Huntly McCarthy, author of *Nurse Benson*). In the article 'Novels with a Purpose', written for the *Westminster Review* in July 1864, McCarthy posited the question whether the enormous influence of novelists could be harnessed to a specific social purpose: 'Is it given to the novelist to accomplish any definite social object, to solve, or even help towards the solution of any vexed social question?' His answer was that a great work of fiction could not be motivated by a message or moral.[69]

Jerome's *All Roads Lead to Calvary* was such an obvious vehicle for the expression of his ideas on social morality that the reviewer in the *Times Literary Supplement* commented that its 'characters are little more than mouthpieces in a succession of symposia...whatever one may think of it as a novel, it would have made a very good lecture...'[70] Even O'Donovan's satire *How They Did It* was, correctly, judged as another 'novel with a purpose' which suffered from the 'defects of its good intentions.'[71] As for Philip Gibbs's *Unchanging Quest*, the *Times Literary Supplement* judged it to be 'not much of a novel as a 'History of Our Own Times' in the guise of fiction.'[72]

The social intent of these writers' imaginative works found even fuller expression in their autobiographies, and, in unfiltered form, in their studies of contemporary England, of literature, of society in general, and of war. In *My England*, Shanks took a truly comprehensive look at the country, its history, literature, institutions and leisure life, going right back to Roman times. The work is prefaced by a quotation by Georges Sorel: 'J'engage avec mon lecteur une conversation familière; je lui sommets des idées et je le force à penser à son tour, pour me corriger et pour me completer...' To make the dialogue with his readers as unambiguous as possible Shanks presented his credentials with a photograph and a short autobiographical note explaining that the work was the result of 'forty odd years partly spent in trying to present to myself in an understandable form the country and the community to which I belong.'[73]

This motley group of non-fictional works testifies to the writers' determination to communicate edifying reflections to their readers. The title of W. B. Maxwell's novel *A Man and His Lesson* reflects what he believed to be the role of the writer: that of the deliverer of a message. In his autobiography he wrote:

> [The writer] has derived a lesson from life and he wants to communicate it, he has found a key to open locked doors, he has seen a glimpse of the only safe road to human progress. Henceforth it is in his message. It need not be stated explicitly. Indeed it rarely is. But it is insinuated into everything he writes. It breathes through every page. It is the spirit and stimulation of his entire work.[74]

The ex-businessman Gilbert Frankau, who acquired considerable wealth from the profits of his novels, throughout his career considered himself motivated by idealism. He defined his reasons for writing the reactionary *Masterson* (1926), a slice of contemporary English life, in terms of the ideal of selflessness bequeathed to him by his war experience:

> Mere royalties were not the main urge. The one white flame had flared again, the one altruistic dream – stimulated maybe by a night in Ypres, where men still disinterred the bodies from the blood-soaked soil – had returned to me while I corrected and recorrected those proofs.

The novel sold 50,000 copies. 'Quietists' called him a 'stunt merchant', 'leftists' accused him of being a 'moneygrubber'. In fact, he asserted, his role in writing the novel was that of an advertising agent for patriotism and freedom of the individual: 'The stunt merchant, for all his stunting, had a creed.'[75]

Another author looking back on his writing career, Vernon Bartlett, traced his 'damned reforming zeal' to the Paris Peace Conference in 1919, which he had attended as correspondent for Reuter's news agency; ever since then his writing had been 'so topical that it was out of date before it could be published.'[76] For Christopher Stone the motivation for writing the novel *The Valley of Indecision*

(1920) was the same that drove the returned soldier, protagonist of his tale, to preach the message he had learnt at the front. 'Over and over again I was forced to wonder why I was spared when others were not...'[77], he revealed in his autobiography. The answer he reached was to disseminate an important message. Stone's social preaching was overt; he introduced the chapter of reminiscences about his radio experience by stating that it was 'quite time that I turned aside from the temptation to reform the world on paper...'[78]

The lessons of war were never far away in these writers' social commentaries. In a truly social presentation of his life, Ronald Gurner wrote an autobiography told solely through the perspective of his teaching experience. At the very outset of his recollections he rejected a Freudian interpretation of his childhood; the simpler truth was the formation of 'that sentiment and idealism of which my vision of the world about me was always coloured.' When he came to the war years he explained why he needed to include them in a history of teaching: 'No one, a schoolmaster least of all, emerged from this war as he entered it'. As all his views on education and on life were 'dominated by that Himalaya of experience', he thought it valuable to recount that 'titanic struggle of life with circumstance' to a younger generation.[79] Back at Marlborough after the war, he compared the 'oleaginous' ideals, be they patriotic or pacifist, of the 'bloodless' stay-at-home schoolmasters to the soldiers' conversations, where 'language was less correct but the contact with life immeasurably greater.' A consequence of this keener sense of reality was his effort to encourage concrete knowledge of the world by starting in the school a society for the study of modern problems.[80]

James Lansdale Hodson, in his *Our Two Englands* (1936), began and ended his analysis by filtering it through two war images. Writing about the unemployed in Cardiff, he remembered how during the Great War they used to joke that 'The first seven years'll be the worst'; on the Pierhead they were using another war expression: 'It's hell.' He concluded by pointing out that the employed were showing the same lack of understanding about the unemployed which the civilians had displayed about the soldiers during the war.[81] Philip Gibbs in the late 1930s posited that the problem of unemployment could have been much helped by the Labour Government organizing the unemployed in 'service battalions' for work, with 'something of the spirit of those who once went singing "Pack up your troubles in your Old Kit Bag..."'[82] In another, similar, social account he described the English industrial situation under the title 'The Front Line of Industry.' The south was 'behind the line', whereas the north represented the 'front-line trenches' and had the 'heaviest casualties.' The landscape of machinery was terrible, 'but not without infernal grandeur.' The way to deal with the problems of this battle was, of course, with the right spirit: humour, courage and the refusal to despair.[83]

Rebuilding – on the same foundations – meant taking into consideration the material with which the old building was made, examining new materials, mapping out the changes; above all, keeping alive the vision of the beauty and strength of the old edifice. Writing about the experience of war necessarily involved the authors in an act of reflection about grave and great matters which too often transcended the power of their literary skills, but which were matched by their earnest enterprise of singling out and re-presenting what was truly valuable in the national life.

Englishness was described anew, in a painstaking imaginative process of discussing the very fibre of the nation. The project of delineation of national identity was complicated by the myth of the English pre-war 'character.' The historian Medlicott still shared in this nostalgia in 1967.

> The year 1914 is roughly the point at which it ceased to be fun to be an Englishman. The racy types, the cheerful Cockneys, the brassy music hall dames, the superb, imperturbable policemen, professors and schoolmasters of an awful, Olympian authority, the great hostesses, the proud clerics: all these people, so self-assured and so dissimilar, had in common during the prewar generations an unreflective belief in themselves as Englishmen or women. It had long been familiar; Charles Dickens has rightly castigated its more arrogant and Podsnappery forms. It had a late flowering among the golden youth of Edwardian England; it went overseas and was buried for ever with the best of Kitchener's army.

The after-war years, by contrast, were a 'lugubrious' age, when self-assurance was replaced by self-consciousness.[84]

Before the war Stacy Aumonier worked as an actor and gave recitals of character sketches of ordinary people. The war interrupted the favourable reception of his act by setting 'his gallery of characters tottering and falling' At the end of 1919 Aumonier told an interviewer that he '... found that certain familiar types which had been thoroughly modern when he first presented them, seemed to grow suddenly old-fashioned; in a year or two many of them seemed quite obsolete.' Together with everything else 'character was in the melting-pot.'[85] The sense of loss of a composite identity made of definite types was countered by inter-war middlebrow writers with the attempt to reconstruct a recognizable model of national character.

Gilbert Cannan ended his *Pugs and Peacocks* (1921) with the note that this novel was part of a series in which he would examine the consequences of the war 'not from any political or sociological point of view, but to discover the light thrown upon human nature by abnormal events and conditions.'[86] The war had reshuffled conventional notions and easy assumptions: they now had to be restructured, a job the middlebrow writers tackled with indefatigable diligence. The reassertion of an immanent, enduring British character was the function that Graham Seton attributed to war histories: they were 'proof that British racial character, whether of the town or of the countryside, nobly upheld the traditions of our race.'[87] 'The Elizabethan spirit' – from a time when England became a world power, individual talent flourished, and literary figures were heroic – was often invoked as a point of evaluative reference. Another important model was the more recent Empire. For the ultimate middlebrow spokesman, Philip Gibbs, who wrote incessantly on contemporary social issues, all analysis came back to the 'spirit of England', and the basic worth of the Empire, where such spirit was tried.[88] Gibbs' role as social educator began early. At twenty-one he worked with Cassell and was in charge of the production of school textbooks; he himself wrote *Founders of the Empire*, which was used as a school textbook for several years.[89]

6 The English Memory of War

Several of the novels of the war boom were compared by reviewers to Remarque's *All Quiet On The Western Front*, in snippets of judgment that help to demarcate the *English* memory of war. One of the most memorable novels of the literature of separation of the late 1920s was *Grey Dawn – Red Night* (1929) by James Lansdale Hodson, journalist, novelist, social commentator, travel writer, playwright, and the author in 1955 of a novel explaining the final involvement in the Second World War of a survivor of the Great War turned pacifist.[90] His 1929 novel, like much of the English literature of the war boom, contains not only an overt indictment of war but also an English view of war that could be easily contrasted with the shrill, romantic condemnation of *All Quiet on the Western Front*.[91] Reviewers praised *Grey Dawn – Red Night* in terms stressing its English quality: 'Worthy many such books as All Quiet' (*Daily News*) and '...worth all the German novels...a permanent addition to English literature'(*Morning Post*).[92] The reviewer of W.F.Morris's *Bretherton* in *The Sketch* found it 'pleasant to have a good war-story written...in the English language by an Englishman, instead of a translation of a German soldier's agonies in the trenches.'[93]

In the introduction to *"Cousins German"*, Oliver Madox Hueffer explained that he had decided to get ready for publication what he had written some time before because of his surprise to hear from contemporary literature 'what a set of blackguard degenerates' soldiers had been. He remembered those years differently. As far as this author was concerned, he was sure that

> ...the years of war were among the happiest, and not perhaps the least useful of his life; that he made more friends and more lovable; that he met worthier men, filled with nobler ideals, than he has ever met since; that, in fact, it was the highest guerdon life could offer to be one of such a gallant company doing real – even if mistaken things – from a noble purpose; that it would not have been a very bad thing, had fate so wished it, to die with and among them.[94]

Before Remarque's book appeared, John Brophy's *Bitter End* (1927) presented, as the title itself reveals, a painful recollection of war. For a correct assessment of his novel one needs to take into account the breadth of Brophy's expression of his memory of war: he edited a prose anthology of the war, a collection of soldiers' songs and slang, and a history of the war, all three with glossaries.[95] This concern with the linguistic, literary, and historical testimony of war reveals a social project of memory which is in control of the meanings and issues involved. In the introduction to his *The Soldier's War*, Brophy described as counter-productive the books – especially the German ones – that only spoke of the 'monotony and misery' of war: as men were asserting all the time in letters to newspapers and in books, they had enjoyed the war.

> It is not a concession for a convinced pacifist to admit that this is true – provided the proper qualifications are made. The War gave to the civilian turned soldier health, adventure (intermittently), a sense of a tangible and valuable task, profound emotional experiences, and comradeship. All these, in the Aristotelian and the ordinary sense of the word, he enjoyed. But these zests are not inseparable from war; if peace denies them to the run of men, then that is a defect of our civilisation that needs remedy. But the deaths of millions, the sufferings of the maimed, bereavements and the anguish of uncertainty, the destruction of property, the loosing of greed, hypocrisy, and selfishness, the shattering of nerves – these are too big a price to pay for a few enjoyments otherwise obtainable. The human – as well as the economic – balance of war is heavily on the debit side.[96]

The measured tones of this condemnation of war, the reasoned consideration of its remembered advantages, and the relation of the argument to the state of civilization are typical elements of the most extreme indictments of war in English middlebrow critique (and the above passage, written in 1929 at the height of anti-war expression, had to be worded strongly).

With his war novels Ian Hay made the only effort in his inter-war career at writing serious works.[97] The author of the wartime bestseller *The First Hundred Thousand*, he wrote in 1921 *The Willing Horse*, an apologia for duty and the moral imperatives dictated by tradition. He also wrote an account of an 'Empire-wide Pilgrimage' to the battlefields and cemeteries of the eastern Mediterranean, which he undertook 'to recapture an ancient and not altogether regretful memory.' The society in charge of this expedition chose for its name that of the 'son of Consolation', St Barnabas. The haste to inscribe the memory of war within the powerful framework of tradition led him to paradoxically base an appeal to 'hope for the future' on the inspiration drawn from locations of massacre: 'The mere fact that to look back upon the past usually does inspire hope for the future is one of the great and sustaining facts of human life. You realize that fact to the full as you stand upon the beaches of Gallipoli.'[98]

James Lansdale Hodson in 1919 wrote a non-fictional war book, *The Soul of a Soldier*, which was dedicated, as was his novel ten years later, to the 3rd Public Schools Battalion. In the preface he referred to the 'simple glory' of those men, 'the greatness and nobility of cause, the straightness and simpleness of the issue...'[99] In this ardent work death itself is transfigured by the cause, and becomes more of a 'consummation' than a 'cutting off of the human life'. Previously the conception of death had been distorted until it was 'all mortuary and no romance, all horror and no glory.' To die now was to die 'in noble company', with Charles Lister, Raymond Asquith, William Redmond, A. F. Wilding, A. G. Pulton, Ivan Heald, Julian Grenfell, Rupert Brooke, Dixon Scott, and Harold Chapin.[100] The contrast in rhetorical pitch between the book and the novel underlines their profound social nature as they adapted their emphases and language to the cultural moods prevalent at different times. What would have sounded like subversive criticism in 1919 was the norm ten years later.

Another example of discrepancy between an early eye-witness account and a novel of the late 1920s is that between Vernon Bartlett's *Mud and Khaki* and *No Man's Land*. The first, a compilation of short press articles published in 1917, stressed the valour of the soldier, his humour, and the concern not to hinder his effort – 'Heaven forbid that, by telling the horrors of war, the writers of books should make pessimists of those at home!';[101] the second emphasized the horror of war and the spiritual dimension of the soldier's ordeal. One was reporting and one was fiction: or was it the other way around? In one of his autobiographies/histories of the twentieth century Bartlett remembered that, having been given the job of composing war sketches, he could not bring himself to interview survivors in hospital and, writing in the park near a Clapham military hospital, would make up stories.[102]

7 'Morality' as a Strategy of Social and Political Renewal

An important element of cultural evidence is that 'morality' which E. P. Thompson has described as the way in which people 'experience' their history, not merely as ideas but as *feeling*, and 'handle their feelings within their culture'.[103] These writers sifted their feelings about the war and the experience of their own times to produce a moral synthesis whose pivot was the nobility of individual choice and action.

Albert Kinross in an early autobiography (told via the history of his interest in cricket) described his discovery of the artistic significance of the manifestation of courage. In 1893, after reading Taine's *History of English Literature*, he realized that the very essence of great literature was courage in the 'moral' sense.

An author, I discovered, need not be a soft wretch full of wind and wheezes. Sir Philip Sidney had died at Zutphen, Ben Jonson had slain a champion in level combat, Byron had died for his adopted country; there were brave soldiers and gallant sailors by the score among my new-found friends. Even Milton had been the equivalent of a Cromwellian staff officer.

When he lay wounded in hospital during the war, hospital staff used to remark with dismay that he seemed 'completely happy.' He was.

One could not explain that one was a British Author...that one had read Taine, and decided that to be a complete writer one must be a complete Englishman or Frenchman or German, and that one must know Death at first hand, and God and the Devil, and have no fear of any one of them.[104]

The moral imperative unfolded by these writers, who conducted their own psychological analyses, precluded what they understood as the 'clever' (an adjective often levelled as an insult) modern creed of psychoanalysis. Phyllis Bottome's interest in Alfred Adler, whose biography she wrote, is explained by his moral stance: 'Adler taught that all neurosis is an attempt to escape from personal responsibility; and that courage is the health of the soul.'[105]

Literary idealism had enjoyed great vogue in the later Victorian period with the sensational success of Mrs Humphry Ward's *Robert Elsmere* (1888), of which Gladstone wrote the review 'Robert Elsmere and the Battle of Belief' in the *Nineteenth Century*.[106] The novel discussed the religious doubts of a minister who in the end gives up the priesthood to help the London poor. This change is brought about by the influence of a philosopher, an obvious portrait of the philosopher T. H. Green, whose idealism countered utilitarianism and dogma with a divinely inspired humanism.[107] Mrs Ward advocated in her work a Unitarian idealistic religion that would achieve progress by substituting for an outdated concept of Christianity a more vibrant and committed one. This novel supplied a model which was repeated often in inter-war middlebrow fiction; the reappraisal of a man's religious beliefs in the light of wider social reconsiderations. Mrs Humphry Ward's war experience included becoming involved in propaganda to encourage American participation and being the first 'official woman war correspondent.'[108] She visited munitions factories and the fleet (in the Firth of Cromarty), went to France, and wrote a trilogy about the war.[109] She was forcefully struck by classes working side by side and by women taking up all kinds of work, but continued opposing women's suffrage. Social change had to be dignified by its insertion in an idealistic model of human redemption:

There will be a new wind blowing through England when this war is done....Men and women, employers and employed, shaken perforce out of their old grooves, will look at each other surely with new eyes, in a world which has not been steeped for nothing in effort and sacrifice, in common griefs and a common passion of will.[110]

Her final comment on the war experience was a novel, *Cousin Philip* (1919), which stressed the exemplary role of the aristocrat, and had the niece of Lord Buntingford working as an ambulance driver in France.

Another woman writer committed to social reform inspired both by religion and by a reaction to Victorian rigidity of values was 'Lucas Malet' (Mary St. Leger Harrison, daughter of Charles Kingsley). A convert to Catholicism, she was 71 years old when she published her thoughtful novel about the consequences of war on young people's attitudes, *The Survivors* (1923). This sympathetic depiction by an elderly woman of the demand by the young for new, more genuine values is one of the most interesting examples of fictional intervention in the post-war social dialogue.

The brand of social idealism which Mrs Humphry Ward was the first to propagandize in fiction influenced even the work of the active suffragette and 'modern' writer May Sinclair. Her role in literature was a distinctive one in the transition between Victorian and modern writing, as she made use of different strands from both towards a new form of fiction. Reputed to be, like Dorothy Richardson, one of the modernist writers, she admired Ezra Pound, James Joyce and T. S. Eliot and wrote on psychology, philosophy and modern literature. Her study of psychoanalysis, however, was linked to the consciousness of a divinely ordained reality, within which she saw the fulfillment of the individual. Her most extensive theoretical writings, *A Defence of Idealism: Some Questions and Conclusions* (1917) and *The New Idealism* (1922), were firmly based on T. H. Green's philosophy.[111] From the mid-1920s she abandoned modern techniques and wrote rather sentimental and conventionally structured novels.[112]

An experience she had while at the Belgian front strengthened her idealistic beliefs. She spent seventeen days in September and October 1914 with the Motor Field Ambulance Corps, organized by Dr. Hector Munro, with twelve other volunteers. In her memoirs she described a mystical experience she had while walking along a road with two Belgian stretcher-bearers, looking for wounded men. She felt that the stretch of road, the tall trees, and the turn it made represented a 'superior Reality', and was aware of the 'possibility of an ensuing agony and horror as of something unreal and transitory that would break through the peace of it in a merely episodical manner'; this sensation intensified to the point of becoming 'ecstasy.'[113] Cicely Mary Hamilton relates a similar wartime experience in her autobiography. Several times while working at the Scottish Hospital in France she sensed 'ghosts'. Her brother Raymond 'came to her' six months after his death. On 18 September 1918, his birthday, she felt his hand through her hair as she knelt praying by the side of a beloved aunt who was dying. Hamilton maintained that the war provided her with a religious certainty which detached her from politics.[114]

The social judgments and analyses of these writers rested very often on spiritual tenets. The appeal was to a religion recast in a more authentic light, to a faith that takes into account the reality and truths learnt in the war. Cecil Roberts in 1931 wrote that it was not surprising that 'God, as an institution, died in the Great War', when the cross of sacrifice had been used to justify so much waste of lives. Yet his account of the armies crossing the Rhine, with Plumer standing at attention for two hours across the Hohenzollern Bridge in Cologne, ended with the memory of his wish, at that sight, for a new faith to emerge from the carnage.[115]

Truth taught by the ordeal of war and spiritual truth were often interchangeable notions, as they made reference to the same myths. Foremost among them was the myth of access to truth through suffering and constant closeness to death. In the introduction to his brother's *The Grey Wave* Philip Gibbs discussed the book's denunciation of the futility of war, its profound bitterness, and the accusation against the Old Men who had traded lives for their own interests. In spite of all this, he was still able to see hope because the young men 'who had stood daily for five years upon the edge of eternity' had gazed into the 'eyes of Truth'. Switching from 'they' to 'we' in a fervour of empathy, he concluded:

> We have proved the power within us because the routine of the world's great sin has established this surprising paradox, that we daily gave evidence of heroism, tolerance, kindliness, brotherhood.
>
> Shall we, like Peter who denied Christ, refuse to recognize the greatness within ourselves? We found truth while we practised war. Let us carry it to the practice of peace.[116]

Often the nature of modern warfare was expressed as 'waiting', a notion which implied at the same time the sacrifice of expecting inexorable horror and the suspension into a different historical time, encompassing the present and skirting eternity. For a close observer such as the war correspondent Cecil Roberts, waiting during the war was linked to tragic fate. After visiting the fleet he described his last glance at it:

> Behind me, slowly wrapped round with silence and darkness, lay the might of a great Empire waiting, waiting, waiting through the hour of destiny. So in the past had waited Babylon, Greece, and Rome, before the inscrutable face of Fate. Truly,

Life is a watch or a vision
Between a sleep and a sleep.[117]

The poem inspiring Edward Noble's title for his war novel *Moving Waters* (1927) was Keats's 'Bright Star, would I were stedfast as thou art' (1819):

...watching, with eternal lids apart,
Like Nature's patient, sleepless Eremite,
The moving waters at their priest-like task
Of pure ablution round earth's human shores.

By such lofty allusions modern warfare and its time element were incorporated into another, ancient rhythm of civilization. It is a short step from this conception of waiting to its inscription into time as meaning and tradition.[118]

To understand the novel *Simon Called Peter* (1921) one must read the introduction Robert Keable wrote to his memoirs. These twelve pages ringing with a sense of mission came under the heading "Standing By". This title, he explained, was based on the act of 'standing by' during the war, so familiar to the soldiers in the trenches waiting for orders, and to the chaplains waiting on the sidelines. These long stretches of life on stand-by meant time for the men to be witnesses of a great event. Keable, as well as many other writers, felt compelled, after witnessing 'the agony and heroism of conflict' and the threat to civilization, 'in some measure to attempt to imprison the *spirit of the thing*...'[119]

War fiction offers endless variations of men and women examining consciously the churning up of history and of their lives. The solitude as well as the conversations of soldiers 'standing by' were invested with deep directions of meaning: 'In their dug-out and ditches they asked of their own souls enormous questions.'[120] The *Times Literary Supplement* praised the chapter dealing with the front in Hugh Kimber's *San Fairy Ann* (1927) for its 'conversations about truth, chances of immortality, and the meaning of things in general.'[121]

In his *The Soul of a Soldier*, James Lansdale Hodson described thus soldiers' thoughts in the battleline:

"Is it decreed whether I shall live or die?" And some find mental peace and rest in a belief in fate embodying "What will be, will be, and I'm done with then"; and some believe in chance or luck and have no rest; and the remainder – the great remainder – think and think and think, now believing – usually in intense danger – that they find the solution in Christ, anon despairing of any solution at all and walking in darkness and crying out in agony, "Why, why, why?" And listening for but hearing no reply.[122]

This anguished question, we will see, seldom goes unanswered in the popular fiction of war.

For Keable the ultimate justification in writing his war memoir (which would be followed two years later by his war novel, one of the most successful of the inter-war years) was the realization that the words of the title of his book had 'a mystic meaning', as they mirrored the words of the Gospel 'They were standing by the Cross of Jesus...' His own memoir, he asserted, had turned into a picture of Christ crucified. Yet the Cross implies Resurrection and hope, great pity and utter nobility: '...standing by the cross I am moved to feel with tears at times, and yet again at others to thunderous acclaim.'[123] The explanation of the war as an experience of suspended testimony; the parallels to be drawn from the mythological wealth of Christianity; the image of a tortured Christ made bearable by the resurrection and the glory of self-sacrifice; the 'thunderous acclaim' of what is also agonizingly painful: these are all semantic constants in the middlebrow memory of war, and powerful antidotes to irony. Edward John Thompson's war poem 'Strange Are His Ways'[124] is the keynote of his war novels, which explore the cruelty of war while finding consolation in religious mystery. One notable exception was Louis Golding, who not only refused to find any inspiration in transcendental meaning but accused God openly of responsibility for the war. In a 1919 poem entitled 'A Thought', Golding imagined entering his room and finding God sitting on his bed, with 'sunken head' and battle-weary features.

> This was the thought and flame that pierced me through:
> If God sat waiting there, anxious and grey,
> Then should I have the charity to say,
> "God, we forgive you; you know not what you do"?[125]

Gurner's novel *Pass Guard at Ypres* reflected closely the author's memory of the town, where he was without interruption from May 1915 to February 1916, as an emblem of meaning. In his autobiography he contended that though Ypres was defended under extraordinarily hard conditions, it had not been in vain.

> But Ypres was not held stupidly or blindly, and, whether we knew it or not, it was deep spiritual as well as political wisdom that was demanding the awful sacrifice. To me at least, though I loathed every stone in its streets, Ypres was full of meaning that the years have only deepened.[126]

The poem he wrote at Ypres in February 1916, 'Tryst', was about the exclusive future memory of war: 'Of hallowed hours of war and woe,/ We will speak very softly, we that know.'[127] Yet it would be a mistake to judge from this wartime poem that his post-war literary work addressed only survivors. In fact the three different reflections of the Ypres experience progressed from the poetry of the soldier of the generation apart, to fiction presenting the meaning of Ypres to all readers, to, finally, his memoirs *I Chose Teaching*, setting the recollection of war within the context of education.

If spiritual laws governed the process of morality, then they must also regulate society. The link between the examination of contemporary problems and the solutions presented by a transcendental dimension of perception was, in several cases, argued in terms which to modern ears used to secular social analysis ring archaic and remote. In *Challenge* ('Dedicated to those who died that Britain might live'), Seton asserted that contemporary political problems in Britain called for 'the application of Christ principles in every sphere of governmental action through a perfected democratic system.'[128] Gilbert Cannan examined the constraints of society in terms of the way in which the tyranny of Victorian economics, based on the authority of the machinery, had superseded the needs and the inspiration of the spirit.[129] Philip Gibbs answered the question of his book *The Day After To-Morrow: What Is Going to Happen to the World?* with the solution which becomes so familiar in reading these works: 'I am old-fashioned enough to believe that ultimately the world can only be saved by getting back, or forward, to the Christian ideal and law of life...' This was a law which demanded obedience, unselfishness and altruistic sacrifice,[130] all qualities which had found inspiring expression in the war.

In the case of two alternative social critiques presented by Kenneth Ingram and Mary Agnes Hamilton, the ultimate solution was a religious choice of life. Ingram wrote an interminable string of 'social works', whose ideas were encapsulated in *Modern Thought on Trial* (1933). He spoke openly and realistically in favour of redistribution of wealth supervised by the State, of an egalitarian society, and of sexual emancipation, even for homosexuals. 'Sex is balanced when sex is allied to comradeship', he postulated in the most daring application of the supreme wartime value. Sexual conduct, however, had to be dictated by character-developing restraint. To this end, he warned, it might eventually be necessary 'to make a bonfire of our neurotic novelists and playwrights', with their self-indulgent obsession with sex.[131] His works attempted to reshape not only England, but civilization itself. In *The Coming Civilization: Will it be Capitalist? Will it be Materialist?* (1935), the second part of which was the enlargement of a series of five BBC talks given in the summer of 1935, Ingram explained that he advocated equality but not a materialist world, and ended with a moral apologia of Christian values. At the conclusion of *England at the Flood Tide*, he admitted that he had been essentially a 'Cook's tourist in Utopia', but defended this magnitude of vision as necessary to grasp the vast pattern of life.

> A thousand years are but a moment of eternity. And, through all the doubt and intrigue and failure of human enterprise, there is that invincible force which true believers call progress, the intuitive knowledge that in the end man will not fail, because the feeblest of his endeavours is inspired by a Divine Spirit, leading forward, ever forward.[132]

Morality is the commitment, and Christianity is the ultimate moral standard: topicality must be subordinated to the eternal cycle of these imposing values.

In a collection of essays about the impending threat of another war, in which different writers drew on their knowledge of the previous war to judge how to prevent the next, Mary Agnes Hamilton, biographer of the Webbs and Ramsay MacDonald, offered the most balanced view. All were agreed about the horror of war, she pointed out; this lesson had gone home well, and everybody wanted peace. But peace could be achieved only by thinking socially, and by transcending the 'old individualistic notions of right and wrong.'[133] Yet her 1944 autobiography, which traces in interesting detail the political developments of the inter-war years,[134] ended with a declaration of political and literary inspiration which is synonymous with her spiritual development. Once again the starting point of the quest for meaning was derived from patriotic courage and endurance. Behind the example of the 'human courage, endurance and faith' of European patriots during the Second World War she perceived 'the knowledge that beauty, goodness, kindness, truth' are not the time-specific creations of men but 'permanent values which reflect in man the spirit of God.' Hence the role of the artist is not to create value, but to 'bear witness to the existence in the universe of something of permanent and vital significance'; in effect, to make ever manifest what Carlyle had called 'Invisible Justice.'[135]

The grandiose tone and scale of such projects put them clearly beyond the scope of politics. Jerome Klapka Jerome, who lectured in favour of a negotiated peace during the war, gave the following reason for never aligning himself with a political party: '...with the years there has come to me the reflection that the future of mankind does not depend upon any party, but upon natural laws, shaping us to their ends quite independently of governments and politics.'[136] For Jerome these laws were ultimately religious ones; for others they were profound character values which had been drawn out by the ordeal of war. The inspiration of the pilgrimage to Gallipoli recounted by Ian Hay had a contemporary prescriptive function. The 'invincible confidence' and cheerfulness of the soldiers, their devotion to duty and tradition, could be the 'talisman' to beat the 'spectre of Distrust' which beset the nation, dividing men and classes.[137] Herbert Asquith extrapolated a similarly vague 'meaning', in the form of personal virtue, from Passchendaele; its memory, symbol of the worst horror of war, stood also for 'a core of resolution.'[138]

Of all the values bequeathed by the war, companionship represented the most frequently exchanged social coin. Communal effort, devoid of political undertones, was portrayed as antithetical to class conflict and associationalism. Harold Spender recalled his work in 1917, when he travelled throughout the country for the War Savings Department, as a time of 'great romance': the concentrated effort of a whole nation lent 'something very splendid about the memory of those years!' But ever since then, people's spirits had flagged, and the very districts where they had carried the 'Fiery Cross' (this term echoing the title of his autobiography, *The Fire of Life*) had 'been riven asunder by hatred and class warfare.'

> That great spirit of unity has disappeared.
> Will it ever return?
> That is the question of to-day.[139]

His son's reaction to this inflated romanticism is quite understandable. Stephen Spender evoked with exasperation his father's idealistic education: 'A game of football ceased to be just the kicking about of a leather ball by bare-kneed boys. It had become confused with the Battle of life. Honour, Integrity, Discipline, Toughness and a dozen other qualities haunted the field like ghostly footballers.'[140]

On a less rhetorical level, the spirit revealed during the war could be made to account for the very permanence of institutions. In Shanks's *My England*, written in 1938, a wartime anecdote was employed to explain the resilience and strength of English institutions. On being asked what she thought would happen if the Germans landed, a woman on the East Coast had replied: 'Why, they'd be taken up!' Shanks surmised that 'if a revolution broke out in England it would be taken up and would go quietly. This was, more or less, what happened to the Chartists in 1848.'[141]

In politics, different allegiances could express the same values. Often a basic conservatism, a fundamental allegiance to traditional values, overlay in the end liberal politics. A. P. Herbert was an Independent member but called himself a 'crusted Tory';[142] Naomi Ellington Jacob, who had once been a member of the Labour Party, and stood as parliamentary candidate for Sevenoaks, later became sympathetic to Mussolini's policies[143] and described herself as 'a Conservative Socialist.'[144] Oliver Onions, once a Socialist, by 1923 called himself a 'Tory with a conscience';[145] according to his friend and biographer Stephen Graham, Wilfrid Ewart told him on the last day of his life that he knew he would always be a Conservative in spite of earlier leanings towards liberal and even radical theories.[146]

Politics was a means to convey a message, but not its motivation. Graham Seton's Liberalism, as he described it in 1931, represented a commitment to justice, family values and anti-socialism.[147] Baxter's conservatism was loyal not to a party but to his ideals about his land of adoption. For a short time in 1929 he interrupted his career at the right-wing *Daily Express* to work as Editor-in-Chief of Inveresk Publications, for a salary of £10,000 a year.[148]

> Liberalism was a declining faith – but what about a new and more robust Liberalism? What about a Liberalism that threw off the shackles of Free Trade in an impossible tariff-ridden world, that would embrace the idea of a Free Trade Empire...a general policy of social reform and Government planning that would attract the younger Socialists and Conservatives because of its pliability, its humanitarianism, and its aggressiveness.[149]

Baxter's account of his Fleet Street career begins with Prime Minister Ramsay MacDonald meeting press editors to announce the sterling crisis, and ends with a dinner at the House of Commons, in the mid-1930s, with other members of the 'lost generation' (Donegall, Melchett, Hore-Belisha, and Edgar Granville) drinking a toast to themselves as ghostly survivors. Yet, as a ghost, Baxter commented, he had '*seen it all and been a part of it all*'. He could say that he had been there when England had borne 'the arrows of war in her breast without cry or boast...'; later he had seen the country 'outraged by the selfishness, the sensuality, and the garishness of the post-war years; and I have seen her rise in her simplicity and dignity to be finer in spirit than ever in her past.'[150]

The most virulently conservative writer was Gilbert Frankau, whose *Peter Jackson, Cigar Merchant* (1920) was a huge success. He was active as a public figure; political journalism always remained the most important activity for him, and his great ambition was to obtain a seat in the House. At a League of Youth address in October 1920, he praised in front of several Indian students the valour of Brigadier General Reginald Dyer, responsible for the massacre of Amritsar the year before. Philip Gibbs was also present and whispered to him: 'I've just heard that you and I, Churchill and Birkenhead are to be the first on the lampposts when the revolution starts.'[151]

Frankau's paternalistic interest in the working class, much in evidence in his novel as Jackson's intense concern for his soldiers, also informed his political activity. Together with a brutal rejection of socialist or syndicalist politics, he professed an interest in labour conditions which was simply a political projection of the ideal officer/soldier relation in the trenches.

During a dinner for press charity, at which Baldwin and Viscount Astor were present, he burst out in an infuriated speech about the betrayal of the Tory Party, which had abandoned protection. His anger was provoked by remembering

> two of my gunners talking in the signallers' dugout at Neuve Eglise. "I'll be glad when I'm back in the old factory", one was saying; and the other, "So'll I. But we're not going to the old conditions." Startlingly, I must have revisualized the men in the dark of the coalpits, the deafening room at a worsted mill, the mufflered figures at the meetings at Bow and Bromley.[152]

8 Safeguarding the Individual Against the Mob

The threat of Socialism telescoped the concern about the disappearance of individualism, the ugliness of industrial development, and the political threat underlying manifestations of mass culture. One word recurred to symbolize all these menacing phenomena: the mob. Among the crudest analyses was that of Cicely Mary Hamilton's *Modern England*. After attacking various manifestations of modernity, from buildings to the Left Book Club, she identified a source of hope in the falling birth-rate. The heights of great civilizations, when individual talent had found full expression, could not be attained by a society in which people were 'members of a herd.'[153] Under the pseudonym 'A Gentleman with a Duster', Harold Begbie in the 1920s wrote a series of books which are in fact treatises denouncing the social consequences of democracy. In works like *The Howling Mob: An Indictment of Democracy* (1922) he denounced the moral corruption of a society that did not rely on principles and ideals but on the prejudices of the Socialist mass.

In *Literature in My Time* Compton Mackenzie concluded his survey by admitting that his brand of conservatism could not stop the transition he was witnessing from a 'pre-machine man' to a 'machine man.' 'We seem to be standing at a point of human evolution when the individual must surrender to the group mind. If Communism can only be fought by the inverted form of it called Fascism, there is no hope for the individual so far as the externals of individuality count.'[154] In a more serious study, George Blake examined the 'vulgarization' of the press, which he dated from 1881, when George Newnes founded *Tit-Bits*, followed by Alfred Harmsworth's *Answers* and *Daily Mail*. Blake's main criticism of the press that catered for a mass reading public with sensational and light reading was a common middlebrow one: its lack of social purpose. Lord Northcliffe's purely commercial spirit 'did not betray the slightest sense...of a moral responsibility' to its public.[155]

Again and again middlebrow social analysis brings us back to the issues of the virtue of individualism as opposed to the dangers of the mass. As Raymond Williams has pointed out, the 'masses are always the others, whom we don't know, and can't know', a way of grouping people in their difference which 'has been capitalized for the purposes of political or cultural exploitation.'[156] Those 'we don't know, and can't know' in middlebrow works are the working-class crowd, while the middle classes are standard-bearers of individualism, that outstanding characteristic of the British island race. Herbert Asquith, the Prime Minister's son, remembered lorries being driven during the General Strike with the notice 'By permission of the T.U.C.'. This expression of regimentation was countered by, paradoxically, the mass response of middle-class individuals, of which Asquith reported a valiant example:

> ...among the crowd of traffic another car was seen, far more typical of the English: it was driven by a private citizen and it bore, chalked upon its bonnet in bold flaming letters, the inscription, 'By permission of my own bl-dy self.' It was a midget car, but it carried a great message, worthy of the land of Drake.[157]

The working class was not seriously thought of as an audience, but it was referred to indirectly, with the same concern, affection, and (when necessary) severity, that the officers had displayed towards their men. The opening quotation of Stephen McKenna's autobiography is an extract from Thomas Carlyle's *Sartor Resartus*, honouring two kinds of men: the Craftsman who toils for his brothers ('thou wert our Conscript, on whom the lot fell, and fighting our battles were so marred') and the one who toils 'for the spiritually indispensable', especially the Artist, 'inspired Thinker', whose work should aim to reward the sustenance he receives from the humble with 'Light...Guidance, Freedom, Immortality.'[158] The effort of post-war reconstruction would be futile without the 'unthinking' work of the lower classes, just as their massive presence had made the war possible. These very basic realities were transmuted by middlebrow social analysts into the following tenet: if the working classes let themselves be guided, then the peacetime task could reproduce the wartime common effort, and justice and harmony would be among its great rewards. Frankau found that the behaviour of the crowd at the 1923 Wembley Cup Final was 'proof that the spirit of self discipline which won the war had not been killed by five years of political squabbles.'[159]

Some writers felt called upon to provide reassurance about the impossibility of a British Revolution. Playing Burke to the Russian Revolution, which he compared to Marat's and Danton's Reign of Terror, Philip Gibbs interwove the chapter 'For What Men Died' with a prescription against Revolution based on the social maximization of the values learnt during the war.[160] In *Some of the English* (1930), a presentation of the English character, Oliver Madox Hueffer stressed the superfluity of political excesses in England. Choosing for his study a borough of a quarter of a who was consulted, agreed and the article was rejected. Aldington was indeed correct in his comment that had he chosen the predictable 'mediocrities' he would have got 'a cheque and a crown of will parsley.'[165]

In an address given to the Literary Circle of the National Liberal Club on 23 November 1928, later published as *The Georgian Novel and Mr. Robinson*, Storm Jameson depicted the exploration of an ordinary man into modern literature in terms of the mapping out of modernity. She likened her own feelings about first venturing into 'the extraordinary complexity of the region' to that of a 'respectable little man of quiet manners who walking through his familiar suburb in the evening is suddenly confronted by the beginnings of a maze labelled variously: *This way to the Bottomless Pit*, and – *To Parnassus*, and – *Danger: Libido Loose Here*.' The modernist writer lived in an isolated, esoteric world of his own; a great author, she asserted, should be great 'in his own times' and reflect the dynamics of the contemporary spirit.[166] A few years later Jameson reiterated her criticism with eloquent conciseness: 'Above all, a writer needs – to achieve complete unspoiled development – the support of a hierarchy of values.' Of those writers who were not committed to such a hierarchy, some manufactured their own system of values, like D.H. Lawrence, while others embraced scepticism, or simply accepted 'disorder and disintegration.'[167]

Most of the writers who did feel part of a vast, unifying network of beliefs were concerned with the dynamics of threat to and rescue of the old traditions within an inevitably modernized social framework. In one of his short manifestos of literary intent, 'In Search of Values', Charles Morgan expressed the aim of estimating 'the ever-changing fiction between what is essential and continuous and what is variable in the development of society'. The 'Blimps' resisted all change and the 'future-gazers' were mesmerized by the possibilities that might lie ahead, but the 'middle truth' was that in society are found both variables and constants: 'what gives to an age its distinguishing character is the relationship, the fiction, between them.'[168] The conception of historical character as a relationship between the old and the new, and of this dynamic as fiction, is a powerful cultural image of literary mediation of value.

Ernest Raymond once defined his literary position within the relationship between the past, the present and the future. In the letter accepting the Presidency of the Young PEN (a 'junior branch' of PEN for aspiring writers under 29 years of age) he presented his ideological credentials by comparing his approach to that of the 'future-gazers', as Morgan would have called them:

> Naturally I think I am with the future rather than with the past, because I think the future will swing back a bit towards old values and old canons of art; but in

4. Author of the bestseller *Lady Audley's Secret* (1862).

5. Herbert Asquith, Vernon Bartlett, Arthur Beverley Baxter, Charles R. Benstead, Anthony Bertram, George Blake, Richard Blaker, John Brophy, Peter Deane, Warwick Deeping, Wilfrid Ewart, Gilbert Frankau, Arthur Hamilton Gibbs, Louis Golding, Ronald Gurner, Ian Hay, A. P. Herbert, James Lansdale Hodson, Oliver Madox Hueffer, A. S. M. Hutchinson, Kenneth Ingram, Robert Keable, Albert Kinross, Laurence Kirk, William McFee, Compton Mackenzie, William Babington Maxwell, Patrick Miller, Charles Morgan, Walter Frederick Morris, Philip MacDonald, J. B. Morton, Bernard Newman, Roland Pertwee, V. W. W. S. Purcell, Ernest Raymond, Graham Seton, Edward Shanks, Duncan Keith Shaw, R. C. Sherriff, Frederick Sleath, Christopher Stone, Gordon Stowell, Edward John Thompson, Hugh Walpole, Francis Brett Young.

6. Stephen McKenna worked in the War Trade Intelligence Department; Harold Spender devoted himself to war propaganda and various war activities at home; Robert Hichens served three years in the Special Constabulary; Stacy Aumonier was in the Army Pay Corps and then chart maker as B3 man; Phyllis Bottome and William John Locke were involved in Belgian relief work; May Sinclair worked in the Hoover Relief Commission; Arnold Bennett worked as director of Propaganda for the Ministry of Information under Lord Beaverbrook; Naomi Ellington Jacob was an officer in the Women's Legion, working as superintendent of a munitions factory; and Noel Streatfield worked as a munitions worker at Woolwich Arsenal.

7. Mary Agnes Hamilton, *Remembering My Good Friends*, 1944, p. 143.

8. Cecil Roberts, *Sunshine and Shadow, Being the Fourth Book of an Autobiography, 1930–1946*, 1972, p. 30.

9. James Lansdale Hodson, *No Phantoms Here*, 1932 (collection of News Chronicle sketches), pp. 287, 161.

10. Of the rest, Frankau founded and edited the right-wing *Britannia* in 1928; A. M. N. Lyons helped Robert Blatchford start the socialist *Clarion* at the beginning of the century; Cecil Roberts was editor of the *Nottingham Journal* from 1920 to 1925; Edward John Thompson was special correspondent for the *Manchester Guardian* in India in 1932; John Brophy was chief fiction critic of the *Daily Telegraph* and edited *John O'London's Weekly* from 1939 to 1945; Anthony Bertram was art critic of the *Spectator* from 1922 to 1924 and of the *Saturday Review* from 1924 to 1927; C.S. Forester was in Spain in 1936–37 for the *Times* and would cover Prague during the Nazi occupation; the populist Helen Zenna Smith wrote special features for the *Sunday People* from 1930 to 1934; Bennet Copplestone (Frederick Harcourt Kitchin) joined the editorial staff of the *Times* in 1895, founded and edited the *Times Financial and Commercial Supplement* (1906 to 1908) and was Assistant Manager from 1908 to 1909; Kenneth Ingram founded and edited the *Green Quarterly* and edited the *Police Journal* in 1929; in 1933 Vernon Bartlett become diplomatic correspondent of the *News Chronicle*, and he was founder and editor of the *World Review*.

11. (At Marlborough College, Strand School, King Edward VII, Sheffield, and Whitgift School)

12. Justin Huntly McCarthy had been a Nationalist MP as a very young man, from 1884, when he was 23, to 1892.

13. Charles Morgan was elected President of the International PEN in 1953.

14. John Feather, *A History of British Publishing*, 1988, pp. 193–4.

15. Alan Swingewood, *The Myth of Mass Culture*, 1977, p. 107.

16. H.E. Bates, *Edward Garnett*, 1950, p. 35. In a typical invective against the modernists, he pointed out that Bloomsbury had not yet become 'an absurd backwater of scandals and beards, introverts and extroverts, mannish women and lily-fingered men, ivory-tower isolations and cocktail parties on the floor...' (*Ibid.*, p. 12.)

17. Richard Findlater, 'What are Writers Worth?', *A Survey of Authorship Prepared for the Society of Authors*, 1963, reprinted in Peter Davison, Rolf Meyersohn, Edward Shils (eds.), *Literary Taste, Culture and Mass Communication*, Cambridge, 1978, vol. 10: *Authorship*, p. 287.

18. *Ibid.*, p. 288.

19. Bates, *Edward Garnett*, p. 77.

20. Michael S. Howard, *Jonathan Cape, Publisher: Herbert Jonathan Cape, G. Wren Howard*,

Harmondsworth, 1977 (first published 1971), p. 12.

21. *Bookseller*, 14 January, 1927, p. 9. Ernest Benn was devoted to flying the anti-Socialist banner and in 1930 published his *Confessions of a Capitalist*.

22. *Bookseller*, 8 June 1922, p. 74.

23. W.G. Taylor, 'Publishing', in *The Book World* (ed. John Hampden), 1935, p. 52. (my italics)

24. Charles Morgan, *The House of Macmillan (1843–1943)*, 1943, pp. 27, 101.

25. *Ibid.*, p. 5.

26. Stanley Unwin, *Publishing in Peace and War*, 1944, p. 11.

27. Ernest Raymond, *Through Literature to Life: An Enthusiasm and an Anthology*, 1928, pp. 52, 34.

28. Marjorie Plant, *The English Book Trade: An Economic History of the Making and Sale of Books*, 1974 (first published 1939), p. 465.

29. Desmond Flower, *A Century of Best Sellers, 1830–1930*, 1934, p. 3.

30. Cecil Roberts, *The Bright Twenties, Being the Third Book of an Autobiography: 1920–1929*, 1970, pp. 152–3.

31. First novels were: Arthur Beverley Baxter's *The Parts Men Play*, John Brophy's *The Bitter End*, David Campbell's *From The Hill-Tops*, A. M. Cogswell's *Ermytage and the Curate*, Peter Deane's *The Victors*, Wilfrid Ewart's *The Way of Revelation*, A. P. Herbert's *The Secret Battle*, A. M. N. Jenkin's *The End of a Dream*, F. B. Keel's *Seven Days in the Line*, Hugh Kimber's *San Fairy Ann*, Shaw MacNichol's *Between the Days*, Patrick Miller's *The Natural Man*, Terence Mahon's *Cold Feet*, W. F. Morris's *Bretherton*, J. B. Morton's *The Barber of Putney*, V. W. W. S. Purcell's *The Further Side of No Man's Land*, Ernest Raymond's *Tell England*, Graham Seton's *W Plan*, Edward Shanks's *The Old Indispensables*, Frederick Sleath's *Sniper Jackson*, F. H. Snow's *No Names, No Pack Drill*, Gordon Stowell's *The History of Button Hill*. For Campbell, Baxter, Jenkin, Cogswell, MacNichol, Mahon, Stowell, and Keel these were their only fictional works.

32. Ernest Raymond, *Please You, Draw Near. Autobiography 1922–1968*, 1969, p. 69.

33. The 1947 Penguin edition of Hinkson's novel sold over 100,000 copies. Brian Cleeve, *Dictionary of Irish Writers*, Cork, vol. 1, 1967, p. 61.

34. Dates of birth were available for twenty-eight out of thirty-seven writers for 1919; and twenty-three out of thirty for 1929–1930.

35. Even Lynn, however, reflected the constant effort of these writers to account for the historical foundation of their work by providing the reader with the 'sources' of their work. The foreword of *Lads of the Lothians* stated that it was the story of the 5th Battalion of the Royal Scots in Gallipoli, based on first-hand accounts, and ended with a historical précis of the Lothian Regiment (The Royal Scots) which dated back to 1633. (*Lads of the Lothians*, 1920, p. 6.) *Comrades Ever* is similarly provided with a foreword which explains that the tale is based on a personal diary and 'certain Government papers', and that A. W. Beves-Northern (of the Nyasaland Protectorate Service) who served in the East Africa campaign checked the story and added to it while on leave in England. A final addendum gives information about the campaign. (*Comrades Ever*, 1921, pp. 4, 352).

36. *Times*, 9 October, 1929, p. 16.

37. *Bookman*, September 1919, p. 185.

38. W.B. Maxwell, *Time Gathered*, 1937, p. 341.

39. John Buchan, *Memory Hold the Door*, 1940, pp. 166–9. John Buchan, whose partner in the Scottish publishing house of Nelson, Tommy Nelson, was killed at Arras in 1915, began the four-year editorial project of *Nelson's History of the War*, the proceeds of which were to go to the families of Nelson employees who had enlisted and to war charities. (William Buchan, *John Buchan: A Memoir*, 1982, p. 138.)

40. Newman Flower, introduction to Hall Caine's *The Woman of Knockaloe; A Parable*, 1923, pp. xi–xii. Newman Flower in 1927 would become owner and managing editor of Cassell.

41. *Saturday Review*, 26 March, 1921, p. 265.

42. Graham Seton, *Footslogger: An Autobiography*, 1931, p. 264.

43. Phyllis Bottome, *The Goal*, 1962, p. 37.

44. Compton Mackenzie, *Gallipoli Memories*, 1929, pp. 392–3. Patrick Shaw-Stewart was killed at Salonica a few months later.

45. George Dangerfield, *The Strange Death of Liberal England*, 1983 (first published 1935), p. 381.

46. Christopher Stone, *Christopher Stone Speaking*, 1933, p. 22.

47. Stanley J. Kunitz and Howard Haycraft (eds.), *Twentieth- Century Authors, a Biographical Dictionary of Modern Literature*, New York, 1942, p. 1401. Thompson was 16 years old in 1918.

48. Sylvia Thompson, Foreword to *The Hounds of Spring*, 1926. (italics in the text)

49. Charles Masterman wrote to the *Daily Express* (September 17) to defend Bennett by adducing the literary example of Disraeli's use of political figures in his novels. (James Hepburn, *Arnold Bennett. The Critical Heritage*, 1981, p. 100.) The novel, published in October 1926, had sold 30,000 copies by mid-June 1927. (*Ibid.*, p. 102) The political scenario of the novel was so recognizable that the reviewer in the *New Statesman* commented that 'its substantially accurate picture of the mentality of our rulers in the spring of 1918 has a definite historical value.' (*New Statesman*, 16 October 1926, p. 18.)

50. Basil Liddell Hart, 'A Personal Note', in Bernard Newman, *Spy and Counter-Spy: Bernard Newman's Story of the British Secret Service*, 1970, pp. 11–12.

51. *Ibid.*, p. 11.

52. Oliver Madox Hueffer, 'Apologia', *"Cousins German"*, 1930, p.8.

53. Edward John Thompson, 'Prelude', *Lament for Adonis*, 1931, p.v.

54. Stephen Graham, *Life and Last Words of Wilfrid Ewart*, 1924, p. 9.

55. Reginald Pound, *A.P.Herbert: A Biography*, 1976, pp. 36–7.

56. Seton, *Footslogger*, p. 371.

57. *Ibid.*, pp. 215–16. *W Plan* (1930) tells of a young Scottish officer who, disguised as a dead German officer – inventor of the W Plan – obtains the papers and saves England from a catastrophic attack.

58. Seton, *Footslogger*, pp. 371–2.

59. V. W. W. S. Purcell, preface to *The Further Side of No Man's Land*, 1929, p. vi. Purcell in the novel gave the name of 7th Northwolds to his own 4th Battalion Green Howards, and the name Blitzburg to the prison camp of Dahön. Like the protagonist of his novel, Purcell went to Cambridge after the war.

60. John Rae, *Conscience and Politics: The British Government and the Conscientious Objectors to Military Service, 1916–1919*, 1970, pp. 207–225.

61. Harold Begbie, *Mr. Sterling Sticks It Out*, 1919, p. vi.

62. Roberts, *Sunshine and Shadow*, pp. 52–54.

63. Warwick Deeping, *No Hero – This*, (1936), 'Author's Note'.

64. Gerald Gould, *The English Novel of To-Day*, 1924, p. 55.

65. *Bookseller*, May 1924, p. 131.

66. Leonard Woolf, *An Autobiography. Vol. 2: 1911–1969*, 1980 (first published in 1964), p. 304.

67. *Athenaeum*, 19 December 1919, p. 1386.

68. Review of Harold Begbie's *Mr. Sterling Sticks It Out*, in *Saturday Review*, 31 May, 1919, p. 528. Begbie's *The Great World* was judged by the *Times Literary Supplement* to be 'good journalism' and 'an indifferent novel'. (15 October 1925, p. 676).

69. Justin McCarthy, 'Novels With a Purpose', *Westminster Review*, 82 (July, 1864), pp. 24–29, 40–49, in *Dictionary of Literary Biography*, Vol. 21: *Victorian Novelists Before 1885*, (Ira B. Nadel and William E. Fredeman eds.), Detroit, Michigan, 1983, pp. 369, 373.

70. *Times Literary Supplement*, 30 October 1919, p. 610. The same complaint about the enforced delivery of a message was passed against Mary Fulton's *The Plough* (*Punch*, 5 November, 1919, p. 400). One reviewer of H. F. P. Battersby's *The Edge of Doom* protested that he had to 'except from commendation the long pages devoted to hackneyed generalities about the war and neutrals, the effect of the war on women, cheap sneers at "the politicians", and so on. Novelists should by this time really curb the desire to vent their views on these matters when they should be giving us real stories and true studies of character.' (*Times Literary Supplement*,

13 November 1919, pp. 652–653.)

71. *Punch*, 14 April, 1920, p. 300.

72. *Times Literary Supplement*, 17 September 1925, p. 598.

73. Edward Shanks, *My England*, 1938, p. 12.

74. Maxwell, *Time Gathered*, p. 333.

75. Gilbert Frankau, *Self-Portrait: A Novel of His Own Life*, 1944 (first published 1940), pp. 236, 238.

76. Vernon Bartlett, *And Now, Tomorrow*, 1960, pp. 249–250. His was a zeal which was ever updated: in this work he gave accounts of apartheid in South Africa and of the position of Asia in world politics.

77. Stone, *Christopher Stone Speaking*, p. 51.

78. *Ibid.*, p. 57.

79. Ronald Gurner, *I Chose Teaching*, 1937, pp. 3, 28. Interestingly, Gurner's discussion of the difference between public schools and free schools parallels the distinction often drawn between middlebrow and highbrow fiction. The former institutions dealt with realities, such as duty and social living, whereas the latter inculcated a self-consciousness and a self-indulgent attitude which in the long run was quite damaging and anti-social. (pp. 180–1.)

80. *Ibid.*, pp. 54–5. Gurner, for all the hope propounded in his enlightened educational theory, ended up an embittered man, tormented by the pain of his war wound and by his memories, and committed suicide. (Hugh Cecil, 'The Literary Legacy of the War', in Liddle, Peter H., *Home Fires and Foreign Fields: British Social and Military Experience in the First World War*, 1985, p. 218.)

81. James Lansdale Hodson, *Our Two Englands*, 1936, pp. 13, 284. His play *Harvest in the North*, first produced at the Manchester Repertory Theatre on 21 January 1935, also mingled the theme of unemployment with that of the war. Set in Chesterford, a small cotton town in Lancashire, it ended with the unemployed's pledge in front of the War Memorial to keep on 'feightin' ' for their children, work, and peace, and with the fifes playing 'Keep the home fires burning.' (James Lansdale Hodson, *Harvest in the North*, 1935, pp. 94–95.)

82. Gibbs, *Ordeal in England*, p. 418.

83. Philip Gibbs, *England Speaks*, 1935, pp. 386–7, 390.

84. W.N. Medlicott, *Contemporary England, 1914–1964, with epilogue, 1964–1974*, 1976 (first published 1967), pp. 79–80.

85. *Bookman*, December 1919, p. 94.

86. Gilbert Cannan, *Pugs and Peacocks*, 1921, p. 288.

87. Seton, *Footslogger*, p. 261.

88. In one of his periodical surveys of the state of the nation, *The New Elizabethans* (1953), he asked whether the English were not losing their 'old individualism and independence of character, asking to be pap-fed by a benevolent State' (p. 19). Gibbs wrote his last book, *How Now, England?* (1958), at the age of 81.

89. *Obituaries from The Times, 1961–1970*, compiled by Frank C. Roberts, Reading, 1975, p. 303.

90. James Lansdale Hodson, *Return to the Wood*, 1955. Hodson joined up as private on 4 September 1914, at the age of 23, went to France in October 1915 with the 20th Royal Fusiliers, 3rd Public Schools Battalion, and was in the trenches at La Bassée and on the Somme for fourteen months. Later he became an officer in the Royal Naval Division and, being found unfit to continue service abroad, worked for the Special Intelligence Branch of the Ministry of Munitions. (blurb of *Grey Dawn - Red Night*).

91. Alfred McLelland Burrage asserted that he could be explicit in his war memoirs without needing to use 'those dirty words which a certain German writer found so essential to his Art.' (*War is War*, pp. 6-7.)

92. Advertisement on book cover of R. C. Sherriff and Vernon Bartlett's *Journey's End*.

93. Cited in blurb of W.F. Morris, *Bretherton: Khaki or Field Grey?*, 1929.

94. Hueffer, *"Cousins German"*, 'Apologia', p. 9.

95. *The Soldier's War*, 1929 (edited with Eric Partridge); *Songs and Slang of the British Soldier: 1914–1918* (edited with Eric Partridge), 1930; *The Five Years: A Conspectus of the Great War*

Designed Primarily for Study by the Successors of Those Who Took Part in it and Secondarily to Refresh the Memory of the Participants Themselves, 1936.

96. Brophy, *The Soldier's War*, pp. ix–x.

97. He was 37 at the outbreak of the war, and served with the rank of Captain in the Argyll and Sutherland Highlanders, earning the MC and the CBE.

98. Ian Hay, *The Ship of Remembrance: Gallipoli – Salonika*, 1927, pp. 5, 7, 41–2. This unironic memory of Gallipoli was also evoked in Ernest Raymond's autobiography. On describing the thrill of arriving at Gallipoli in August 1915, at W Beach, he attributed the power of this memory to the fact that the campaign 'had a glamour, a tragic beauty, all its own.' In fact, amidst those legendary places, the campaign soon assumed 'the perfect pattern, the Attic shape, of a Greek tragedy'. (Ernest Raymond, *The Story of My Days: An Autobiography 1882–1922*, 1968, p. 127.)

99. James Lansdale Hodson, *The Soul of a Soldier*, 1919, pp. iii.

100. *Ibid.*, pp. 113–14.

101. Vernon Bartlett, *Mud and Khaki: Sketches from France and Flanders*, 1917, p. 13.

102. Vernon Bartlett, *I Know What I Liked*, 1974, p. 18.

103. E.P. Thompson, 'The Poverty of Theory' (1978), in *The Poverty of Theory and Other Essays*, 1978, pp. 363, 366–7.

104. Albert Kinross, *An Unconventional Cricketer*, 1930, pp. 65–8.

105. Phyllis Bottome, *Search for a Soul*, 1947, p. 317.

106. Kunitz and Haycraft (eds.), *Twentieth-Century Authors*, p. 1473.

107. Hrisey Dimitrakis Zegger, *May Sinclair*, (Twayne's English Authors Series, no. 192), Boston, 1976, pp. 19–20.

108. Esther Marian Greenwell Smith, *Mrs. Humphry Ward*, Boston, 1980, pp. 42–43.

109. *England's Effort: Letters to an American Friend*, New York, 1916; *Towards the Goal* (with an introduction by Theodore Roosevelt), New York, 1918; *Fields of Victory*, New York, 1919.

110. Mrs. Humphry Ward, *England's Effort*, p. 37, cited in Smith, *Mrs. Humphry Ward*, p. 120.

111. Zegger, *May Sinclair*, p. 18. In *The New Idealism* Sinclair discussed her strong interest in mysticism. *(Ibid.*, p. 107.)

112. *Ibid.*, p. 142.

113. May Sinclair, *A Journal of Impressions in Belgium*, 1915, pp. 193-194.

114. Cicely Mary Hamilton, *Life Errant*, 1935, pp. 227–243.

115. Cecil Roberts, *Half Way: An Autobiography*, 1931, pp. 162, 191–2.

116. Philip Gibbs, introduction to Arthur Hamilton Gibbs, *The Grey Wave*, pp. 270–1.

117. Cecil Roberts, *A Week With the Fleet*, 1919, pp. 93–4. (Reprints of articles written during the war).

118. Edward Noble was 70 years old in the year of the publication of his novel.

119. Robert Keable, *Standing By: War-Time Reflections in France and Flanders*, 1919, pp. 3–5, 8–9. (my italics)

120. Philip Gibbs, introduction to Arthur Hamilton Gibbs, *The Grey Wave*, p. xiv.

121. *Times Literary Supplement*, 10 November 1927, p. 812.

122. Hodson, *The Soul of a Soldier*, pp. 107–8.

123. Keable, *Standing By*, pp. 10–12.

124. In Edward John Thompson, *Collected Poems*, 1930, p. 104.

125. Louis Golding, *Sorrow of War: Poems*, 1919, p. 33.

126. Gurner, *I Chose Teaching*, p. 36.

127. In *Ibid.*, p. 37.

128. Graham Seton, *Challenge*, 1935, 'Foreword', p. 11. (my italics)

129. Gilbert Cannan, *The Anatomy of Society*, 1919.

130. Philip Gibbs, *The Day After To-Morrow: What is Going to Happen to the World?*, 1928, p. 236. Here Gibbs discussed with unashamed versatility the work of different scientists, eugenics (with separate sections for the thyroid, thimus and pituary glands), and philosophical, spiritual and political forecasts.

131. Kenneth Ingram, *Modern Thought on Trial*, 1933, p. 243.

132. Kenneth Ingram, *England at the Flood Tide*, 1925, pp. 220–21.

133. Mary Agnes Hamilton, 'No Peace Apart from International Security: An Answer to Extreme Pacifists', in *Challenge to Death*, 1934, pp. 273–4.

134. In particular, she discussed the increased national interest in international affairs which dominated the elections of 1918, 1922 and 1924, and, to a great extent, 1929, the spirit of hope in reconstruction, and the grave mistakes committed by all, including herself, in continuing to clear Germany of all responsibility. (Hamilton, *Remembering My Good Friends*, pp. 98–9, 101–102.)

135. *Ibid.*, pp. 308–310. One writer whose left-wing politics did not look for any religious reference was Carmel Haden Guest. Her son was David Guest, a mathematician and philosopher and Communist soldier who died fighting in Spain in 1938. She edited a memoir called *David Guest: A Scientist Fights for Freedom (1911–1938)*, 1939.

136. Joseph Connolly, *Jerome K. Jerome: A Critical Biography*, 1982, p. 127.

137. Hay, *The Ship of Remembrance*, 1927, pp. 42–3.

138. Herbert Asquith, *Moments of Memory: Recollections and Impressions*, 1937, p. 309.

139. Harold Spender, *The Fire of Life: A Book of Memories*, 1926, pp. 218–19.

140. Stephen Spender, *World Within World*, 1977 (first published in 1951), p. 8.

141. Shanks, *My England*, p. 99.

142. Kunitz and Haycraft (eds.), *Twentieth-Century Authors*, p.106.

143. James Norbury, *Naomi Jacob: The Seven Ages of 'Me'*, 1965, p. 113.

144. Kunitz and Haycraft (eds.), *Twentieth-Century Authors*, p.100.

145. Hugh Cecil, 'The Literary Legacy of the War', in Peter H. Liddle, *Home Fires and Foreign Fields: British Social and Military Experience in the First World War*, 1985, p. 206.

146. Graham, *Life and Last Words of Wilfrid Ewart*, p. 252.

147. Seton, *Footslogger*, pp. 310–311.

148. Inveresk was owned by William Harrison, who in 1928 had bought the liberal *Daily Chronicle*. Harrison was a Conservative and a strong supporter of Tariff Reform. (Arthur Beverley Baxter, *Strange Street*, 1935, pp. 254–5.) A different kind of partnership was that started between Harrison and Frankau in 1928, when they founded together the sixpenny weekly *Britannia*, devoted to the protection of industry and the interests of the Empire. The venture, under Frankau's editorship, proved very expensive and folded by the end of the year. Frankau's reasons for joining this project was the belief that the right political choices could transcend party politics. (Frankau, *Self-Portrait*, pp. 283–302.)

149. Baxter, *Strange Street*, p. 255.

150. *Ibid.*, pp. 280–1. (italics in the text)

151. Frankau, *Self-Portrait*, 1944 (first published 1940), p. 194.

152. *Ibid.*, p. 226.

153. Cicely Mary Hamilton, *Modern England: As Seen by An Englishwoman*, 1938, p. 14. Evelyn Waugh deplored her argument for assuming 'that the lives of men usually engender ugliness'. (*Spectator*, 22 April, 1919, p. 716.)

154. Compton Mackenzie, *Literature in my Time*, 1933, pp. 244–6.

155. George Blake, *The Press and the Public*, (*Criterion Miscellany*, no. 21), 1930, pp. 6–7.

156. Raymond Williams, *Culture and Society, 1780–1950*, Harmondsworth, 1984 (first published 1958), p. 289.

157. Asquith, *Moments of Memory, Recollections and Impressions*, p. 364. (my italics)

158. Cited in Stephen McKenna, *While I Remember*, 1921, p. 9. The choice of Carlyle's work was particularly apt, with its combination of imaginative, autobiographical and essayist elements. Fiction and fact are barely distinguishable in McKenna's own work. *Sonia Married* is prefaced by a dedicatory letter to Walter Francis Roch which discusses the moral and political near-bankruptcy of the nation, and the kind of solutions attempted by his idealistic protagonist, Charles O'Rane. (Stephen McKenna, *Sonia Married*, 1919, pp. 7–9.) Stephen McKenna occupied a special space amongst the social commentators. A nephew of the Liberal statesman and banker Reginald McKenna, whose biography he wrote, he was a wealthy man who knew intimately the high social and political circles he portrayed so topically. During the war he could not serve because of weak health and worked for the War Trade Intelligence Department from

1915 to 1919; in 1917 he was part of the Balfour mission to the United States. (Kunitz and Haycraft (eds.), *Twentieth-Century Authors*, p. 882)

159. Frankau, *Self-Portrait*, p. 207.

160. Philip Gibbs, *Realities of War*, 1920, pp. 342–352.

161. Oliver Madox Hueffer, *Some of the English: A Study Towards a Study*, 1930, pp. 40–50.

162. Wilfrid Ewart, 'Young Men of England', *When Armageddon Came*, 1933, p. 334.

163. *Times Literary Supplement*, 8 August 1936, p. 647.

164. Alec Waugh, *My Brother Evelyn and Other Profiles*, 1967, pp. 115–6.

165. Richard Aldington, *Life for Life's Sake*, 1968 (first published in New York, 1940), pp. 200–201. Aldington was in constant contact with Eliot between 1919 and 1928, when the poet was trying to establish a name for himself, and he witnessed the backlash provoked by his work from 'the defenders of the *status quo* in literature – the amorphous mass of Georgians and the formidable rear-guard of Victorians'. Eliot was dubbed 'drunken helot' by one reviewer, and even Holbrook Jackson, founder of the excellent magazine *To-day* (1917–1923), rejected Aldington's request to write an article about his friend with the comment: 'But Eliot's a wild man.' (*Ibid.*, pp. 199–200.)

166. Storm Jameson, *The Georgian Novel and Mr. Robinson*, 1929, pp. 1, 71.

167. Storm Jameson, 'Novels and Novelists' (1932–1933), in *Civil Journey*, 1939, pp. 91–2. The sardonic contempt for highbrows of A.P. Herbert, who in 1931 wrote *Ballads for Broadbrows*, was notorious. He just could not accept the opening lines of *The Waste Land*: 'Try as I may, I cannot see what it is that entitles this passage to the name of poetry.' (Cited in Pound, *A.P.Herbert: A Biography*, p. 95.)

168. Charles Morgan, 'In Search of Values', *Reflections in a Mirror*, 1944, p. 2.

169. Raymond, *Please You, Draw Near*, p. 43. (italics in the text). Young PEN was started in 1928; its first president was E.M. Forster, followed by Lady Rhondda and Bertrand Russell. (*Ibid.*, p. 42.)

170. Gibbs, *England Speaks*, p. 409.

171. Albert Kinross, 'England, My England!', *The Atlantic Monthly*, May, 1921, p. 694.

2 The Invisible Hand of The Cause

In *The Parts Men Play* the author, Arthur Beverley Baxter, interrupts the narrative after the outbreak of the war to offer explicitly and in italics his personal comment:

> *In a war in which every nation was the loser, Britain can at least reclaim from the wreckage the memory of that glorious hour when the Angelus of patriotism rang over the empire, and men of every creed, pursuit, and condition dropped their tasks and sank themselves in the great consecration of service.*
>
> *What is the paltry glory of a bloody victory or the passing sting of defeat?*
>
> *War is base, senseless, and degrading – that was one truth that Selwyn did recognize; but what he failed to see what that in the midst of all the foulness there lay some glorious gems. When battles are forgotten and war is remembered as a hideous anachronism of the past, our children and their children will bow in reverence to the stone set high in Britain's diadem – THEY SERVED.*[1]

The passage is lengthy; the authorial intervention is forceful; the words are high-flown and the sentiments vigorous. The direct, rhetorical style seems to imply a precise awareness on the author's part of his own attitude to war. Yet in trying to define clearly the terms of Baxter's judgment of the experience of war, one finds that this passage does not yield them easily. War, in this statement and throughout the novel, is condemned as brutal and futile, and yet is glorified indirectly for the inestimable human value of the response of the British people to their country's call for help. The outbreak of war is an important focus of meaning because it represents the response of unquestioning sacrifice. The emotive, prompt, archetypal response is a historical moment to be treasured as a reference of value even when the motivation – war – is negatively qualified.

Most popular novels about the war present the reader with the same analytical impasse: the contradiction between a wealth of overt moral, philosophical and social comments and a blurred focus of judgment. It is a challenging paradox, as these novels seldom shy away from evaluative comments and often seem to have been written under the compelling need to offer an assessment of the common tragic experience of war, and to communicate and reinforce essential social values. The language is frequently highly emotional, charged with feelings of grief, regret and fear of the future

Notes to Chapter 2 can be found on page 84

which give the lie to the rational pretence of the author's judgments. But if the novels are intellectually formless, they are full of the feeling of experience and of the need to understand it through narrating it and explaining it.

What is the meaning of war? What is the attitude to be adopted towards it? The writers feel compelled to address these questions and their novels abound in scenes of reflection and debate. Soldiers exchanging remarks and doubts about their experience while resting in billets; an officer musing on life minutes before a night raid on the enemy trenches; a civilian interpreting the disaster which he can observe lucidly from his safety at home: the authors' views are presented in varied guises but as openly as the fictional mode will allow. As Leed has argued: 'The war experience is an ultimate confirmation of the power of men to ascribe meaning and pattern to a world, even when that world seemed to resist all patterning.'[2]

The rich site of values in this fiction needs to be interpreted for a more complete understanding of the experience of the survivors of the First World War. There are several 'layers' of meaning to be unearthed; by beginning with the more overt judgments about the war, it is possible to chart the patterns of evaluative reference which need to be analyzed.

1 Patriotism

The 1919 novels about the war are characterized by stress on innate patriotic feeling and on the willingness to do the job at hand without complete understanding of the aims and principles involved. The memory of the war is very young and the authors make an obvious effort to tie the loose ends of a trauma in order to exorcise it, an attempt which necessitates their belief in the existence of a cause sustaining even those men who were unaware of it. Unquestioning incomprehension becomes the mark of sacredness. *Love Lane* traces the patriotic dedication of a greengrocer who does not understand the purpose of his intense commitment. The meaning of his sacrifice is revealed after his death at the thanksgiving service held in his town in November 1918; his involvement was part of a process through which the 'God of Righteousness' had made manifest the 'omnipotence of the moral law.'[3] In W.B. Maxwell's *A Man and his Lesson* (1919) everyone feels involved in a crusade for world freedom, and statements about 'the cause' become increasingly noble in spite of the weariness and the horror. The terrible rhythm of violence and death does not negate the underlying motivation which supports the men through their ordeal, but on the contrary enhances its meaning. The officer Jim Chaytor, protagonist of *The Edge of Doom*, at the end of 1916 has no reticence in calling the war 'a dreary mechanical business of slaughter, as different from the old exhilarating art as making sausages was from riding pig.'[4] Yet this forceful image of repugnance represents the instinctive human reaction to inhuman conditions, not a condemnation of the purpose of the conflict.[5] The duality is ambiguous and explained, with all the assurance of noble principles, in terms of the strength of the cause:

> Under the dull daily routine the cause dropped out of view; you could not pretend it was sustaining you. Yet, had it been a question of not seeing the thing through, it would have been the cause that barred the way, the cause that was bound up so clearly with the real brotherhood of man. It was because his country stood for that, because she was out to punish the accursed thing – the slavery of the sword, the feudal right of compulsion over the souls of men – that he had taken a hand in the hateful business. It did come back to that in these bad hours when the flesh was weak, and achievement looked so interminably far away. This was not a fight for gain or glory, but of man's faithful spirit with the powers of evil.[6]

These attitudes to war are expounded in a verbose, turgid language which modern cultural perceptions translate as 'idealistic'. Idealism is indeed a strong presence but it is always approached obliquely, defined indirectly. The patriotism of the protagonist of *If Winter Comes* is conveyed through a sudden, powerful emotion. Mark Sabre watches the local regiment leave at dawn soon after the outbreak of war. He cannot join them because of a weak heart and is overwhelmed with feeling as he sees his friends leave: 'This bursting sensation in all his emotions!' The author, who has just devoted four pages to a survey of the social climate of 1913, and who has made his character a man aware of social issues, can only express the importance of the moment through a prolix but imprecise metaphor of meaning. Mark's mind goes back to his school days when, during a very important match between the school and the town, he had felt the same overwhelming emotions and had cheered until his throat ached. The cry then had been 'Schoo-oo-ool! Schoo-oo-ool! Schoo-oo-ool!'; his heart now was crying 'England! England!'[7] The bombastically idealistic *Tell England* also never focuses on a specific motivation. At the outbreak of war Ray 'felt the brilliance of being alive in this big moment; the pride of youth and strength. I felt Aspiration surging in me and speeding up the action of my heart. I think I half hoped it would be my high lot to die on the battlefield.' These feelings have been prompted by the patriotic outburst of the Colonel who interviews Doe and Ray when they enlist. He tells the boys they have timed their lives 'wonderfully' to be eighteen in 1914, protagonists of this glorious moment. Ray is stirred by this magniloquence: 'I saw dimly the great ideas he was striving to express.'[8] But 'the great ideas' about the war are unidentifiable amidst the florid rhetoric of the passage and what stands out is the vague expression of a momentous consummation of the two men's youth and breeding. For the schoolboys of *Tell England* war is an ineffable experience of pure ideals – unexpressed.

In *The Edge of Doom* (1919), H.F.P. Battersby defines war as a fight of right against wrong. Yet this experienced observer of the reality of war[9] does not attempt to attribute the courage of the soldiers to a consciousness of lofty ideals. 'With everything on their side that might inspire heroism', Officer Chaytor's men 'were heroes for no reason at all.' He explains this heroism in terms of its Englishness. As a source of inspiration the soldiers go into battle not with the cry of "God defend the Right!" or "St George for England", but kicking an old football and shouting "Pass!", "Play up!", "Play the Game." Discussing the attitudes to war of different nations, another officer comments that for others war is not a game: for the French it is a great, fine ordeal; the Russians die for the Tsar and for their faith; the Italians 'to redeem their country'; the Germans for 'a big idea'. In spite of the fact that they all have to die whether they 'take it seriously or make a sporting jest of it' the French resent the English lack of ideals. Chaytor laughs, and explains that whereas the French have 'the dramatic instinct...we can only be reconciled to doing a fine thing by making a jest of it.' There is an 'un-English' strain in him that would like to see a more immediately uplifting impulse, but he is confident that the cause *is* there even if not in full view.[10]

In 1935 N.P. MacDonald edited a book of essays entitled *What is Patriotism?* which included contributions from a philosopher, a scientist, Churchmen, members of the services, and two popular novelists (Ernest Raymond and Storm Jameson). While the essays, written after the 1932 Oxford debate on patriotism, reflect a common concern with finding a definition of patriotism which will not smack of militarism, the motivation for fighting is still discussed as an undefinable, if very powerful, force. Cynthia Asquith pointed out that the soldiers, the people who offer the most direct expression of love for their country, are also those who give this love the least definition. She quoted from E.B. Osborn's introduction to his 1917 compilation of war poems *The Muse in Arms*:

> The soldier's love of his land...is something inexpressive, never to be directly intimated, much less anatomized, in terms of 'ise and 'isms...The soldier instinctively feels that, as soon as love of one's country and all that inhabits there is thought of as 'patriotism' the best of its spiritual flavour is beginning to be lost. It is then as a flower entered in a botanist's museum; a quality once soul-compelling and inexplicable which must now be explained and justified; a thing to be dried, dissected, lectured upon, argued about.[11]

In these novels, similarly, patriotism is addressed mainly as a concrete expression of deeply embedded values. As a theory it could be dismantled too easily by the horror of the war and the increasingly clear threat of another conflict. Analyses, slogans, patriotic clichés are judged as empty artifacts which miss altogether the meaning of the soldier's world. Also, they are related to the political arena, from whose formidable organizational framework pours forth a constant stream of dry investigations and peremptory commonplaces. In *The Edge of Doom* one of the philosophical outbursts is about the vapid patriotic verses dished out to harness the support of the masses.

> I suppose you must have a gull like that, some sort of ring through its nose, to drag that dull beast Democracy into action. I used to mouth about the brute myself, in the far off days of two years ago when I was still an unrepentant Liberal. Oh, Democracy, what drivel is talked in thy name...[12]

The enormous sacrifice of the war can never be justified with a rational argument. The articulate patriotic argument, be it the fiery speeches of recruiting officers, the ruthless rationalizations of headquarters or the glib glossing over of tragedy by the press, is despised for making a mockery of an experience which cannot be contained by any theoretical construction.

In its magnitude the significance of war defies and defeats politics. Commitment is about awareness, choice, involvement; duty is about acceptance, tradition, endurance: politics and patriotism fall into these two fields. Patriotism is an absolute which man is unequipped to define in words; whatever it is, it is *not* politics.[13] In *The Querrils*, immediately after the declaration of war Edward Grey's speech is condemned vehemently by the family. But the disgust is directed towards the political situation and towards the man of politics, both representing all that tarnishes the Querrils high-minded attitude to life. For these narratives to uphold value intrinsic to the war experience they must avoid direct analyses in their quest for meaning. In 1929 Ernest Raymond still insisted on the unspoken characteristic of English patriotism: 'For the Englishman out of uniform can sometimes talk patriotism; in it, never; he had rather by far talk sedition. It is his strange inverted poetry.'[14] With a neat phrase, within the context of the story of the development of the protagonist's idealism through the war, subversiveness is reabsorbed into a patriotic pattern.

W.H. Hindle, in an article on war literature in the *Bookman*, affirmed that to understand the 'spirit of the Englishman in war time'

> one must go not to Mottram or Williamson but to MacGill and Frankau. In them we find what from our national character we might expect – a consciousness of the evils of this greatest evil done by mankind, but a consciousness dimmed by sentimental regard for some vague ideal imagined in a non-existent beyond; a racial adaptability to appalling conditions; a sometimes humorous, sometimes disgusted tolerance of them; in a word, the romantic mind.[15]

While the romantic mind never focuses its attention on politics, it draws heavily for meaning on 'Englishness', the most ambiguous and ubiquitous assumption of value. The ultimate crisis of civilization – war – is the experience which in so many novels provides the chance to equate civilization with England and to dwarf political issues with the urgent relevance of immanent national qualities.

Often the memory of a corner of idyllic rural England or the thought that were it not for the defence of the English shores their land would resemble the devastated French countryside makes instant sense of the soldiers' ordeal. England is transfigured by the physical and emotional displacement of war into a tangible ideal; all sacrifice can be justified in the name of the land from which all derive their sense of identity and tradition. The dashing secret agent of Buchan's *Mr. Standfast* believes that an acre of the soil of England ('old and kindly and comforting') is 'cheaply bought by the best of us.'[16]

When it comes to describing the attitude of the common soldier even the awareness of an underlying ideal is considered unnecessary. A standard attitude is presented again and again as the most viable mental framework for the lower classes; the war is a job, something that must be got through without thinking about it too much or trying to explain it. In *The Barber of Putney*, Curly has this advice to give to Tim Himrick, who is shocked by the horrible death of his friend, killed by a shell on their first day in the trenches:

> Look 'ere, son. I know just how you're feeling. Fit to howl. I bin through it. Just take a tip from an old 'and. Don't never think. Don't never think. There's no good in it when it comes to war. You'll see worse things than this yet. Bags of worse things. Keep doin' something. It's the only way. When you 'aven't got a job, sleep. When you can't sleep, get a job.[17]

The cause may not be apparent to the soldier, but it is there all the time, like an invisible hand guiding the men through chaos to a meaningful outcome. The emphasis is on the constant willingness to work, not on the pitch of the motivation. In *A London Lot* an officer compares unfavourably the courage of the 'hot foot recruit' to that of the 'more lagging and colder-hearted men' who make up the New Army. These soldiers stayed behind as long as possible to do their job at home with the same tenacity they are now showing at the front. As a consequence, the brand of their courage is more reliable: '...he who fails to become excited because his vicar has waxed red in the face, and is waving a flag, may display equal imperturbation when "the big stuff" cometh over. Enthusiastic people, on the other hand, are apt to find the big stuff monotonous.'[18] The underlying cause all are fighting for, even when not aware of it, is all the stronger and more validated for its power to keep the soldiers faithful to a job of such horrible danger. In these novels written by middle-class writers, such portrayals of the working-class stoical attitude to a predicament they cannot fully understand imply an expectation of a similar acceptance of their role in society.

The ideologically equivalent term to 'the job' for the upper classes is 'the game.' Ernest Raymond told Berta Ruck about the formal conclusion of the game for an officer friend of his. In November 1918 he paraded the men and read them the wire sent by Headquarters: 'Hostilities will cease to-day at eleven a.m.'.

> Being British Tommies they did not fly into any wild excitement, nor weep, nor babble of their country, nor turn and kiss each other on both cheeks. Only the Sergeant stepped forward, saluted very smartly and asked politely:
> 'EXCUSE ME, SIR, BUT WHO'S WON?'[19]

After four years of doing his job the Sergeant needed to put this courteous question to the officer who had been playing the game and was acquainted with the complexities of its procedure.

No expression suggests better the obliqueness of English idealism. It is replete with social meaning, it is a linguistic cornerstone of continuity, and at the same time represents a strong resistance against analyzing cultural and social meaning. This turn of phrase provides instant social identification and evokes a traditional code of values which need not be articulated but merely acted out. The charismatic and happy personality of Sim Paris, the protagonist of *One Increasing Purpose*, is illustrated in its determination by a characteristic habit he had when playing rugby or cricket at school and at Sandhurst of making a gesture which meant 'Can I? By gad, I will!'. It is exactly the same gesture he employs when leading his men over the top in France: 'Can we? By gad, we will!'[20] In *The Parts Men Play*, the 'part' played by the protagonist, the American Austin Selwyn, is to graduate from a reasoned, rationally-based pacifism to an emotional support of war, and finally to enlistment, through the education of unspoken values. In a conversation with Lord Durwent's eldest son, Malcolm, a perfect public-school gentleman, he asks him how he can seriously expect the small English force to stop the huge German army. Malcolm has a ready, calm reply: '"Ever play "Rugger?" he asked. "Rugby? Yes." "Then you've often seen a little chap bring a big one an awful cropper."'[21] In Edward John Thompson's *These Men, Thy Friends* the gallant example of an officer who carries the soldiers through the attack in which he dies is related to his innate flair for cricket. He can tell whenever the soldier's spirits are beginning to lag and, by his forceful and gentle presence, succeeds in averting the consequences of such mood.[22]

Gilbert Frankau's bestseller *Peter Jackson, Cigar Merchant* pivots around the aggressive assertion of a patriotic imperative, which is articulated through reference to icons of class value. This is one of the most noteworthy novels of 1919 as it was the first novel of the post-war years to sell more than 100,000 copies and therefore one which must have struck an important note of recognition in the reading public's consciousness. After the outbreak of the war Peter Jackson becomes aware of a compelling sense of duty when he begins reading the casualty lists. But all he can say when he announces the decision to his wife is: 'Pat...I don't think I can keep out of this thing any longer. It wouldn't be – he fumbled for the expression – quite playing the game.'[23]

The spirit which is so willing to do the right thing is at the core of the utterly homogeneous attitudes which he encounters in an officers' mess in a huge gutted French farm in 1915. The men all look identical, with the 'same carefully curled-up moustaches, the same modulated voices.' They address each other with nicknames. The atmosphere is unmistakable to Peter: 'merely glorified Eton.' This is the backbone of England. Its hallmark is understatement; everyone is pretending not to indulge in emotions, not to know or care much about his role in the war. If questioned by an outsider as to why they were fighting they would have answered with the lift of an eyebrow which meant: 'My dear fellow, I was at Eton (or Winchester, or Haileybury, or Harrow, or a hundred others of the foundation which pacific intellectuals affect to despise) and *one does, don't you know, one just does.*'[24] This display of the strength of deep cultural roots implies an entrenched class system which is the truly unmentionable political dimension.

The 'ordinariness' of characters such as the lower-middle-class protagonists of *The Barber of Putney, Love Lane, William – an Englishman* and *Sorrell and Son* reinforced the blind loyalty of those playing the game. Their values are described as the purer ones for not having the least hint of modern 'cleverness' about them. *The Sword Falls*, written in 1929, argued an understated patriotism through the pathetic endurance of the clerk Albert Robinson. Like Bill Hollis (*Love Lane*), he is a very innocent, sensitive man, who fancies himself a poet.[25] His world collapses during the war; his son is killed (after which tragedy he enlists), his house is bombarded, and his wife dies. Afterwards he returns to work and tells his employer who asks him about the 'bad time' he had: 'Oh nothing really, sir. It was a very interesting experience in many ways. All that sort of thing broadens the mind so, I always think.'[26] He has lost everything except the unshakable balance intrinsic to his class. The lower middle class was held up in middlebrow literature as a model of middle-class values, which they cultivated more rigorously than the middle class itself, motivated as they were by aspirations to the social stratum immediately above them. The precise distinction they made between themselves and the working class, through the keen fear of social slippage, served to delineate sharply the middle-class territory.

The vaguely artistic leanings often ascribed to these protagonists are a function of their class, which implies a degree of power to perceive the meaningful aura surrounding experience. 'Imagination' is an important keyword, often used to imply a world of culture, of emotions and meaning which is denied to the working class.[27] Working-class endurance is portrayed as noble but much more limited in scope and vision. In *Paper Prison* Mark Tuyler joins a working-class battalion. His appraisal of the men distinguishes between the crassness of the working-class man and the worth of the private soldier, in a social view which splits into a political and 'human' perception of the lower class.

> The "Bill Browns" who remained in the ranks were ignorant, uneducated, stupid men of incredibly narrow outlook and interest, and very many of them amazing by-products of our system of free and compulsory education. Let me hasten to add that they were splendid fellows, the salt of the earth, staunch and sound, solid and reliable.

Among them he was 'utterly alone.'[28]

Perhaps the most realistic and sombre portrayal of warfare, George Blake's *The Path of Glory* (1929), set in Gallipoli, has as protagonists two privates, the Clydeside shipyard workers Macaulay and Macleod, who are pipers in a Highland regiment. When they discover that although they joined as pipers they will not be playing, they brave the blow with the strength of their dullness: 'They did not complain, these two, for they had the ox-like brains of the Highland peasant, incapable of enterprise.' The enchantments and cultural resonances of foreign lands as they travel to Gallipoli leave them unaffected: 'It seemed that no environment, however startling, could interest them. Their minds and lives were narrow; they asked but food and sleep and, when it could be got, the relaxation of drink. They would have played Nap in the shadow of the Sphinx.'[29] As working-class men their predicament is ironic because their situation is already socially 'degraded' (to use Northrop Frye's terminology). They have none of the middle-class protagonists' control over their situation because they lack the innate emotional and mental means of deriving moral significance from the war.

2 The Enemy

Vehemence of feeling against the enemy lends confident fluency to the patriotic sentiments of some of the earliest war novels. The defeat of Germany ranges in importance from the paving of the way for a truly democratic society to a successful crusade against the legions of evil. A few episodes of intense violence and anger towards the enemy display a rare frenzy of retribution. In *Tommy of the Tanks* the regiment reacts to the crucifixion of a British soldier by deciding not to take any more prisoners and kill all the Germans they capture.[30] In *Sniper Jackson* a German assassin stalks no man's land at night and stabs English soldiers, laughing horribly; the retaliation in kind of two privates is told without a hint of criticism.[31] Generally, however, English hatred is directed not towards individuals but towards the German army as the loathed, contemptible enemy.

Anti-German animosity is the emotional centre of *Peter Jackson*. The focus of the novel is reiterated throughout with almost brutal clarity; the English are fighting to put down the 'two-legged Beast' threatening their country. Peter Jackson rants about the role of 'the Beast', the fight against which he interprets in universal, transcendental terms. God has created the Beast for a clear purpose; without him 'man's finest attribute – the very manhood of him - would atrophy. He would become flabby, emasculated: and in his flabbiness he would perish.'[32]

The denunciation of an evil enemy informs also *John Brown: Confessions of a New Army Cadet*, written by R.W.Campbell, who was a member of the British Territorial Force and trained cadets during the war. This work, in which the silly pranks of trainee officers serve as the pretence of a plot, reads like a series of lectures on what war represents for the New Army. The modern military cause is clear-cut: defeating the Germans. To lend emotional force to this aim the enemy has to be portrayed as morally dangerous, and Campbell refers to the German 'blind reliance on bluff, bombast, rapine, terror, corruption, and assassination for the intimidation of neutrals', as well as to the deeply corrupt nature of an oppressive regime. They are opposed by peace-loving Britons, 'home-loving, shopkeepers in arms', who find themselves at the front because the Germans have created this 'vile' and 'hellish' place.[33]

Early novels written by civilians about the home front are particularly heavy-handed in imputing the war to the intrinsic evil of the German nation. A deceptively mild example of this attitude is represented by the 'Love Spinner', the gentle, elderly spinster who unlike many others does not shun her German neighbour, a woman married to an English soldier, and speaks to her in terms which make a clear distinction between her feelings for her as an individual and for the Germans in general: 'I hate German ways! I could kill Germans, I think – yet, my dear I'm fond of you!...To torture prisoners – butcher the non-combatants – it cries for vengeance! My forefathers were soldiers, not savages: I and all here, we cannot understand the German mind.'[34] Instinctive, emotional response is always self-justifying. Compton Mackenzie has a Benedictine monk explain the English participation in the war through sentiment alone; he hears France 'screaming like a woman' and sees 'Belgium being knocked about like a little girl.'[35]

In *A Widow's Wooing* the apparently liberal attitude which seeks just treatment of the Hartmanns, mistakenly believed to be Germans and therefore ostracized by the small town in which they live, receives an unexpected twist when the young Ronald Hartmann affirms that this treatment would be fully justified if they really *were* Germans: 'Once a Hun always a Hun, and the greatest scandal of the times is the way in which naturalised and unnaturalised Huns are allowed to go free to do what mischief they can to us.' Ronald's sister has horrible nightmares about the unspeakable sights she has seen in a village taken over by the Germans. She hopes they may suffer a thousand-fold what they have inflicted on others: 'The beasts! The beasts! And then people talk of peace with them, before we have smashed them to the mud! Talk of brother Germans! And I saw That! That!'[36]

Berta Ruck's *The Land-Girl's Love Story*, prefaced by Kipling's racialist poem 'Our Germans,'[37] is not surprisingly imbued with an extreme distrust of Germans. A farm owner's humane and generous attitude towards the German prisoners working for him is proved misplaced when they set fire to the harvest. It may be hard to relate the honest face of the young German peasant to the atrocities committed by his nation, but individual innocence is irrelevant since

> ... it is when such thousands of these harmless souls are moulded and driven by these fiends who have cankered a once merely decent, sentimental, dreamy nation – it is then that the atrocities are made possible – the atrocities for which they all alike are paying now – too lightly![38]

There is a disturbing discrepancy between the content of the novel and the author's real experience of the enemy. In her autobiography Berta Ruck relates meeting young German prisoners and praises them for being excellent workers; her parents had German prisoners lodged in the house and stood up to local protests that they were 'much too nice to their Huns.'[39] This account is in direct opposition to the events and attitudes of her 1919 novel, heavily loaded with popular propaganda. Her autobiography, written after she had embraced her friend Storm Jameson's ideas on disarmament,[40] does reflect guilt about her earlier professions of hatred for the Germans.[41]

The debunking of the myth of German evil began immediately after the war. Two of the earliest examples are to be found in novels written by women. In *Living Alone* two witches, one English and one German, meet in the sky and fight with their broomsticks, only to realize in the end the ridiculousness of hurling the same accusations at each other and of fighting

Evil with brutal force.[42] Much more directly, in *A Servant of Reality* the young soldier dining at home on his first evening back after demobilization shocks his wealthy parents by rationally and calmly questioning the wartime British judgment of Germans. When his father reacts violently to his tale of his experiences as a prisoner of war and shouts that the Germans – 'Damned bullying blackguards!' – are not human beings, he replies:

> It's very funny your saying that, Sir...They struck me as very human always, and very like some of our own people. It occurred to me that we might be treating Germans just the same, if we thought of them what they thought of us. I often used to wonder if we weren't. War makes people's minds untruthful.[43]

With each year war novels became more concerned with being 'truthful' about the question of the enemy. The most notable exception to the process of understanding Germans as fellow-victims was the indomitable Frankau, who in 1935, in the novel *Three Englishmen*, defiantly reiterated all the most truculent statements of his 1921 bestseller. He again referred collectively to the Germans as 'the Beast' and accused 'the bleatings of all the pseudo-intellectuals, and all the muck-rakings of all those who...have sought, for some twenty years and more, to besmirch every fair shield of knightly achievement...'[44]

The earliest novels to be concerned exclusively with a moral truce with the enemy were two tragic love stories. Philip Gibbs's *Back to Life* (1920) has as its theme an English officer making the controversial gesture of marrying a German woman in the name of universal brotherhood; she dies before the end of the war. The novel presented the hopelessness of doomed love between 'enemies' as an absurd consequence of war. Hall Caine's message in 1923 was more explicit. In *The Woman of Knockaloe*, another tragic love affair between an Englishwoman and a German interned in a camp for alien civilians, he made the first open plea for brotherhood between Germans and English. The writing of the novel was prompted, as the foreword explained, by the bitter realization that far from ending all wars the war had 'strengthened and inflamed' its spirit.[45] The novel's first edition of 50,000 copies was sold out immediately after publication.[46]

By the end of the Twenties the vast majority of novels about the Great War depicted English and German soldiers sharing in the same predicament: as the officer-protagonist asserts in *Young Orland*, they were all fighting against a 'Third Thing' – Destiny.[47] The evolution of attitudes about the Germans is clearly exemplified by the plots of *W Plan* (1930), *"Cousins German"* (1930), *Blood Relations* (1935) and *Bretherton: Khaki or Field Grey?* (1929), which all revolved around cases of English/German blurring and merging of identities, through spying, marriage, and amnesia. In the 1934 novel by John Brophy, *The World Went Mad*, the fate of German and English is intertwined as closely as possible. The German soldier who dies at the feet of a young Englishman he has been helping turns out to have probably been his step-brother, from an affair the English soldier's father had had years before with a German woman.

3 Disenchantment in the Novels of the Late 1920s and 1930s

As the disappearance of anti-German feeling eliminated the only rallying point of patriotic righteousness, disillusionment came to the fore in the discussion of the experience of war in the novels of the late 1920s and 1930s. The change of emphasis from earlier novels is strikingly illustrated by *The Jesting Army* (1930), written by the author of *Tell England* (1922), that exercise in high-minded public-schoolboy patriotism. Although *The Jesting Army* is also a sentimental novel, its stress is on the cheerful and brave attitude of the men, not on the intense solemnity of experience of the earlier work. Ernest Raymond was a padre in the war, and a religious element is present in both his novels. But while the religious fervour of the *Tell England* schoolboys dictates their patriotic perceptions of the war, the protagonist of the 1930 novel abandons the conventional idealism of his religious education and befriends the cynical Hugh Anson, who has no time for military glorification. His attitude is openly irreverent:

> I'm quite clear that war's a crime, but also that, like all other crimes, it's a colossal sport. But when it comes to hanging up my sword on my study wall, after the war, and being proud of it – well, I'm not going to be such a humbug as that... I'm going to have a ring fixed to its point, and I am going to attach that ring to a chain that dangles from a certain little cistern in a certain little retired room in my house; and I shall be able to pull the handle of my sword every morning after breakfast.[48]

The predominant memory of most narratives of disillusion is the burden of extreme suffering of one generation. *Pass Guard at Ypres* (1930) is the moving account of the process of bitter disenchantment of platoon leader Freddy Mann of the first battalion of Loyal Southshires, until his death at the siege in Ypres. By 1917 he believes that what his friend, private Bamford, once told him about the war is true: 'What's the use o' thinking in this 'ere war? Either we'll be cold mutton tomorrow, or we won't.' There is nothing to think about in a war which kills, maims, and denies humanity. Colonel James Wingate tries to resurrect Freddy's patriotic interest in a well-meaning talk with him about God, England's cause, the honour of the regiment, and the British soldier. But Freddy is totally absorbed in and isolated by his apathy and utter lack of belief in anything: 'I'll carry on, sir, and do the bombing. It doesn't matter, as far as the bombing is concerned, whether I believe or not.'[49] There is a sad dignity in his ability to carry on in spite of the war stripping him of his armour of belief.

Yet in spite of his pronouncements about war being such hell that the only thing to do is not care, he does care about 'Wipers'. This city, which has witnessed the end of his belief in war and the death of so many of his company, exudes 'glory in the guardianship.'[50] War is too horrible and destructive an experience for Freddy to believe in the fight for the salvation of his country. He is isolated from his past and alienated from an England which completely misunderstands the reality of the front. All his emotional strength is concentrated on the physical background of his disillusion, which provides him with an ideal within meaninglessness. As he lies mortally wounded, he hears clearly the Voice of Ypres asking him what has been taken from him. All? All. It then asks him whether he has learnt the high lessons of Ypres:

> "Courage."
> I have learned much of Courage.
> Faith?
> Yes, Faith – but I had forgotten.
> Friendship, too, so great that before it death is a little thing?
> I have known such friendship – Robbie
> Sacrifice, also: have you learned to give?
> I have given all.
> And Pain: is Pain your master?
> No
> Or utter Weariness?
> I have fought Weariness and overcome.
> Death, then. Is death yet fearful?
> I am prepared to die.
> These are high lessons: have you learned them all?
> A little: I have tried –
> O mighty Voice of Ypres triumphant, speak!
> "PASS ON, THRICE TRIED, TO
> BE FOR EVER OF THE
> BROTHERHOOD!"[51]

In the foreword to the novel, which consists of his poem 'To Youth', Gurner makes an appeal to contemporary youth – 'living in a world now free' – to listen to a tale of agonies foreign to them in the name of slain youth whose cries he can still hear, and who sometimes still speak to him.[52] It is the poem of an ex-soldier who feels keenly the isolation of his generation and whose claim to be heard rests on what the soldiers conquered for the youth of today, and on the presence he feels of those who have died. The transmission of values learnt in the war was the subject of a later novel by Gurner, which sadly had echoes of his own life. *Reconstruction* (1931) shows a schoolmaster, Roger Carbury, inflexibly Calvinistic and with little sense of proportion, returning to Croyle College after the war and trying to teach his students the lessons of the war. The reaction to what those around perceive as his fixation destroys him, and he loses his job and his family.

The novels of the late 1920s and 1930s very often relate the futility of war to contemporary problems. The wide and vague scope of these bitter terms of criticism of the follies of contemporary 'civilization' deflects the focus of condemnation from the political dynamics which can make war possible. In *Retreat* (1930) the Irish doctor O'Reilly thinks it funny that people should have ruined such a perfect blueprint for harmonious coexistence as Christianity to the extent of needing the Hague Convention, 'a Convention governing human slaughter!'[53] Men alone with death, martyrs of their age, become illuminated with a wisdom which, no matter how bitter, contains by virtue of its detail the prescription for a better world. In *No Man's Land*, after a raid on the German lines, Stevenson, a young officer, is left dying in a shell-hole on the Ypres Salient. In the day of life left to him he reflects with intense bitterness on the purpose of war. The terms of his analysis are vast: he considers civilization itself the issue at stake, and argues that 'Le jeu ne vaut pas la chandelle' because they are fighting and dying horrible deaths for 'a mockery of civilization.'[54] On leave in London, he recalls, he had seen people queue up in front of hideous picture-palaces, 'with their imitation marble, their stucco work', to watch absurd stories acted by glamorous people in order to relieve the monotony of their drab lives. In the same street people were marching alongside two policemen who were taking a drunken woman to the police station. He was disgusted by the scene, which in his last hours prompts him to conclude: 'What had a civilization that produced such scenes in its largest city deserved but a war which would lead to its own destruction? What else could you expect in a world that believed only in symbols, that lost Christ in its dispute over ritual, that forgot the finer qualities of patriotism in cant about flags and armaments and glory of war?'[55] The artificiality of contemporary civilization is a sign, in his opinion, of people's refusal to face the truth about their slums, their distorted patriotism, their manipulation of Christianity to keep the poor resigned, and the pettiness of their education and ambitions.

The awareness of these attitudes in society does not allow him to harbour any illusions about how the memory of the war will be treated. He knows what should be done: 'It may not be memorials and monuments that they ought to erect after this war, as they had done after its puny predecessors, but mountains of chloride of lime. And you'd never again be tempted to go to war.' But he knows that people, wanting to glorify war, would strut to church carrying their swords, which looked more attractive than a rifle-grenade or a jam-tin bomb. Children would not be told about how soldiers dug latrines and covered corpses with chloride of lime, because such tales would be considered a bad influence on them; but they would be allowed to boast about and treasure the sword or the hat-badge.[56] Stevenson's hope for mankind is projected far away in the future. He believes there might be other world wars before men, finally revolted by war, would 'strive for perfection' and become worthy of the spark of life which gave them the capacity to appreciate what was fine and beautiful.[57]

The evils of war are exposed in a way which throws into relief the lessons learnt by men during this ordeal. In *Retreat* the message is most sombre. The empty patriotism and brutality of war distorts standards and creates false superlatives: 'A little exotic knowledge forced up in a hothouse – that's the product of War.'[58] For those who have the strength to pursue it, the core of meaning lies in a courageous and profound spirituality. Other novels offered a much more buoyant reference of meaning. Morris's *Behind the Lines*, published in 1930, the year after his bestseller *Bretherton*, was a tale of segregation from the life of the trenches through desertion imposed by a fortuitous set of circumstances. When Peter Rawley finally rejoins his unit in March 1918 he is happy to be reintegrated into what is a unity in a particularly vital sense:

> ...Rawley was content; he was even happy. Once more there was an object in life, something that demanded all one's strength of body and of will....he was back again with the pack, inspired by the contagion of human effort concentrated to a single purpose. One might suffer hunger, thirst, fatigue, pain, death, and fear, but one suffered neither futilely nor alone. Consciousness of a noble purpose spurred one's flagging efforts; hardships borne in common fed the warming fire of comradeship.[59]

In his autobiography, W.B. Maxwell qualified thus his recollection of the men's depression of spirits in the autumn of 1916: 'It was not that the uplift had gone. That never left. The unselfish surrender to a very terrible necessity was no less complete. The flame burst clearly, although not so visibly.'[60]

Grey Dawn – Red Night mirrored the war experience of its author James Lansdale Hodson. Dedicated 'To Those of the Third Public School Battalion who went to France with me and did not return', it reads as if Hodson was describing his ordeal as one who had not survived. John Hardcastle is also in the 3rd Public Schools Battalion and in the end is killed by a shell. The novel is a thorough, sensitive description of the various facets of his *alter ego*'s experience, from the training at Aldershot to the muddy, cold despair of the Somme, and it conveys the author's profound knowledge of the fear and the companionship of the trenches. The cover of the novel displayed instead of an illustration, some writing clearly spelling out the novel's intention even before the book was opened: 'In what other war novel, English or German, is the degradation and corruption of the trenches so honestly and so terribly rendered, *and yet at the same time* with so much balancing description of good humour, loyalty, good health and other "compensations" of the life?'[61] The word 'balancing' in this passage is loaded with hope, as it refers to that process in the middlebrow memory of war which constantly counters degradation with human value.

4 Personal War

The titles alone of some these works reveal a concentration on the experience of the individual, the source of all that is morally worthy and beneficial to society: *Mr. Sterling Sticks it Out, The Man Who Went, God and Tony Hewitt, Young Orland, John Brown: Confessions of a New Army Cadet, Mrs. Fischer's War, William – an Englishman, Grope Carries On, A Man and his Lesson, Lord Raingo, The Barber of Putney, Mrs. Marden, Sniper Jackson, The Woman of Knockaloe, A Widow's Wooing, A Servant of Reality.*[62] Civilians' experiences cover an extensive range of cases: the ordeal of the pacifist (*Mr. Sterling Sticks it Out*, 1919); the intellectual challenge of the problems of war for a Cambridge professor who believes that effective protest has always been made by individuals, never by the mass (*Pugs and Peacocks*, 1921); the ostracism endured by the Englishwoman whose German husband enlists in the German army (*Mrs. Fischer's War*, 1919). Under the test of war, men, and sometimes women, acquire a new, more intense degree of understanding. In novels which necessarily address momentous social problems and consequences – war and reconstruction – the reflection is anchored in the perspective of personal development, which contains the answers for all levels of existence.

In *William – an Englishman*, a London clerk does not really notice people because, as a rather amateurish Socialist, he is only interested in them as members of organizations. He and his wife are alike in not having anything to do with those who think differently from them. This, the narrator explains, is due not to unkindness but to their having 'lived for so long less as individuals than as members of organizations – a form of existence which will end by sinking charity out of the sweetest heart alive.'[63] With the outbreak of war, patriotism challenges William's political conscience and wins out. By joining up, his better instincts reawakened by the patriotic call, William stands up as an individual and consequently finds himself. His old socialist creed is replaced not with a rationale of patriotic commitment but with a new way of living and believing without the need to explain to himself and to others precisely in what or why. Instinctive morality triumphs. The blurb aptly described the content of the novel: 'The Romance of an everyday Englishman who awakens to the great things of life.' William's conversion to this new human faith of individualism never wavers. His new horror of the constraints imposed by organizations informs also his criticism of military life: 'We've been made to do things for so long....we've all of us been taken – and bent and twisted into things we never meant to be...'[64]

The protagonist of *No Hero – This* (1936) criticizes society for the violence it perpetrates through war against the individual instinct for self-preservation, the strongest in man.

> We must fight for our clan and our country, and no high metaphysical argument will save us from being damned and scorned as cowards if we dare to value the one self more than the stark need of the many. Societies must protect themselves. But they will help us to dress up our own cowardice in shining and noble armour, and call it by high-sounding names, patriotism, sacrifice, the pride of a manly self-regard.

The acknowledgment that the 'crowd man is right when one of these crowd catastrophes ravages the earth'[65] by its terminology draws even more attention to the issue of the threatened individual.

Although war thwarts the expression of the will of the individual and requires him to subordinate his life to military organization on a national, and even international, scale, the forced involvement in such a vast social machinery is discussed in moral and personal terms which leave the value of individualism intact. To Peter Blaven, the protagonist of *The Natural Man*, war brings strong confirmation of individual worth. The beginning of the novel sees this young man entering the war in 1916 full of hope that it will rescue him from his narrow life and unfold his powers as a human being. The war experience does come up to his expectations by endowing him with a new and confident understanding of himself: by the end of the war he has become an individual 'on his own feet,' 'a despot over his own affairs.'[66]

In *Out of Darkness* Charles Feversham's flouting of society and retreat to a private world of his own in the French countryside is a function of an idealistic, slightly eccentric character: 'The English spirit doesn't get its chance. It buds at the public-school and flowers at the 'Varsity, and then it marries and settles down and becomes ineffectual. It hasn't got an inspiration.'[67] Middlebrow novels provided a model of middle-class values, presented as ideals and revealed as 'inspirational.' The factor which is indispensable to operate this ideological translation is individualism, a constant which precludes the authors from conceding social and moral legitimacy to the working-class. The multitude of the working class, prone to clinging together in political groups, represents an innate negation of private values which can attract the crudest judgments. 'I hate the people,' comments a young lady in *Time and Eternity* about the crowd she sees in the street. 'They can never be anything but a mob.' Her boyfriend explains to her that they are 'listless' and 'characterless' because they are frightened of poverty and exploitation; when they will not be afraid any longer, they will be 'tired and stupid.'[68]

In his 1915 bestseller *The First Hundred Thousand* Ian Hay had asserted that the class animosities fomented by Union leaders were dying in the trenches and that the war was creating egalitarian and peaceful modes of social coexistence by establishing the right moral qualities with which to safeguard society from class upheaval. This ideal of continued harmonious coexistence between the officers and the soldiers once out of uniform provided a pattern of natural subordination; Waites has shown that the possibilities for a classless society which could be glimpsed from the war years only served to foster the 'image of a more deeply divided society.'[69] In *John Brown* the narrator reminds the readers that it will be worth listening to the upper-class cadets of his novel when they become war veterans because they are the guarantors of a stable society. Their love of comradeship is described as 'the true Democracy, for "the Boys" have no social measures, only the simple standards of Faith, Hope, and Charity.' This training has equipped them to 'develop the finest, fairest Democracy this world has ever seen. Far better to have the Democracy of the trenches than the Anarchy of Trotsky. *For Heaven's sake, be wise!*'[70]

One 1919 novel reveals in detail a common model of discussion of the interaction between individualism and a social role. Stacy Aumonier's *The Querrils* describes the effect of the war on an English middle-class family. The Querrils are a very charming, happy and liberal family, totally absorbed in their devotion to one another. Their work at the 'Settlement', where they help 'problem' working-class youngsters to become rehabilitated into society, is a personal attempt to solve the problems of 'poverty, misery, and vice' through 'suggestion and "atmosphere".'[71] The outbreak of the war finds them detached and disapproving, but their attitudes change as they become aware of the need to be involved in this great social and moral question. The eldest son, who was for a while an active pacifist, enlists and dies in France. The plot of *The Querrils* depicts the transition from the idyllic security of domestic happiness to the obligation of social involvement, therefore apparently away from individualism. But a consideration of the language in which this evolution is described tells a different story.

The family devotion is selfless to a degree which jeopardizes independence of action. Their American friend MacDowell criticizes their attitude because it neglects the fact that 'in all big things in life one has to act alone. In every adventure, in every experience, there comes a moment when one has to suddenly weigh a chance, make a quick decision, and one has to do that alone....this mutual self-effacing business is bad for a race. Unselfishness becomes selflessness.' It is again the American who enlightens the Querrils about the causes of the war. These are love and fear: love for the people one cares about and fear about their safety – with love the predominant factor. 'And, sir, it's not the gauzy, universal brotherhood-of-man, grape-juice and potash brand of love that counts. It's the intense individual love....It's that makes you do things, fool around, and go to war because you're frightened. It's your story, and the story of the gay little earth.'[72] The involvement (they call it 'interference') to which the Querrils become converted is in fact the determination to take a strong individualistic stand and not to act as a unit; by the end of the story the family is dispersed, as all the children except the youngest one have left and gone far away to lead their own lives.

An old friend of the Querrils thinks about them after the end of the war, and enters a long soliloquy about the peculiarly Anglo-Saxon gift for 'interference.' This term is divested of pernicious political connotations by being placed in the context of personal choice rather than that of world affairs; yet the subject of this disquisition is nothing less than imperialism. The Anglo-Saxon, the elderly gentleman reflects, loves to explore and roam free and wide in the world. Once home he starts worrying about things he has seen, like women throwing their babies in the river Ganges in religious rituals, Malay slaves working for Chinese masters in salt mines, and people mutilating themselves.

> And one night when the Teuton and the Slav – and even the Latin – is sleeping soundly in his bed he wakes up and thinks: "No, but damn it all! Babes in the Ganges! A bit thick!"' This disturbs him so much that he decides he must return to change things, and being a practical man he thinks he may as well take some tea to sell to the native population. Even though the power of 'Interference', greater than himself, drives him to act, that is not the reason why he goes back, since he does not like interfering and detests a 'situation.' He goes because he represents 'a landmark in evolution, the conscience of mankind...A decent chap![73]

The personalistic term 'conscience of mankind' is an appropriate resolution for an argument of global political scale reduced to the personal idiosyncracies and decency of 'a decent chap.'

Sanford Sternlicht adopts the correct framework of investigation in discussing C.S. Forester's attitude to war against the backdrop of the author's conception of individualism. Forester's *The General* (1936) is deservedly well known for its portrayal of one of the GHQ managers of disaster. In order to understand this novel it is necessary to consider Forester's earlier, now forgotten, *Brown on Resolution* (1929). This novel depicted the heroism of Albert Brown, sailor in the Royal Navy and illegitimate son of a naval officer. Taken prisoner by the German cruiser Ziethen near Resolution (Galapagos Islands), he escapes to the island after stealing a rifle, and for two days holds off the ship from landing and making necessary repairs; this gives a British ship the time to arrive and defeat the Germans. Sternlicht argues that in this novel Forester began to consider 'the meaning and ways of war' as 'innumerable small actions of individual human beings, which ultimately determine victory or defeat despite the plans of great leaders.'[74] Forester's judgment of the nondescript Albert Brown is not one of unqualified glorification. In a final interpretative gloss, he states that the credit for Brown's action belonged not to him but 'to the Navy, the tremendous institution which had trained him and disciplined him.' After acknowledging the wider institution, Forester concludes with a panegyric of the value highlighted by his narrative:

> ...but at the same time the argument hands over to Brown all the glory and honour for what he did on Resolution, and to Brown as an individual must be given the credit for the eventual destruction of Ziethen. For he acted on Resolution without orders, on his own keen initiative, under conditions where neither discipline nor training could help him.[75]

In his next novel he would castigate, in the figure of General Sir Herbert Curzon, the obtuse leaders who relentlessly stifled all such 'keen initiative.'

The directions of meaning of these novels are idealistic and apolitical in a way which implies immutable significance; the next two chapters will examine the nature of these unchanging, pervasive values and discuss how they were employed as a language of personal and national definition.

Notes to Chapter 2

1. Arthur Beverley Baxter, *The Parts Men Play*, 1920, p. 247.
2. Eric J. Leed, *No Man's Land: Combat and Identity in World War I*, 1979, pp. x.
3. John Collis Snaith, *Love Lane*, 1919, p. 275.
4. Henry Francis Prevost Battersby, *The Edge of Doom*, 1919, p. 322.
5. Only one novel in 1919, the sonorously patriotic *Tommy of the Tanks*, contained no references to the changed nature of modern warfare. All of the protagonists are alive at the end of 1918, after having fought the Huns, ('pig-eyed, high-cheekboned', 'stern-faced, fierce-eyed men') without ever relenting in their hate and ardour. Given the bias of the novel, the foreword seems singularly superfluous. 'The Great European War was entirely of Germany's making', it begins, and goes on to explain the murderous responsibility of a people now 'loathed and

despised by the whole civilized world.' (Escott Lynn, *Tommy of the Tanks*, 1919, pp. 82, 86.)

6. Battersby, *The Edge of Doom*, p. 322.

7. A. S. M.Hutchinson, *If Winter Comes*, 1921, p. 189.

8. Ernest Raymond, *Tell England: A Study in a Generation*, 1922, pp. 167–8. The cover of the novel, showing red rose petals falling on flames, rendered melodramatically the sacrifice of war.

9. Battersby had received military training and had been a war correspondent during the war.

10. Battersby, *The Edge of Doom*, pp. 204–5, 227–8.

11. in N. P. MacDonald, *What is Patriotism?*, 1935, pp. 278–9.

12. Battersby, *The Edge of Doom*, p. 242. Cicely Mary Hamilton condemned the increasingly great part played by politics during her lifetime, 'for to live politically, to think politically, is almost inevitably to become less honourable, less kindly – and, in many cases, less intelligent.' (Cicely Mary Hamilton, *Life Errant*, London, 1935, p. 245.)

13. As Lynne Layton observes, Vera Brittain's novel *Not Without Honour*, written in 1924, still reflected the strand of idealism which had helped her pull through her war experience. One of the protagonists, Christine Merival, after reading in Oxford the dying letter at Gallipoli of her teacher and lover realizes that 'the dramatic surroundings of a great deed or a great ideal were the necessary response to human nature's need for the interpretation of Truth into symbols.' (p. 314, cited in Lynne Layton, 'Vera Brittain's Testament(s)', in *Behind the Lines: Gender and the Two World Wars*, New Haven and London, 1987, p. 77). Brittain's political radicalization led to the pacifism of her 1930s writings. *Ibid.*, pp. 80–81.

14. Ernest Raymond, *A Family That Was*, 1929, p. 447.

15. W.H. Hindle, 'War Books and Peace Propaganda', *Bookman*, December 1931, p. 159.

16. John Buchan, *Mr. Standfast*, 1919, p. 27.

17. J.B. Morton, *The Barber of Putney*, 1919, pp. 52–53.

18. A.M.N. Lyons, *A London Lot*, 1919, pp. 97–99.

19. Berta Ruck, *A Story-Teller Tells the Truth: Reminiscences and Notes*, 1935, p. 142.

20. A.S.M. Hutchinson, *One Increasing Purpose*, 1925, pp. 13–14.

21. Baxter, *The Parts Men Play*, p. 190.

22. Edward John Thompson, *These Men, Thy Friends*, 1927, pp. 272–3. Philip MacDonald's *The Patrol* (1927), a tale of extreme heroism, endurance and hardship, centres around the strategy of a terrible game, with a platoon surrounded by Arabs in a desert oasis in Mesopotamia being killed one by one, and in turn killing the attackers, until all are dead.

23. Gilbert Frankau, *Peter Jackson, Cigar Merchant: A Romance of Married Life*, 1919, p. 389.

24. *Ibid.*, pp. 516–17. (italics in the text). Francis Brett Young in *Jim Redlake* describes the 'intrinsication of the much-condemned public spirit' present in the regiment as the reason for its soldiers' unconscious heroism. (Francis Brett Young, *Jim Redlake*, 1930, pp. 535–36.)

25. In this respect he is remarkably like R.C. Sherriff, the lower-middle-class author of the public-school war play *Journey's End*. The cover of *The Sword Falls* shows a typical lower middle-class interior, complete with aspidistra, and an angel holding a sword.

26. Anthony Bertram, *The Sword Falls*, 1929, p. 277.

27. Sherriff's description of Trotter's lack of imagination in *Journey's End* serves to define the terms of different memories of war along specific class lines. See chapter 5, pp. 153–5.

28. Percival Christopher Wren, *Paper Prison*, 1939, pp. 131–2.

29. George Blake, *The Path of Glory*, 1929, pp. 21, 130.

30. Lynn, *Tommy of the Tanks*, pp. 105–6.

31. Frederick Sleath, *Sniper Jackson*, 1918, pp. 97–107.

32. Frankau, *Peter Jackson*, pp. 680–1.

33. R.W. Campbell, *John Brown, Confessions of a New Army Cadet*, 1919, pp. 62, 145–6.

34. Clara Turnbull, *The Love Spinner*, 1919, p. 246.

35. Compton Mackenzie, *Heavenly Ladder*, 1924, p. 321.

36. James Blyth, *A Widow's Wooing*, 1919, pp. 94, 206–7.

37. 'The Stranger within my gates,/ He may be evil or good,/ But I may not tell what powers control –/ What reasons sway his mood;/ Nor when the Gods of his far-off land/ May re-possess his blood.' (Cited in Berta Ruck, *The Land-Girl's Love Story*, p. 294.)

38. *Ibid.*, p. 309.

85

of *Chances* (Arthur Hamilton Gibbs, 1930), an old Oxford running blue who spends one night a week doing religious work in Whitechapel slums, are reflections of a kind of middle-class social intervention which had its origin in the late nineteenth century. In 1869 Edward Thring, headmaster of Uppingham School, founded the first settlement; this experiment was so successful that by 1900 there were twenty-four settlements in London, mainly in the East End. Oxford House in Bethnal Green and Toynbee Hall in Stepney were started in 1884, following meetings in Oxford colleges responding to the publication of *The Bitter Cry of Outcast London* (1883). The first was principally a religious community, whereas the second represented 'a centre for social work and social observation.' (Ian Bradley, *The English Middle Classes Are Alive And Kicking*, 1982, pp. 111–113.)

72. Aumonier, *The Querrils*, pp. 89, 217.

73. *Ibid.*, pp. 268–270.

74. Sanford Sternlicht, *C.S. Forester*, (Twayne's English Authors' Series, no. 320), Boston, 1981, p. 59. His *The African Queen* (1935) is also a highly individualistic wartime tale of adventure and courage, bringing out the woman in Rose Sayer, and the man in Charlie Allnutt.

75. C.S. Forester, *Brown on Resolution*, 1929, pp. 127–8.

...he had to be here, scratching about in a hole in the earth, following the irrelevant profession of death, a hundred miles away in space, the whole breadth of existence in every other dimension. It was as if some stooping sub-human creature, from a pre-historic age, with a brute jowl and brute fears and suspicions working behind its wrinkled receding forehead, had leapt forward through time and begotten a child on a woman gracious with all that civilization had achieved at its zenith – and then the creature had been sent back through the centuries to sprawl among the banes and terrors of its cave, tormented by faint, uncapturable memories, as of a dream beyond its scope. But he wasn't a troglodyte, he wasn't merely a muddied mechanic of pawl and detonators and rifle-bolts, he was Eleanor's lover, her husband, the father of her child.

This officer, doomed to die before the birth of his son, is also tormented by the way in which war is reducing him to a series of automatic reactions; it has put on him 'an armour of discipline and duty and weariness' under which his personality has 'shrivelled away.'[4] In quite similar language, John Hardcastle remarks that on certain days he felt that the advance of 'millions of years' was as nothing: your club had become a rifle, your skins were turned into jerkins and waterproof capes and tin hats, and you were stalking about after your prey.'[5]

The landscape itself is not of this world or of this age. In *The Natural Man*, for the young gunner subaltern coming in sight of Lake Zillebeke the landscape presenting itself to him is one 'that could not have been made by any natural forces, or else the forces were suddenly working backwards, tearing the world to pieces.' He 'reads' the landscape as visibility of what until then had been only literary pictures of grotesquely dream-like quality, images from the 'great epics', Doré's horrors, and Blake.

> Blaven felt as if memories he had never been conscious of were rising in him, and also were outside him. Men themselves could actually create or expose to the eye, upon their own very earth, the unimaginable.[6]

The unimaginable in this instance finds meaning by being related to fantastical literary memories.

The intimate world of companionship, the one tangible help that soldiers could rely on, and the one gain which even the most cynical observer could not discount, held together the pieces of a shattered world. Companionship is most often portrayed as the powerful bond between men inhabiting a world which no outsider can understand or visit. Only another soldier could understand the reality of trench warfare and by this very terrible knowledge alleviate its horror. In *Peter Jackson,* after the Somme offensive the men, aided by their officers, labour for three hours to clear the ground and bury the dead. Two men, after that horror, sit to breakfast together.

For the moment, the reticences of civilized life were in abeyance. Each of these two knew, as he crouched over the bacon-box in the sodden, broken chalk-trench, that he was hanging on by the eye-teeth to his last remnant of sanity. Each still saw the same bestial vision: smashed pit, half-buried gun, slithering soil, mangled men writhing and groaning, mangled men lying deadly still, Charlie Straker's face white and drawn in the light of the hurricane-lamp – and the Head that watched him, the Head that still grinned under its shrapnel-helmet, the Head which had been Pettigrew...Once again sanity trembled in the balance. Their haggard eyes met across the candle-flame; and from those eyes naked soul looked at naked soul.[7]

Naked souls: stripped of all the self-deceptions and the props and securities that made them easily functional in peacetime, they had to cope with unspeakable knowledge which they could share only with their comrades. This is the 'truth' that emerges clearly for everyone confronted with the reality of the trenches.

In these novels war is often portrayed as bringing the men to a better knowledge of themselves through prolonged intimate knowledge of the most brutal existence and through the profound authenticity of their world apart. John Cornelius, in the homonymous novel, is happy to go to war because he thinks he will finally learn about reality. He does, but the way in which reality is opened up to this writer with little experience of life is through a mystical experience, the most powerful direction of truth. This spiritual event remains to the end of his life his most 'real' experience, overshadowing 'all his earlier realities, his personal ambitions, his anxiety for his material happiness.'[8]

Reality is indeed one of the keywords in these novels about change of identity. For two clergymen, the war experience is a chance to acquaint themselves unequivocally with life, after being shaken out of the complacency of their well-defined world: 'I mean to try and get down to reality myself and try to weigh it up';[9] 'He had the queerest feeling of his old life falling from him, dropping round his feet like the outworn scales of a serpent...Had they [his tasks and duties] ever been quite real? Well, he had shed them now, and was to move out into life illumined by the great reality – death!'[10] The *Times Literary Supplement* remarked about the novel *A Servant of Reality* that such a title indicated that the book was gloomy.[11] Indeed it is, as the reality described is war and the way in which it affects a young surgeon by shattering his previous aloofness and confidence. But even though he learns of cruelty and pain he has a newly-found vision, born of his searing contact with reality, to help him make sense of what he has learnt. Until the war he had lived by a very honourable moral code which allowed him to keep life at a distance. War destroys this security: 'Anthony had not allowed for a life that was a hideous nightmare beneath the place of self-control, not for a moral chaos without rules.' In a familiar attempt at re-evaluation he realizes that if he can patch up their bodies, he cannot give soldiers the spiritual comfort they desperately miss. The answer is religion, which he describes as something indefinite, made of 'human ties, traditions, and the obligations of love.'[12]

Fear The severest test set by the encounter with the reality of war was the soldier's confrontation with his capacity to deal with the onslaught of brutal danger. The frightening unpredictability which characterized the lives of soldiers and mirrored their suspension of control over their inner resources was a function not only of external circumstances but also of the level of courage with which men met them.

> That the temper and compass of a man's courage should vary from day to day was one of those intimate and surprising discoveries that many a man made for himself during the war. The 'I' in him blew hot and cold; it shivered one day and laughed the next; nor did it take its mood from the environment of the moment.[13]

The battle with fear and with one's nerves played havoc with men's balance of body and mind. Identity became a double gamble with the notions of duty and sanity. Disintegration of control over the self was evoked by Blaker with lucid horror in *But Beauty Vanishes*. On leave in March 1916, Stewart tells his mother-in-law about intense fear, those moments beyond reasoning when

> your scalp felt as though your hair was being carried about upon it by ants or lice; when your cheeks and lips were sagging loose, looking like cheese mildewed with the colour of a beard suddenly sprouted to a full day's growth; when your stomach flopped about within you like an empty bag of wet parchment because the air was suddenly ripped asunder and the earth jerked away in a deafening crash...

At times like these thoughts were not about survival, but about the most trivial aspects of trench life, like the whereabouts of a knife or Field Cashier's day.[14]

Fear was also a vital component of the dynamics of companionship, as courage was necessary to others' survival. James Lansdale Hodson noted in his novel that in trench friendships courage was one of the most valuable assets – 'A brave man was beyond price and beyond praise.'

> For such who failed, you found yourself entertaining some contempt: not a contempt you were proud of, because in your sympathetic moments you knew the

fellow couldn't help his fear. But when he permitted it to show...then irrationally and illogically, and perhaps cruelly, you found yourself despising the fellow. For to be decently unafraid was the common standard reached by nineteen out of twenty: or, at least, if you were afraid you said, "My God, I'm frightened to death: wind up like blazes," and you grinned and got on with the job.[15]

The war here is seen as a task which tested to the limit all physical and psychological resources: part of a soldier's duty was to reinterpret his identity in terms of a common effort of endurance. In *Sniper Jackson* the familiar theme of the unpreparedness of imagination for the shock of fear, for 'the awful physical terror which had gripped him at the first German volley', is 2nd Lieutenant Ronald Jackson's brutal initiation into the war. What controls his terror is his encounter with an equally frightened young recruit in tears, who tells him he wants to leave. Jackson comforts him gently: 'This is nothing at all. It will be over in a minute or two.' His words calm both soldier and officer, whose understanding of the importance of his responsibility 'banished the last vestige of his fears.'[16]

In several novels the trauma of a drastic change of personality engendered by the destructive effects of fear is depicted with moving openness. There is no reticence in describing how the pre-war conception of courage as a powerful male ideal was shattered and then redefined by trench warfare.

Horrible! That unaccountable fear. Makes you sly – almost. All the decent, honourable feelings you've grown up with seem to drop like water out of a burst paper bag. You're just a cunning, shivery creature ready to bolt into a hole – and leave someone else to do the dirty job.[17]

The first, and by far the best, novel to portray this personal devastation was A. P. Herbert's *The Secret Battle* (1919). Other novels with fear as the central element are May Sinclair's *The Romantic* (1920), Terence Mahon's *Cold Feet* (1929), Charles R. Benstead's *Retreat: A Story of 1918* (1930), Naomi Jacob Ellington's *"Honour Come Back"* (1935) and Warwick Deeping's *No Hero - -This* (1936). They are alike in their close examination of a man's personality struggling to deal with what is felt as an emasculating emotion. Even Gilbert Frankau's determinedly virile novel *Peter Jackson* includes an unselfconscious account of his own experience of shell shock.[18]

These narratives are characterized by an effort at psychological analysis which is generally lacking in other popular novels. Terence Mahon's *Cold Feet* presents a close psychological study of a man whose abject fear of danger cannot be concealed any longer once he finds himself in the trenches; he is court-martialled and sentenced to death. The narrative is interwoven with recollections of the man's traumatic public-school days, and of the woman he loved but lost after her discovery of his reluctance to join up. He talks to a chaplain before dying, and, even though he is an agnostic, the night before his execution he has a very strong mystical experience. Miraculously, a man walks into his locked cell. His physical features resemble those of an old school-master who alone understood him as a child; his speech and kindness are those of Jesus. He comforts him and reassures him about his personal worth. The next day, moments before his execution, the condemned man saves the lives of the firing squad and others around him by deliberately attracting onto himself the attention of enemy aircraft. He is awarded the Victoria Cross posthumously and his courage is vindicated in the eyes of all who knew him. The interweaving in this novel of the soldier's military experience with recollections of his life before the war highlights trenchantly the tragic consequences inflicted by the dramatic, sometimes grotesque, transmogrification of that fear which had been manageable in his pre-war daily life.

Within the context of a very realistic picture of the retreat of the Fifth Army, *Retreat* tells the story of the complete psychological defeat of a middle-aged Cambridgeshire padre who, afflicted with uncontrollable fear, cannot adapt himself to the conditions of war. His inflexible religious devotion admits of no rethinking; he lacks imagination and commands no respect from the soldiers or the officers. The novel traces the progress of the tragic collapse of an identity which will not reshape itself against the new reality of war. Another study of the wartime male predicament of a sense of identity dissected by fear was written by a woman. The title of May Sinclair's novel, *The Romantic*, refers to a man who is admired for his strength and dashing idealism, but who in the course of the war, working in the Ambulance Corps, reveals the worst kind of cowardice, involving cruelty both in its consequences and in the attempt to blame others for it. After his death a psychoanalyst explains to his fiancée the origin of his behaviour. The *Athenaeum* recognized the sincerity of the author but 'deplored' her allowing the love of her craft to 'suffer the eclipse of psycho-analysis';[19] the *Spectator*, on the other hand, praised it as 'a notable achievement in psycho-analysis'.[20] As will be seen later, the achievement of Sherriff's *Journey's End* was the intimate portrayal of the soldiers' world through their experience of fear. James Agate, the aggressively middlebrow critic who contributed to the play's success with his enthusiastic radio talk following the first performance, judged the film version to be superior because of its starker portrayal of the horror of war. The facet of experience Agate stressed to reinforce his point about the necessity of portraying the horror of war was fear.

General Crozier has described an execution for cowardice. But what he has not told us is that the lad who was hanged on the butcher's hook entered the war with as noble and high a courage as the rest. None of us slinks into battle. Some can stand it when they get there, and some can't.[21]

The brand of courage that soldiers did acquire in the trenches was a very different matter from the heroic gallantry of old. Hugh Kimber's novel *San Fairy Ann* presented the philosophy encompassed by the anglicized rendering of the French sentence 'ça ne fait rien' – 'it does not matter' – as the main lesson learnt by the soldiers. In the end this turns out to be a valuable asset for the post-war survival of the soldiers: 'Death, grief, spite, ugliness – it mattered not, humanity would progress....say "San Fairy Ann" and be courageous...' Thus, for the protagonist Richard Steele, the relegation of pain and the worst obstacles of life to the realm of the insignificant represents not 'the banner of pessimism, but a message of hope.'[22]

Communion with the Dead Most soldiers became conversant with death. Stephen Graham, in his account of a tour of France and Belgium in 1920, spoke familiarly and with no hint of squeamishness of the remains of soldiers.

> Lying in an old trench behold a skull! It is clean and polished – a soldier's head, low and broad at the brows, high at the back. There is a frayed hole in an otherwise perfect cranium. The simplest way to pick it up would be to put a finger in an eye-hole and lift it. You must put both hands together and raise it fearfully if it be the first skull you have ever found...[23]

The moment of death is depicted as unheroic, agonizing, and ugly. The protagonist of *No Man's Land* describes men falling 'not in the dramatic way men fell on the films...but just staggering forward, carried on by their momentum, and then giving way at the knees, like dying beasts in the bull-ring.'[24] The death of friends is related as the tragic violation of the profoundest human value in war, and as a tormented, unbreakable link between the dead and the surviving soldiers. The dead of the war may meet their end belatedly, like Wilfrid Ewart, who died at midnight on New Year's Eve in Mexico City, hit by a stray bullet: 'As if some bullet of the war had never ceased to fly in the air and still searched for him! As if the angel of Death had sent out a gleaner after the harvest had been gathered in and had picked him off and added him to the rest! He was not to be allowed to survive.'[25]

The trenches and the memories of men are haunted by the ghosts of dead comrades, reinforcing the terrible closeness that at times exists between the soldiers and an afterworld on whose threshold they live. The novel *Sniper Jackson* is punctuated emotionally by the presence of dead soldiers. On the eve of an attack at Ypres in 1917, as a Colonel listens to soldiers singing during a service, he also hears the voices of their dead comrades, whose spirits, he knows, 'were still quickening in the breasts' of the men around him. Lieutenant Jackson feels the evening breeze full of hummings and whisperings, the voices of his dead friends trying to cheer him up; and when he walks by an estaminet and sees inside it men talking quietly and sombrely he immediately recognizes that they are talking of 'the chums they have lost.'[26] In an authorial aside entitled 'In the Night', Frankau, after the chapter on the Somme offensive in *Peter Jackson*, sums up thus what remains of that time: 'Only memories, bitter memories that waken men o' nights' and make them relive what keeps them awake, 'so that they walk once more, naked and alone, among the careless ghosts of men they knew'.[27]

Communion with the dead underlines most poignantly the concept of a race apart, a generation which is doomed to live within the emotional confines of an experience which can be understood only by those who lived through it. When the American writer Selwyn, protagonist of *The Parts Men Play*, returns home he finds he cannot work because he is haunted by memories – and by the dead. One night he throws open the door to let some air in, but he is made even more restless by the quiet of the night, and the droning sound of the sea.

> Beneath the canopy of that same sky the dead were lying. Across the seas a breeze of spring was stealing about the graves, as now it played about his face.
> What was his pact towards them – to mourn, and fill his life with useless melancholy? To forget, and turn his face towards the future?
> Forget...?
> 'There are times...when I long for the power to reach out for the great truths – hidden in space – and in the silence of the night.'[28]

But the need for truth, and the search for it, are inextricably bound up with the dead who populate the quiet night.

The experience of contact with dead friends often has strong mystical connotations. In *Love Lane*, Billy Hollis, invalided home from France because of his wounds, is summoned out of the house in the middle of the night by the voice of his dead friend Stanning.[29] In the name of what that friendship meant to him, he decides to return to the front, where he joins his friend in death. In later novels this mystical note is all the stronger because of the significance with which time invests the role of dead comrades. In *Life Without End* the curate Hugh Richmond, estranged from the Church and his family and racked by religious doubt, returns to Bazentin, nine years after being wounded there, in the hope of receiving a sign from God. Here he meets with an otherwordly solution to his existential morass as the ghosts of thousands of dead soldiers rise before him and tell him to return to his place in life.[30]

Salvation through the intervention of the dead is also the dramatic conclusion of *The Red Horse*, in which a war ghost saves the protagonist from suicide. His dream of active work towards world peace in tatters, abandoned by his wife, ostracized by society, Owen Seaforth is about to shoot himself when in a sudden vision he sees a ghostly figure astride a red horse, holding a bloody sword. He raises the revolver to his forehead, looking in the mirror, and at that moment the mirror reflects a figure from his past. He recognizes in the 'knightly-looking man' his friend Gareth, the friend 'he had loved more than anything in life'[31] and who had died in the war. He throws the weapon away, saved by the meaning of the past from an apparently meaningless life.

Spiritualism hardly ever features in these novels, since the notion of the spiritual dimension of war is always related to a confrontation with *reality*. In *Mrs. Marden* Robert Hichens tells the story of the grief of a mother who resorts to spiritualism to contact her son, only to learn that true Christianity alone could reconcile her to her loss. The text that helps bring her to religious comfort is Ernst Haeckel's very popular *The Riddle of the Universe*, which propounded a metaphysical approach to evolutionary materialism.[32]

Spiritual Language　The values of a separate world, and the presentation of the significance of the memory of war on the level of strong emotions but unstructured ideas, found congenial expression through spiritual images and transcendental solutions. Several book jackets showed the sun, rays, or dawn in a stylized expression of the quest for light they contained. Among the most striking were the covers of *San Fairy Ann* with black bayonet blades against the sun and of *God and Tony Hewitt* with the silhouette of a naked man with arms stretched towards the dawn. The cover of *One Increasing Purpose* depicted simply a glorious sunrise.[33] With most soldier-authors it is as if, although survivors of the war, they had died in the trenches to their old selves, and were now striving to perpetuate a sense of profundity and authenticity about their experience. As a colonel in *Retreat* tells Padre Elliot in 1918: 'Standards are different here. A lot are inflated, a few artificial, but a number nearer to the absolute than any, I should say, except in 1914.'[34] Values which are absolute have the unassailability of religious principles, and like them are a territory which enjoys immunity from political probing.

Twelve novels have openly religious titles: *All Roads Lead to Calvary, Saint's Progress, The Seventh Vial, The Valley of Indecision, The Way of Revelation, The Willing Horse, Simon Called Peter, The Woman of Knockaloe; a Parable, Heavenly Ladder, God and Tony Hewitt, The Red Horse, Prelude to Calvary*. In a few more the major theme is spiritual. Religion is not portrayed as the sanctuary to which soldiers turn. The old religion offers no comfort and is spurned as a civilian institution which cannot reach the men in their predicament. Spirituality is a perceptual framework for those men who – retrospectively and via the novelist's pen – reflect about the meaning of their new world and of their drastically changed personalities.

Religious references provide a ready reservoir of images with which to illustrate the awesomeness of the war experience; they are the most suitable for writers who need to adopt a language which reflects the intensity of the men's ordeal. The theme of *Pass Guard at Ypres* is that of the loss of all belief. Yet the narrative is suffused with a spiritual aura which bestows a transcendental quality to Freddy Mann's suffering. In the winter of 1916 Freddy's company is billeted in the Monastery of St Sixte; the apparently alien world of the monks is linked to that of the soldiers by the destiny of sacrifice.

> For them [the monks] the bell, the watches at midnight, the via dolorosa and the peace unspeakable: what is it to them if their bell calls to other hearts besides their own, if a peace falls sometimes within their walls upon others, who, carnal perhaps and unregenerate, nevertheless must make offering, they, too, of their bodies, and tread like them the way of pain?[35]

The parallel between the spiritual nature of the lives of the 'silent brotherhood', unchanged through time and detached from external circumstances, and of the sacrifice of the fighting brotherhood, brought together by a contemporary catastrophe, serves to lift the soldier's predicament to a loftier level. When Derrick in *This, My Son* makes up for fighting on Germany's side (his country of origin) by taking the place of his identical twin Stephen, an English officer who is to be shot the next day, he turns to religious language to ask for England's forgiveness:

> By the cross upon my forehead you shall know me, England, for one who in the person of another did take your cross upon my shoulders at the last. Greater love hath no man...when you have found me, give one sign of that forgiveness which, unknown to all but the spirits of your Dead, I died myself to gain...[36]

The New Testament provides references of suffering, salvation through death and self-sacrifice in the Gospels, and images of struggle in the Apocalypse. The symbol of Crucifixion is closely tied to the concept of Redemption and to the understanding of history as deriving from, and moving towards, a consummation of meaning. The evangelical theme of 'greater love hath no man than this, that a man lay down his life for his friends' (St. John XV, xiii) honours and glorifies the soldier's death; that of the seed needing to die before being born invests the annihilation of the old identity with the promise of ultimate meaning. The image of the pain and fear of Jesus Christ in the garden of Gethsemane while his disciples are sleeping is a powerful parallel with the soldiers' suffering and the civilians' obliviousness. How could one find a more appropriate expression for the young man about to leave for the front than: "'Oh God, if it be possible let this cup pass from me!" Gethsemane!'?[37] 'Better any settlement than this Golgotha'[38] is an equivalent cry of supplication for torment to be lifted. In *Grey Dawn – Red Night* this prayer of desperation of an officer being shelled at the Somme is followed by the second term of spiritual reference of the garden of Gethsemane: acceptance of God's will. "'Lord, if it be possible let this pass from me. Nevertheless, not my will..." He grew calmer; life rested not in his hands, nor any man's. If God saw fit...Strange how simple the question had suddenly become.'[39] Acceptance and meaning become inseparable.

The Red Horse takes its title from the Revelation horse, which signifies war: 'And there went out another horse that was red. And to him that sat thereon it was given that he should take peace from the earth: and that they should kill one another. And a great sword was given to him.' (VI, iv). The title and the moral of *The Seventh Vial* are also gleaned from the Apocalypse. The seven golden vials are 'full of the wrath of God' (XV, vii): 'And I heard a great voice out of the temple, saying to the seven angels: Go and pour out the seven vials of the wrath of God upon the earth.' (XVI, i); 'And the seventh angel poured out his vial upon the air. And there came a great voice out of temple from the throne, saying: It is done.' (XVI, xvii). The novel's interpretation of this passage is that the seventh vial was not poured out in vain. As Bill Cunningham explains to his friends after reading these verses from the Bible, the vials of wrath symbolize periodical excesses in 'selfishness and inhumanity'; God, Bill speculates, 'arranges' for wars as a punishment or as an opportunity for mankind to prove its worth.[40] The novel is divided into three parts: I. The Heroes – The Book of Ignorance; II: The Warriors – The Book of Sacrifice III: The Conquerors – The Book of Rewards. The protagonist, an utterly idealistic artist, has a vision before the war of Mary and Child at Albert; three years later he sees the statue of the Virgin Mary topple over the martyred town.

The Way of Revelation, whose title is an overt reference to the text by which it is signposted, is preceded by the quotation which so aptly describes the new kind of warfare introduced by the Great War: 'And he gathered them together into a place called in the Hebrew tongue Armageddon.' (XVI, xv-xvi). The progression of the novel reveals life in the trenches as purgatory: suffering related to the ultimate attainment of the spirit.

It was always a crooked and a twisted and a torn and a broken memory in after-years, yet starred with strange intervals of lucid, unexpected peace, during which men saw visions of a wondrous ultimate purity and splendour – else, must surely have perished. It was as though souls had to be tested through denial of the life of the mind, of the realm of the soul, of the celestial human thing. Beauty and Death allied....Men lived, physically and mentally, in the dim contorted regions of the anti-Christ. But they saw visions – yes. And if men lived and died in the nether-world, losing sense of individuality and time, they came back every nine, ten, or eleven days to meadows vivid with the lush green of new grass, riotous with wild flowers, instinct with the upward pushing growth of the spring. And if existence itself became a purgatory, there was peace still, and hope, in the faces of the dead.[41]

In *Ermytage and the Curate* the author uses a powerful biblical metaphor to render the older generation's sacrifice of its young. Ermytage is struck painfully by a letter from his mother saying she has been praying for his full recovery from his wound, thus unwittingly hurrying 'the return of her only son into the valley of the shadow of death.'

He thought of Abraham offering up Isaac on the bloody altar of sacrifice...Ah! How little people in England, even one's nearest and dearest, realized what one was feeling out here, and how earnestly you prayed that the cup might pass from you...![42]

Religion also provides solutions in the post-war years for some men who deliberately recast the mould of their lives in the light of what they have suffered and learnt. In *Simon Called Peter*, *If Winter Comes*, and *The Valley of Indecision* the resolution is identical: the repudiation by Christ-like protagonists of a vacuous world through real faith, real divine inspiration. After four years in the war, Sim Paris (*One Increasing Purpose*), shaken and distraught by the death of his friends, finds 'absolute knowledge' one night in a dug-out through spiritual contact with his dead mother. He asks her the question that has been tormenting him for a long time: why is he the only one of his original battalion to have survived death or mutilation for so long? He receives an answer.

Immediately with his cry to her, alone in that dark and airless dug-out, he had within him the absolute knowledge that, through those perilous years and among those thousands more gifted and more worthy who had fallen and who yet would fall, he had been spared, and would be spared, because he had been selected, reserved, set apart, for an especial purpose.[43]

The purpose for which he has been saved is to help others. After the war he travels the country preaching the gospel for a year.[44]

The Valley of Indecision is about the spiritual quest of a 25-year-old ex-soldier, Peter Currage, who has seen his father die at the Somme and on that night devoted his whole self to Christ.[45] There is an interesting exchange of ideas between the young man and his friend General Hayling, who agrees that a new world must be built out of the war. His beliefs astonish the idealistic Peter because of their similarity to his own.

> The world has been in an uproar. New conditions, new objects, new standards, new everything. Every able-bodied man, and nearly every woman, has been through the mill. What have they learned? That the best way to get warm is to work hard; that the man who shirks or malingers or tries to down his pals is soon found out; that money doesn't matter, nor physical comfort, nor food – not so much as we used to think; that loyalty to a good leader is the finest thing in the world; that you can't be too quixotic; that there are good and bad men all round us, and that the bad ones aren't worth strafing...It's only in the services that a man learns that self-sacrifice – constant self-sacrifice – is positively practical.

This is a remarkable manifesto of the *practical* lessons of war, all derived from the soldiers' exercise in self-obliterating virtue. For the General these lessons are crystallized into the objective of 'Patriotism, Imperialism, Culture', and the doubling in size of the British Empire.[46] For Peter the goal must be purely religious. Yet the distance between his pure goals and General Hayling's more specifically political ones is short indeed, as is made clear by the way in which Peter defines the dangers to be combated in society. In his first public speech this modern apostle of God invites his audience to take note of 'the signs of the times': 'Unemployment, profiteering, anarchy, mob-rule.'[47]

The protagonist of *The Theatre Queue* elaborates on his girlfriend's glib statement that war had changed everything by opining that understanding the lessons of the war holds enormous potential for the future. He considers companionship, 'by which the most imminent dangers appeared to vanish because they were shared', and 'the mutual forbearance and respect, that made all effort both possible and glorious upon the field': would they represent the positive fruits of victory, would they last in a way that would show the war to have been the instrument of releasing truth? 'And under the touch of truth, set free, what new forms of beauty might not be born! What new aspirations! And might not suffering itself be seen to be no longer a mystery, but indeed "a revelation"?'[48] This final paradox – that the Great War may turn out to free Truth from its peacetime shackles – is not specious rhetoric. The soldiers had been living the greater paradox of profound brotherhood and love during war with another nation. In order to distil meaning from war, authors like Wallis needed to believe that the values they portrayed held long-term social possibilities. Religion provided them with the rhetorical apparatus with which to confer on the human values learnt at the front just such legitimacy.

2 Home Front

The question of identity finds definition through terms of comparison and antithesis. Home is often referred to dissociatively in relation to the soldiers' experience. The word 'civilian' is used almost exclusively as a disparaging label; it groups non-combatants as people excluded from any understanding of front-line life. Whatever their denomination – '"brass hats", "people at home", lawyers, politicians, pro-Germans, the FO'[49] – they are devoid of the sensitivity acquired by the soldiers in tragic circumstances, and their relation to the war ranges from indifference to profiteering.

The civilian lives out his own self-conscious war experience mainly through reading and believing the reports in the papers, airing loaded views about the conduct of the war, and hating the Germans. The soldier cannot talk about his experience at the front because he knows he could never convey what he has been through, nor be ever understood. If this lack of communication isolates the soldier even further it passes unnoticed by those at home, who think they already have an informed view of the war. Far from being synonymous with joyous reunion with the familiar, homecoming is painfully complicated for the soldier by home being perceived by him as alienated from, and even antagonistic to, the attitudes which are at the basis of his experience. *Labels* is a sensitive account of the two kinds of war waged by the soldiers and by those at home. Sir Thomas Wickens, a stockbroker who has received a knighthood for his patriotic activities, is well-meaning, proud of his contribution, and incapable of any real insight into the ordeal his son Dick, a captain in the artillery, has been through. On the evening of his son's homecoming, he is pained to hear him say that the war was not a good job. He could understand such pronouncements if they came from Ramsay MacDonald or Bernard Shaw, he says, but how can a soldier speak like this?

> Didn't we contribute men and money as few nations have done in the course of history? Didn't our women give up everything and go out and nurse you right up to the cannon's mouth? Didn't we civilians, in our humble way, back you up morally and physically to the utmost extent of our powers? Wasn't Lloyd George an outstanding example of the highest type of statesmanship and patriotism? Weren't Haig and Foch a better team than anything the enemy could bring up against us?...Think of the ethical side of it too – of our high ideals, of what we achieved for civilization by disproving with our very life's blood the inherent falseness of the brutal Germanic culture! Don't you call that doing a good job?

This passage is a little gem of rhetorical condensation of all the tenets of civilian patriotic fervour. The punctuation of the speech with 'we' and 'our', and the words 'our very life's blood' claim active participation in the war; the glib recital of the components of this experience indicates the illusion of a well-rounded mastery of its issues. Yes, it's all true, admits his son, 'but it doesn't mean anything.'[50]

By stages Dick learns that the deep lack of understanding between him and his father is due to their referring to two disparate experiences. There have been two wars, the actual one in which he was involved and the imaginary one the civilians lived. His reasons for believing the imaginary war the more terrible of the two reveal that he understands the gulf between soldiers and civilians in terms of the former's emotional intensity of experience and, consequently, finer sensibility. The superhuman effort and suffering of the soldiers had made them more aware of the possibilities of life and had given them a full understanding of the worth of brotherhood, whereas the civilians' suffering was as imaginary as their war, it had failed to teach them to overcome hatred and suspicion and had affected them with its insanity.[51]

The boundary between the world of the soldier and that of the civilian is graphically portrayed in *Magnolia Street*, which centres on another, racial, dichotomy. The novel tells the story of a street in Manchester which is inhabited on one side by Jews. The war years are the only ones in the history of this street when the two groups forget their differences – 'gentile pavement fused with Jewish pavement'.[52] The constant anxious worry about the absent young men becomes the emotional common denominator of Magnolia Street. Still, the notion of a common experience excludes the fighting-men; when the author discusses the return of a soldier, again he must resort to the image of two different worlds. The young man who has come back is like a ghost who does not belong to the world that used to be so familiar to him. Even though while he has been away he has known physical love for the first time and encountered horror he did not know existed, he is somehow more innocent than he was before. He has confronted ideas like God, Eternity, and Death for the first time.[53] Golding gives him no name and his family is not mentioned: he is a solitary figure who has re-emerged from a world no one else knows, and now occupies an undefinable dimension between life and death.

In Gilbert Frankau's bestseller the two male protagonists only see the fighting-man: 'To them, non-combatants were traitors, shirkers, 'conchies', self-advertisers, money-grubbers: always ready to betray the fighting-man, to cheat him and rob him, to preach to him first and leave him in the lurch afterwards.'[54] The more culpable civilians are all powerful people who fraudulently and with much show project the image of efficient managers of the war: government officials, politicians, profiteering businessmen. As the narrator remarks in *Special Providence*, the most dreadful aspect of war was 'the council-chamber, the newspaper office and the drawing-room', where people regarded 'sacrifices they exacted from others as though they constituted a merit of their own.'[55]

In these popular novels meaning is often identified indirectly through a strong condemnation of politicians and civilians, who distort the value of war and sabotage its potential positive effects for the future. Edmund Leach elaborates on Mary Douglas's concept of the social implications of notions of what is soiled and impure[56] by arguing that to protect their own individuality people build boundaries to reinforce their moral security and keep out the dirt of what is different. Nevertheless, individuals are connected to one another in a structure of power and domination which entails the crossing of boundaries: power, therefore, 'is located in dirt.'[57]

The 'purity' of a determinedly apolitical discourse was elaborated in antithesis to the great political alarms of the pre-1914 years. The memory of war had as its political backdrop such events as the suffragettes' movement, syndicalism, the Irish problem, the rise of Labour. As Leed has argued, the image of the returning soldier lent itself to a 'conceptualization' of social organization that transcended political conflict.

> Those, both socialists and conservatives, who conceived of modern society in terms of estrangement, privatization, self-interest, and class conflict saw the veteran as a "Comrade", a man of community. He had been formed amidst the "natural" solidarities that underlay the artificial divisions of class and status. He thus constituted the best hope for a resolution to those tensions that defined capitalist society.[58]

The presentation of this idealized image in middlebrow fiction did not preclude the recognition of the difficulties of reabsorption into society which returning soldiers experienced.

William McFee's *Command* is the only novel to demystify in aggressive fashion the values used as buffers against a political analysis. The protagonist, a second officer in the Navy, soon comes to understand that the other officers, 'with their closely-guarded privileges and esoteric codes, were fighting much more for their class than for England, that an England democratized and ravished of her class system would be to them a worse place than an England defeated by a class-conscious enemy.' He spends the war years on a freighter in the Salonica region, acquiring through his experience a better knowledge of himself and a disillusioned view of his society. Back in London after the war, he observes the officer class in civilian clothes and thinks about their complete lack of understanding of their

Empire. In describing their attitude he uses the image of dirt which, as we have noted above, Leach and Douglas employ to describe people's perception of what lies beyond their boundaries: 'Indeed, they were very fond of saying those words "rotten" and "putrid" for alien things they did not like.'[59]

Three novels discussed, in very different ways, the plight of the unemployed ex-soldier. *Peace in Our Time* (1920) considers three generations – pre-war, war, and post-war – through three different characters. The novel ends with an artificial solution for the demobilized officer and his friends who start a dancing club, and includes a prayer for each generational representative. For the 50-year-old it is '*I know that my Redeemer liveth*';

> ...for those luckless ones, contemporaries with none but themselves, who were being pressed out from life and its joy between two generations – "*Yea though I give my body to be burned –*"....for the younger generation still, in whose unknowing hearts lay all hope to come – "*Wherewithal shall a young man cleanse his way?*"[60]

The Victors relates the tragedy of the suicide of a young unemployed officer in the early Twenties. Guilt is laid heavily on the unconcern of the comfortable, mainly old, individuals who followed the war from their club armchairs. Although the novel revolves around the question of unemployment and lack of assistance for ex-officers, politics only makes an appearance when an ex-officer who is working as a bus conductor – a 'public school boy and a *sahib*' – talks of harassment by the Trade Unions, which do not like people of his social extraction.[61] Harold Spender's *The Man Who Went* tells the story of the difficulties met by a war veteran who, promised a better future by the recruiting officer when he had enlisted, now cannot find a job. The novel is resolved by the love of a woman who urges him to be patient and to stick it out together with everybody else, 'big 'uns and little 'uns.'[62] It is a call for social unity by a writer who had been fired by the expression of solidarity showed by people during the war.[63] The subdued optimism of the resolution of this novel is not merely a function of the author being a civilian himself; it hinges rather on a solution which substitutes for rancour the wartime spirit of comradeship.

The values revealed by the contrast between the soldiers' world and that of the civilian were later frequently championed by ex-civilians themselves. In *Lord Raingo* Arnold Bennett offers an interesting portrayal of the highest levels in Whitehall, including a thinly-veiled description of a demagogic and ruthlessly efficient Lloyd George. John St Loe Strachey, editor of the *Spectator*, quite correctly pointed out that Halifax's comment that 'the art of Politics is a very coarse one' was echoed throughout the novel.[64] When Lord

Raingo's son comes home after escaping from a POW camp, he is unimpressed by his father's world, 'a crew of circus-performers, liars, warmongers and millionaires.'[65] Politics represent the upheaval of the present and the change is blamed on the politicians.[66] The title of Gilbert Cannan's *Pugs and Peacocks* (1921) comes from the comment the Cambridge professor Melian Stokes makes when he sees pugs chasing the peacocks in the garden of his aunt Lady Rusholme's house: 'those pugs were like modern politicians yapping at the most venerable traditions, to try to make them furl their tails.'[67]

Politics rest on a class awareness which is petty and contemptible next to the unity of effort at the front, an effort which is impeded by trade unions' demands, or, as a young man at the front complains, by the strike of the man who has taken the soldier's job.[68] The criticism levelled against the crassness and greediness of self-seekers and against politics as a moral social model can only mean in practice the condemnation of the political class activity of the workers. For this denunciation to carry sufficient force without engaging in a language of class conflict which would defeat the terms of the argument, the focus is on the obvious targets of people who during the war contradicted the spirit of the soldiers' world: bureaucrats and profiteers. In England, states the protagonist of *The Seventh Vial*, there were 'the same old profiteering, munitioneering troubles of the lesser breeds who had enough and wanted more, the while these men were drinking in the bitterness of sacrifice and its strength.'[69] The resentment against such people is still expressed very shrilly in 1936 by Naomi Ellington Jacob in *Time Piece*. Claudia Marsden is at the head of a munitions factory, as Jacob herself had been, where workers go on strike because the tea trolley is always late in reaching them. With the force of her contempt and anger, and with the threat of locking them out, she persuades the 'gutless rats', the 'poor blasted fools', the 'damned, bloody murderers', the 'slobbering, doddering old wives' to go back to work.[70] In *The Willing Horse*, the novel Ian Hay wrote six disillusioning years after his eulogy of wartime social harmony, an officer explains that the scarcity of troops is due to the politicians satisfying the demands of the 'Labour bosses' and not relinquishing people from civil employment.[71]

Wartime civilian activities are the subject of four satires,[72] a literary medium particularly suited to express the ridicule and contempt warranted by home propaganda. The protagonists of these satires are inept human beings who, like fluttering moths, are attracted by the bright light of the war and keep circling around it in a continuous flurry of empty activity. A member of the Circumvention Branch of the Circumlocution Office (an institution drawn from Dickens's *Little Dorrit*) details thus a typical day of bureaucratic activity during the war:

And meanwhile the two wars went on simultaneously....The English advance was arrested at Lens and the French were thrust back from the Chemin des Dames; but Mr. Harper had been invited by Mr. Towle to lunch at his club. London lay defenceless before menacing squadrons of German aeroplanes; but Mr. Burnet detected a fallacy in the financial criticism by Mr. Polperro and drove his point home. It was determined to bring all England's man-power into the struggle by means of a new combing-out; and Mr. Harper found a job for Cyril that kept him at work all night.[73]

John Galsworthy's *The Burning Spear* is a comic indictment of war propaganda through the portrayal of its effects on the pathetic John Lavender, an extremely mild and innocent elderly man who, fired by the articles he reads in the papers, applies for a commission from the Ministry of Propagation (of mass hysteria) to set out on a tour of patriotic propaganda. Through the quixotic antics of the elderly bachelor ("If I had fifty sons I would give them all"),[74] Galsworthy turns upside down the principles of the most fiery topics of his speeches, and time after time the old bachelor's simple and kind temperament wins over the stupidity of the patriotic creed which should be driving his actions. Much to his own shame Mr. Lavender helps a conscientious objector against an attack by four men, and he fails to do his patriotic duty of interning a German because he is moved by the obviously deep love between him and his wife.

In Galsworthy's novel warm-hearted individualism operates as a moral antidote to the heartless attitude of organizations. In *How They Did It* David, after working for a while for the War Office, realizes that 'the real horror of war was not the physical hell at the Front but the spiritual and moral bankruptcy at home', which makes a mockery of 'the spiritual and moral triumph' which sustains the soldiers. The theme of the novel is the corrupt and selfish running of the war, which 'has fallen into the hands of those who stayed at home, into the hands of every type of man from the second-best to the worst.'[75] When David is told by a friend that his vision and his experience will enable him to write about the meaning of the war once it is over, he replies that he is becoming sceptical about his power to change things because of the crippling influence of greediness and selfishness amongst those at home. Selfishness is the moral, irrefutable focus of criticism. In 1919, in *Sylvia and Michael*, Compton Mackenzie asserted that the

selflessness of those who died is terribly stained by the selfishness of those who have let them die. Yet the younger generation...will have the compensation when it is all over of such amazing opportunities for living as were never known, and the older generation that made the war will die less lamented than any men that have ever died since the world began.[76]

As for the profiteer, he is the very opposite of all that the soldier is and fights for. Whereas the soldier is selfless in his service to the country, the profiteer is greedily egocentric; the soldier's life is as uncomfortable as the businessman's is luxurious; the soldier's experience borders on the spiritual while the profiteer thrives on materialistic speculation and accumulation. In *Fairy Gold*, Sir Caleb Fuller, who has been granted a knighthood for producing a very successful patent bomb, and whose son escaped the front by getting a useless home job which earned him an MBE, exposes the narrowness of his soul when he fussily regrets the end of the war: '...speaking for myself and some of my colleagues we were really a tiny bit disappointed when the war came to an end just when it did.'[77] Compton Mackenzie's crushing contempt clearly breaks through.

The descriptions of those who benefit from the war are almost grotesque. The soldiers all have the physical grace and beauty of their youth, in sharp contrast to the 'old men' who caused the war or are now benefiting from it. Physical descriptions linger on the ugliness and grossness of some civilians:

> ...bloated and coarse, he carried his sixty years as though he had not in all that time known one hour of strenuous exercise or of clean joy in the open. Overeating...was stamped on his face...A dead thing he seemed to me; dead more truly than any of the lads who had flung their happy lives away for the cause of the world while he and his like 'lived.'[78]

In *The Victors* the injustice of the destitute ex-officer's predicament is driven home by the physical vignette of 'an old gentleman asleep unbeautifully in a deep chair by the fire' in his London club: 'He was very ugly, with his mouth open and his enormous stomach heaving as he snored.' While observing him in his lazy surfeit of food and drink, Michael muses that he must have lived this life all through the war, while he and his friends were risking their lives for such people.[79]

General Headquarters, the 'brass hats', occupy a separate niche of guilt in the eyes of the soldiers. Although physically close to the men, they are civilians in military disguise whose decisions reflect not so much complicity with a political network of power at home as lack of understanding of the real nature of the war. This unawareness of what the soldiers know so intimately, the nature of modern warfare, is the particular indictment against GHQ, who through their obstinate attachment to old patterns of fighting keep sending the soldiers to slaughter.

The General is an accomplished portrayal of a general of the old school. The exposure of the profound guilt he shares with his colleagues is all the more shocking as it unfolds against the background of their obstinate belief in the validity of tried military methods. Forester had been too young to fight in the war, but the sure hand with which he handles this central question of the mismanagement of the war, and the fluency with which he weaves in and out of different wartime psychological predicaments reflect how much had been learnt by non-combatants about the experience of the war through the debate and the literature of the inter-war years.

In many novels the condemnation of GHQ's blundering provides incisive anecdotes: in *Pass Guard at Ypres*, for example, a military strategist who has never been near the frontline works out with mathematical precision the time and casualties to be gone through until the German front collapses;[80] in *No Hero - This* the protagonist is angered by a brass hat who calls 'scalawags' the men who are sick because of the predicament he himself put them in.[81] There can be no illusions about the 'gods with feet of clay',[82] who think of the soldiers as ninepins in their game.

Conscientious Objectors   Conscientious objectors might be expected to be the group of people at home to attract the most bitter degree of disapproval from the war novelists, yet almost the reverse is true. Even though one finds isolated examples of violent antagonism, for the major part references to conscientious objectors are characterized by understanding. In *The Jesting Army* a man, revolted by his wife's hatred of the Germans, infuriates her by calling the conscientious objectors 'heroic fellows'.[83] The conscientious objectors' attitudes are respected, even when not shared, for arising from a sensitive and idealistically committed nature. Thus, if the civilian cannot understand the 'conchy' and will not forgive him, the soldier sympathizes with his inner spiritual struggle, and feels that they are sharing in the same non-materialistic world of values which other civilians cannot penetrate.

As early as 1919 Harold Begbie, that prolix upholder of conservative values, produced an apologia of the conscientious objector's choice in *Mr. Sterling Sticks It Out*. Christopher Sterling is an almost saintly man who will not let war divert him from his aim of devoting his life to helping and re-educating the poor. He is a Quaker, and, as he explains at length, for him politics *is* religion. Although a rabid anti-Socialist, Begbie was able to paint a positive picture of Christopher's life in his anti-capitalist world, since the religious motivation behind his renunciation of all material goods deflected all political threat. In a letter to Lloyd George written on 9 March 1918, Begbie supported his request that the novel be allowed to be published, in spite of its controversial subject matter, on the grounds that its concern was 'simply a contrast in religious temperaments. There is one character who dies on the battlefield for England in a kind of ecstasy (Rupert Brooke) and there is his brother who goes to prison for his religious convictions (Stephen

Hobhouse).'[84] Christopher is profoundly committed, but not to a political cause; he believes that the most *political* event in history was the life of Jesus, because of the sense of continuity it has lent to the centuries.[85]

Religious convictions are what motivate this wealthy banker's son to renounce his wordly position and to move to an unidentified 'slum' to educate and help the poor. He refuses to take part in a war which appalls him with its violent consequences. Two of his brothers who go to the front understand him and accept him; his youngest brother confides to him his most intimate thoughts about a war which he finds terrible but just. Christopher pays the highest price for his convictions, and dies from the treatment he receives in prison. The brother who stayed home with an 'indispensable' government job, and who has a brilliant political career in front of him, proves to be the most intolerant of Christopher's choice and is the only one to come to his deathbed wearing a military uniform.

Another 1919 novel, Jerome Klapka Jerome's *All Roads Lead to Calvary*, includes a strong defence of a young man, Arthur, who refuses to fight from religious motives. When his friend Joan learns that he is a pacifist she dreads the consequences: the Press would call him a 'conchy', 'the spiteful screamer who had never risked a scratch' would denounce him as a coward, the 'local Dogberry of the tribunals' would pontificate about Christianity and would not listen to him, screaming crowds would follow him about. She can foresee his predicament so clearly (Arthur is killed by a mob) because since the war started she has been observing 'the fighters with their mouths', 'the savage old baldheads', the 'sleek, purring women', the 'shrieking journalists'. They all had in common a glibly violent readiness to sacrifice the young men, while the latter felt no hatred towards the German soldiers. Interestingly, Arthur's death links Joan more closely to the soldiers' experience by providing the motivation for her to go and work as a nurse in France; the hatred shown against her friend makes her want to fight for peace and freedom of conscience. The conclusion, to help a war that will end war, is not at all paradoxical in the context of the novel, where the only feelings of gentleness and of tolerance of the enemy are to be found at the front: 'patience, humour, forgiveness, they had learnt from the war.'[86]

Martyrdom is often the consequence of the pacifist's choice. *Mr. Standfast* contains a sympathetic portrayal of the pacifist Lancelot Wake, who joins a Labour battalion and dies for his country. In a novel written eleven years later, A.S.M. Hutchinson's *He Looked for a City*, an equally high-minded conscientious objector dies as a consequence of his imprisonment.[87] The general hate and persecution which tormented the young poet and his family during the war years turns by the late 1930s into general tolerance for his pacifism, which is now viewed as the attitude to be expected from a man of his intellectual brilliance. The vicarage which during the war had been shunned because of the young man's choice is now a centre of excited interest. But this is no consolation to his sad father, who considers that this change of attitude is merely a sign of time having swept away all the conventions of the past, regardless of their worth.

Defining English Identity against German Character Englishness in these novels frequently finds definition out of confrontation with the enemy, the Germans. Hatred is a civilian domain, an aberration all the more distasteful for being un-English. The protagonist of *Pursuit* during his month in captivity writes the novel *Clipped Wings*, which equals the success of *The First Hundred Thousand*. It is the first book not to depict the Germans as brutal villains; while 'it appealed to that section of the British public who liked a handshake after a row, it seriously offended the "let's go on hating" brigade.'[88] Fair play is the quality which allows the English to come to regard the enemy as a patriot in circumstances equal to their own. Richard Grenville admits that the German treatment of prisoners is fair, even though he himself would have no compunction about exterminating the whole country. Still, his English sense of moderation does not allow him to act upon such feelings. His tolerance is couched in terms of a characteristic national sense of fairness; the protagonist is 'English of the English, and it is not in his blood to hate his enemies.'[89] Compton Mackenzie strikes a religious blow against hatred in *Heavenly Ladder* by having the curate Mark Lidderdale maintain that the hate-inflated talk of parsons is contemptible and un-Christian; it is not *decent*. He invests this quality with the masculine gender: 'We are such a decent nation, we English, so much the most civilized masculine nation, that it really would be a mundane catastrophe if the war succeeded in turning us into Germans.'[90]

Love of animals is a characteristic expression of English sensibility. In *This, My Son* British soldiers, after entering a village from which the Germans have just retreated, find a kitten crucified to a door, still alive. They attempt to rescue him, but as the first nail is removed a bomb explodes which kills them all. 'I tell you, the German who nailed down that kitten paid the greatest compliment possible to the British character in fixing the bomb behind it'[91] is their moral requiem.

A number of novels compare English and German personality through a plethoric consideration of racial characteristics. The Germans are depicted as intellectual, authoritarian, autocratic, humourless; the English, by contrast, are tolerant, gentle, and undogmatically fair. Germany stands for an imposed order and discipline, while England is free and its system stems from the individual's heart.

The Germans who live in England choose to do so because of its free society. Thus the German baker Pommer, who lives in Walworth, says that he feels more an Englishman than a German because he is a democrat: 'England is a good country for free people.'[92] Similarly, Mrs Fischer's German husband, revolted by 'the system of tyranny and repression' which for him is synonymous with Germany, has opted to live in England. 'England, he adored her! England always for him. England, right or wrong.'[93] The dying German soldier, son of an Englishwoman, whom the protagonist of *The Arches of the Years* meets in hospital, 'adores England.' 'He was half English in blood, all English in mind. He cared for England, cared for her tremendously; and he had to fight her…'[94] This effusively emotional language of commitment to a foreign land pays the ultimate tribute to its worth.

The implications of national differences are the subject of eight novels.[95] The most exhaustive treatment is in *Children of No Man's Land*, an account of the life of German aliens during the war. The father of the two young protagonists leaves Germany because his gentle nature – which again makes him an Englishman at heart – makes him rebel against the choices imposed by a despotic father. In England he lives very happily with his English wife and two children until the outbreak of the war, when he and his family become victims of a climate of extreme anti-German feeling. Although Stern's depiction of the aliens' problems is concerned and sympathetic, as in most other novels the only Germans who are really accepted are those sensitive individuals who come to England for the free and tolerant environment it can offer. Those who came merely for business reasons do not escape the stereotypic Teutonic characterization, as in the grotesquely comic portrait of the financier Otto Rothenburg and his family. Out of pure funk, Rothenburg strives to be as English as the English after the outbreak of the war, whereas up to that moment he had ruled severely over a very German household. His frantic attempt at an English metamorphosis involves a change of family name to Redbury, while the children's names change from Hedrig, Lenchen, Konrad and Gerhardt to Hedda, Nell, Con, and Hardy.[96] These attempts at English cultural camouflage show up these individuals as all the more German in their unimaginative conception of what an Englishman is, and stress the fine uniqueness of English identity.

In the other novel whose theme is the experience of German aliens, the largely autobiographical *Mrs. Fischer's War*, the trauma of psychological and sometimes physical persecution reads like a love relationship with England threatened by the prejudice of people who in the hysterical climate of the war betray the spirit of their country. Still, the persecuted Germans' feelings towards their adopted country do not change, as England for them is not its people, but a higher, unchangeable entity.

Women and War   Terms of contrast between the world of the soldier and
that of the civilian determine the discussion of identity in relation to the
home front, the Germans, and conscientious objectors. To these must be
added the frequent examples of a reversal of feminine and masculine
stereotypes of sensitivity and roles. Women get jobs and assume new
financial and organizational responsibilities; they express a fervid hatred of
Germans; they hold a disenchanted and pragmatic view of religion. The
men, on the contrary, have lost control over their day-to-day material
circumstances; they are offended by the fierce hatred of the enemy expressed
at home; they live in a dimension which is laden with the spiritual and the
mythical. Also, the narratives about the war written by men display an
openness about the personal expression of emotions and feelings which is
more commonly associated with women's responses.

If the ordeal of the conscientious objector is shown to parallel in
important respects that of the soldier, the wartime experience of women, by
contrast, is often ascribed to that selfish and vulgar area of life corrupted by
its utter alienation from the predicament of the man at war. The wives in *If
Winter Comes, God and Tony Hewitt*, and *The Red Horse*, for example,
underline with their petty materialistic concerns and their obliviousness to
the soldiers' ordeal the gap between the distinct worlds they and their
husbands inhabit.

Often a veiled accusation of prostitution labels the activities of wartime
women, whose corrupting freedom is set against the ennobling
imprisonment of the men at the front. Idealism is a male quality, in vivid
contrast to the uninspired and often pernicious materialism of women.[97] In
Gilbert Frankau's *Martin-Make-Believe* (1930), the wife of the extremely
idealistic Martin Kenterton betrays him with a friend of his. Before the
formal end of his marriage he goes back after ten years to the scenes of his
war experience at the 'Gethsemane of the Somme', as if to recapture,
together with the sense of pain and death, the idealism which has now been
vilified: 'back to those towns, those fields, where once, long ago, he had
lived, for all the filth of them, cleanly.'[98] The degradation of Rosemary
Meynell in *The Way of Revelation*, through her disloyal affair with a young
civilian and her self-indulgent life of pleasure, serves to highlight more
dramatically her fiancé's spiritual journey. In other novels there are three
episodes of men feeling disgusted at the loud and coquettish behaviour of
women in public places.[99] The worst sin of all is unfaithfulness with a
profiteer. In *Rachel Fitzpatrick* the 'painfully smart' young woman who
makes enquiries in a government office about her missing soldier husband
pretends to dab her eyes with a scented handkerchief, and climbs into a big
limousine where an 'odious old man' is waiting for her.[100]

The playing down of carnality in trench narratives, within the context of the soldier's absorption with greater issues, sometimes intensifies into a deliberate rejection of women. The protagonist of *No Hero – his*, who has a platonic and idyllic relationship with a Frenchwoman, goes so far as to assert that relationships between men and women should be based on spiritual values rather than on sex.[101] Patrick Miller's *The Natural Man* (1924) traces the process of self-knowledge in the war of a young officer who does not want women or drink because they could not quench his high-minded aspirations. His mother had taught him that the 'natural man', to whom is entrusted the task of procreation, is coarse. One question bothers him: 'was the war a business of natural men?' He does not find a specific answer, but his own war is lived according to perceptions other than those of a 'hot-blooded' animal.[102] The *Times Literary Supplement* reviewer aptly remarked that 'War, as Blaven finds in Paris, is a mistress more seductive than any of the *demi-monde*, and here her features and her adornments are described by a lover.'[103] Similarly, J.B. Priestley commented that Miller 'loves war and woos it as a mistress.'[104]

In *The Red Horse*, the night Owen's close friend Gareth dies, Owen goes to a brothel: there could be no starker expression of the dichotomy of the purity of male friendship and the squalor of relations with women. Sex in this novel of terrible survival is antithetical to the positive realization of ideals. The failure of Owen's ideals after the war provokes an excess of lasciviousness in his life. The degradation of complicity in business immorality, following the collapse of his grandiose dreams of starting a peace organization, brings him to constant thoughts of women and a mad physical desire for his wife's sister, a 'sex-madness' which he confesses to his wife and Irene in an hysterical, accusing outburst.[105]

Women's religion is often depicted as prosaically conventional, in opposition to the painful immediacy of the men's otherwordly understanding. In *Simon Called Peter* the narrator comments that Peter Graham's fiancée has in common with Napoleon the belief that Christianity means more 'as the secret of social order than as the mystery of the Incarnation.'[106] In a number of novels man's religious or pseudo-religious process of change is set against the woman's practical approach to religion.[107] There are four instances in 1919 novels in which women's religion is described as a ritualistic means of comfort and an enforcer of social rules.[108] How can one follow Jesus, argues Christopher Sterling's mother: 'The advance of civilization would become a rout and a disaster.'[109]

Except for a few novels written by women, the overall impression about the war experience of women is one of separateness from the men's world; at the same time the very description of this distance reveals the effort to bridge it as one of the main concerns of this didactic fiction.[110] Phyllis Bottome's *A*

Servant of Reality addresses in particularly lucid terms the distance separating women from the soldiers' war. Just after the Armistice a young man reflects that his two young sisters, who have worked as VADs, have survived the war utterly unscathed.

> Nothing had finished for them, nor had they ever seen the betrayal of illusion.
>
> The war had been a great call on their young and unawakened energies; they had met it dauntlessly, protected from all its horrors, and free from its indelible stains.
>
> All that had come to them and all that they had given up had developed and enriched them.
>
> They had never been terrified or beaten down, or come to the end of their tether.[111]

The word 'terrified' more than any other reveals the perceptiveness of the author's comments; as we have seen earlier,[112] Bottome's witnessing of the shattering fear of a soldier at Folkestone represented the turning point of her perceptions of the men's ordeal.

In some instances there is a rewriting of past positions. The protagonist of *Special Providence* looks back with shame at her eagerness to participate in 'herd emotion' at the outbreak of war, and identifies the failure of her imagination and conscience, and the embracing of the patriotic principles, with 'ancestral promptings' which equated the painful with the right and encouraged the obligation to think the same as everyone else. By a 'universal sleight of mind', she now recognizes, the enemy had been made to embody the evil of war, and hatred of the Germans had become an essential function of serving the right ideals.[113]

The few novels which show women as protagonists of the tragedy of the lost generation were all written in the 1930s, after the men's story had been exhaustively told.[114] The 1919 novel *The House of Courage*, by Mrs Victor Rickard, was purportedly about the ordeal of women during the war, and their peculiar brand of courage. The experience of women, however, is presented as merely the reflection of the men's: their courage is a function of their support. There is an obvious glorification of the virility inherent in war by this author who used professionally her husband's full name.[115] When the newly-married Hilda Grove finally reveals to her husband that she is perturbed about his not enlisting, unaware that he is reluctant to burden his wife with the responsibility of the estate, she bursts out: 'If I were a man...no consideration would keep me from going – If I were a man – oh, if *only* I were a man.'[116]

The novel written by Pamela Hinkson thirteen years later also followed the progress of the war through Irish and English families, but here women were portrayed as victims of war in a way which uncovered the particular identity of their suffering. The cover of *The Ladies' Road* (1932) declared in big letters that in this work 'for the first time man's active and woman's passive parts in the war are treated with equal sympathy and equal truth.'[117] The novel portrays the anxiety of women as powerless love, the tragically vain attempt to follow the men down their own roads of pain. Fear exercises its tyranny over a group of women who, although they live together while doing war work in London, are each totally alone, constantly locked into a terrible world with their absent husbands, a world which may be shattered any minute by death. In their minds they walk down the endless roads across the flat French countryside which lead their men to the front, in an effort to be near them and understand their predicament. When one of the women's husbands is killed, sympathy proves to be a terrifying experience. The young widow holds her friend's hands as if to pull her into her barren existence, and gazes at her with pity: the widow now is in a position of horrible safety from uncertainty, while her friend has to go on challenging death every moment of her life.[118] There is another moving description of bereavement in a man's novel, John Brophy's *The World Went Mad*. In the chapter 'Widow's Bed' he tells intimately of the feelings of a young widow sleeping alone, with her baby son next door.

> But even more subtly Julian would be with her, his living body that was now shattered and dead in Palestine, lingering alongside her body in these moments for the night-time, between sleep and waking, when she dare not close her eyes for fear the sweet, delusive memory of his arms should come creeping around her waist and shoulders, and in a frustrated hallucination she should feel her loins drawn into his, awakening and warm and joyous. It was mad and wicked and futile to yield to the importunities of desirous memory. She must not do it! She must learn to forget, to let Julian's body die away from her, perish and crumble from her breasts and her arms and her thighs, as it was perishing and crumbling in the far-off foreign earth. His kisses must fade and falter, he must take on the placid abstraction of an idea: he must become a character, a composition of mentally conceived qualities, whom his son would be brought up to revere.[119]

In this passage, written in 1934, the memory of war has come to a maturity which allows this ex-soldier to depict the bereavement of a woman.

Two popular novels, of a very different literary standard, were written in the 1930s depicting the experience of women near the battle-line in the Great War. The earlier of the two, Helen Zenna Smith's *Not So Quiet on the Western Front* (1930), is a badly-written novel which overwhelms the reader with a battery of aggressively negative platitudes and a determined effort to shock with its explicit content.[120] Helen Zenna Smith (Evadne Price) worked for the Air Ministry during the war but never went to France. Yet, for all their manufactured appeal, there is something authentic about these pages of provocative language, and the anger rings true.

The author makes no effort to portray her heroine as attractive. She is a rather plain, unhappy girl who during her experience as an ambulance driver in France loses all illusions about her class and her sex. All that is feminine, poised and conventional is denied; she has stepped into a world of violence and pain which forces her to perceive the emptiness and hypocrisy of the world of her middle-class parents and the repressive injustice of conventional morality. The horror she witnesses is never communicated with expressions of compassion but only with shrill complaints and bitterness.

Smith pursued her overworked, unconventional theme of a woman's extreme alienation from her middle-class world in the sequel *Women of the Aftermath* (1931), where the tragic consequences of the war were brought to an extreme of controversial provocation. Nellie marries an old boyfriend who, as a consequence of terrible wounds received in the war, is deprived of the use of his legs and is sexually impotent. The decision to marry him owes little to generous compassion, but is rather a gesture of indifference to any dream she may have previously nurtured about married life. She soon grows impossibly tired of her parents' and her in-laws' pride in their war hero, and finally cannot bear the devastation that his tragedy works on her husband's personality. She leaves him to live with a photographer who is charmingly selfish; this parenthesis of fun and happiness, however, proves to be again an illusion, as her lover jilts her carelessly. In the end Nellie finds a source of great comfort and freedom in flying a small aeroplane, literally getting away from a sordid reality.

In Irene Rathbone's *We That Were Young* (1932) the thematic focus is made immediately familiar by the title: that of a generation that has sacrificed its youth to four and a half violent years. This is a poignant account of a nurse's experience first in London and then in France, reflecting the author's own experience. The tone is sombre and quietly desperate. Joan loses her adored young brother, who has survived the war, to the Spanish influenza, and there is no resort to the usual romantic resolution to redeem this sadness. At the end of the novel, middle-aged at thirty-four, she is dominated by the sense of the loss of her generation's youth, a feeling she tries to convey to a young niece:

> Can you believe...that *we* were all young once? You can't of course....No other generation ever was so young or ever will be. We were the youth of the world, we were on the crest of the life, and we were the war....Youth and the war were the same thing – youth and the war were us.

The identification of war with her youth makes it for Joan an object of nostalgia: '...although it was so every-dayish at the time, and we were sickened with it, it seems, now, to have a sort of ghastly glamour.'[121] This 'ghastly glamour' is an attribution of meaning which finally unifies in many narratives the experience of men and women as they look back at the war across years which have robbed them of their youth and of a desperate intensity of purpose.

3 A Generation Apart

The author of *The Victors*, Peter Deane, in the article 'The Tragedy of the Survivors' (1930), supported the common criticism that war literature depicted the experience of war inaccurately. The real tragedy was that of the living:

> It is true that a good many of the survivors look back upon those years as the best of their lives.
>
> At that time, certainly, although at any moment they might have to leave it altogether, the world belonged to them. They have never, since the War ended, felt their feet securely on the earth for which they fought.[122]

In the longest war narrative, Richard Blaker's *Medal Without Bar*, written in 1930, the detailed story of a middle-aged gunnery officer and a thorough account of a field-artillery battery, the epilogue stresses the survivors' feeling of being a race apart. Captain Cartwright offers this sad contemporary footnote to his experience at Passchendaele and in Palestine:

> Women...can now be heard to say, "No. Things haven't changed at all. It hasn't done a bit of good. There is something about it all that men must have liked – and would like – egoism – or you wouldn't think about it the way you do; and read those books; and talk about it–" The sons and daughters begotten of these survivors...say rightly – "After all, ten – twelve years – it's a long time you know." ...These are the things they say, and rightly, for they have seen only the badness of the execrable job. Those who saw not only the job's badness but the best, also, that was made of it, pause. They have no answer. For they are the generation of the broken hearted. Pausing, they behold the ghosts that rise from the tide's inscrutable blackness; and they look upon the shadows of them whose mighty fellowship made misery tolerable.[123]

Sometimes only a few years constitute a generation away. In *The History of Button Hill* Eric's wife-to-be, ten years younger than he, accuses him 'of being extravagantly sentimental about the war.'[124] At the end of the war the protagonist of *Farewell to Youth*, with the disillusionment of his hasty pre-war marriage and the sense of hopelessness for survivors intensifying the anguish of the loss of time and opportunity, at twenty-six years of age feels old, tired in mind and body. His father is aware of the painful, accelerated growth of his son: 'He felt young and less experienced than his son, as if in the past four years Nat had taken a short cut and now stood at his elbow.'[125]

In the 1930s, as the memory of war recedes, generational distance acquires new intensity. Stephen McKenna in the introduction to his *The Way of the Phoenix*, explained that the aim of this novel was to show how the effects of the war in the past fifteen years, seen through the Dermott family, had 'made the oldest and the youngest of us uncomprehending and incomprehensible strangers trespassing from different centuries.'[126] In Irene Rathbone's *They Call It Peace*, Lorna, who lost her husband in the war, is terrified for her young son, as she fears the imminence of another conflict. But his son anticipates with gladness not having 'to feel inferior any more to the beglamoured crowd of you – killed and living – that were "in the war."'

> You with your memories and your silences!...Your sense of apartness – of being specially singled and stricken by the gods!...Your hitherto conviction that 'it' couldn't happen again!...'The old men let us in for it,' you used to say among yourselves. But what have you done – you, the now middle-aged – to prevent us, or yourselves or your children, from being left in for the hellish next?[127]

Similarly, in *Vanessa*, the young Anstey Veasey bursts out during a dinner party with the absurd claim that his generation is also entitled to the 'adventure' of war: 'I've heard lots of fellows say it was the best time in their lives.'[128] There is a terrible contrast between the vacuous empathy of these words and the uncontrollable, tearful reaction of Maurice, who has not missed out on war and has been perpetually scarred by it. Storm Jameson's *That Was Yesterday* is a narrative which parallels some of her own experience during the war. Even when everyone has become a conscientious objector ('except some politicians, some parsons, most of the newspaper proprietors, and a few respectable morons of both sexes'), the protagonist is honest with the memory of her war in telling how, after the Somme, she withdrew from the group 'Friends of the Peace' because she saw that although she hated war she was in the war, as was the whole of her generation: 'It will blot us out. After this we shan't be *in* life at all.'[129]

The different strands of definition of the collective experience and of national character highlight the frictions and ambiguities, the manifold nature of the memory of war. The use of religious language was one way employed by these novels to channel diversity into a unitary stream of significance. The next chapter will examine reference to tradition as the most powerful means of access to an ultimately meaningful process of history.

Notes to Chapter 3

1. James Hilton, *Random Harvest*, 1941.
2. Richard Blaker, *Medal Without Bar*, 1930, p. 485.
3. Gilbert Frankau, *Peter Jackson, Cigar Merchant: A Romance of Married Life*, 1919, p. 542.
4. John Brophy, *The World Went Mad*, 1934, pp. 115, 113.
5. James Lansdale Hodson, *Grey Dawn - Red Night*, 1929, p. 176.
6. Patrick Miller, *The Natural Man*, 1924, p. 118.
7. Frankau, *Peter Jackson*, pp. 610–11.
8. Hugh Walpole, *John Cornelius*, 1937, p. 522. Walpole considered this novel of his extremely special, in a way his own autobiography. (Rupert Hart-Davis, Hugh Walpole, 1985, pp. 358, 385.)
9. Robert Keable, *Simon Called Peter*, 1921, p. 181.
10. John Galsworthy, *Saint's Progress*, 1919, p. 320.
11. *Times Literary Supplement*, 30 October 1919, p. 613. H.G. Wells praised *The Yellow Pigeon* for its sentimentality interspersed with comedy, and declared that he would put it next to a couple of other books in his 'library of the realities of the Great War.' (Blurb of Carmel Guest's The Yellow Pigeon, 1928.)
12. Phyllis Bottome, *A Servant of Reality*, 1919, pp. 27, 29. In the case of one novel, *Kif* (1929) by 'Gordon Daviot' (Elizabeth Mackintosh), the qualities of nerve, courage and daring which the young Kif learns in the war fit him for the crime of burglary in his post-war life, and lead to his execution for murder. A very light story, it was nevertheless presented as a weighty narrative; the blurb referred to Kif's journey towards his 'awful fate' as having 'the inevitability of a character in a Greek tragedy'.
13. Warwick Deeping, *Kitty*, 1927, p. 148.
14. Richard Blaker, *But Beauty Vanishes*, 1936, p. 300.
15. Hodson, *Grey Dawn – Red Night*, p. 187.
16. Frederick Sleath, *Sniper Jackson*, 1918, pp. 24–5.
17. Deeping, *Kitty*, p. 135.
18. Ronald Gurner also suffered from shell shock. Ronald Pertwee wrote his first novel in the neurasthenia ward of the Third London General Hospital (Stanley J. Kunitz and Howard Haycraft (eds.), *Twentieth-Century Authors, a Biographical Dictionary of Modern Literature*, New York, 1942, p. 1096).
19. *Athenaeum*, 22 October 1920, p. 552.
20. *Spectator*, 13 November 1920, p. 641.
21. James Agate, '"Journey's End" Again', *Around Cinemas*, 1946, p. 67.
22. Hugh Kimber, *San Fairy Ann: Ça Ne Fait Rien: A Love Story of the Great War*, 1927, p. 261.
23. Stephen Graham, *Life and Last Works of Wilfrid Ewart*, 1924, p. 3.
24. Vernon Bartlett, *No Man's Land*, 1930, p. 108.
25. Stephen Graham, *The Challenge of the Dead*, 1921, p. 28. A man digging for bodies told him; "'S a funny thing though – the British dead keep much longer than the Germans. If I put a spade through something and it's soft, I know it's a Jerry." *(Ibid.*, p. 27.)
26. Sleath, *Sniper Jackson*, pp. 296, 302, 297.
27. Gilbert Frankau, *Peter Jackson, Cigar Merchant*, 1919, pp. 609–10.
28. Arthur Beverley Baxter, *The Parts Men Play*, 1920, pp. 437–8.
29. John Collis Snaith, *Love Lane*, 1919, pp. 263–65.
30. Graham Seton, *Life Without End*, 1932, p. 279.
31. Duncan Keith Shaw, *The Red Horse*, 1928, p. 227.
32. Haeckel was a German biologist (1834–1919) who achieved great popular fame throughout the world with this work (1899, translated into English in 1901). (*Makers of Nineteenth-Century Culture 1800–1914*, Justin Wintle (ed.), 1982, p. 268.) In his autobiography, Hichens related how his novel had 'greatly offended the devout believers in spiritualism'. (Robert Hichens, *Yesterday: The Autobiography of Robert Hichens*, 1947, p. 265.)

33. Fussell has discussed the moral significance attributed to the sky within the context of the literary tradition dating from Ruskin's chapter 'Of the Open Sky' *in Modern Painters*. (Fussell, *The Great War and Modern Memory*, pp. 51–63.)

34. Charles R. Benstead, *Retreat: A Story of 1918*, 1930, p. 315.

35. Ronald Gurner, *Pass Guard at Ypres*, 1930, p. 156.

36. Douglas Pulleyne, *This, My Son*, 1927, pp. 292–3.

37. Shaw, *The Red Horse*, p. 93.

38. A. D. Gristwood, 'The Coward', in *The Somme*, 1927, p. 147.

39. James Lansdale Hodson, *Grey Dawn – Red Night*, 1929, p. 258.

40. Frederick Sleath, *The Seventh Vial*, 1919, p. 120.

41. Wilfrid Ewart, *The Way of Revelation: A Novel of Five Years*, p. 288.

42. A. M. Cogswell, *Ermytage and the Curate*, Arnold, 1922, p. 56.

43. A. S. M. Hutchinson, *One Increasing Purpose*, 1925, p. 23.

44. Even one of the most unconventional protagonists of war fiction, the eccentric artist Charles Faversham, who refuses to enlist because of pacifist ideals, is in the end reconciled to his fate in the war through faith in God and the belief in a wider scheme of purpose. (Kenneth Ingram, *Out of Darkness: A Drama of Flanders*, 1927.)

45. The words of the title are a biblical allusion to the 'valley of decision' (Joel, III, xiv). 'Valley of indecision' are also the concluding words of Battersby's *Edge of Doom*: love was the reward for all that the protagonist had endured in it. (Henry Francis Prevost Battersby, *The Edge of Doom*, 1919, p. 350.)

46. Christopher Stone, *The Valley of Indecision*, 1920, pp. 188–9, 190–1. The novel is dedicated to Brigadier-General Randall Bannett Barker DSO 'who was killed within a few feet of me and whose death made me more utterly miserable than at any other moment in the war.' (Christopher Stone, *Christopher Stone Speaking*, 1933, p. 48.)

47. Stone, The Valley of Indecision, p. 17.

48. Arthur J. Wallis, *The Theatre Queue*, 1920, p. 319.

49. Henry Francis Prevost Battersby, *The Edge of Doom*, 1919, p. 237.

50. Arthur Hamilton Gibbs, *Labels*, 1926, pp. 36–7, 38 (my italics).

51. *Ibid.*, p. 51.

52. Louis Golding, *Magnolia Street*, 1932, p. 113.

53. *Ibid.*, pp. 296–7.

54. Gilbert Frankau, *Peter Jackson, Cigar Merchant*, 1919, p. 658.

55. Mary Agnes Hamilton, *Special Providence: A Tale of 1917*, 1930, p. 108.

56. Mary Douglas, *Purity and Danger: An Analysis of the Concepts of Pollution and Taboo*, 1984 (first published in 1966).

57. Edmund Leach, *Culture and Communication: The Logic by Which Symbols Are Connected*, Cambridge, 1976, pp. 61–2.

58. Eric J. Leed, *No Man's Land: Combat and Identity in World War I*, 1979, pp. 195–6.

59. William McFee, *Command*, 1922, pp. 117, 311.

60. Oliver Onions, *Peace in Our Time*, 1923, p. 274.

61. Peter Deane, *The Victors*, 1925, pp. 94–95.

62. Harold Spender, *The Man Who Went*, 1919, p. 308.

63. See page 54.

64. *Spectator*, 9 October 1926, cited in James Hepburn, *Arnold Bennett*, 1981, p. 465.

65. Arnold Bennett, *Lord Raingo*, 1926, p. 188.

66. In one novel the target was the world of finance. In *They Call It Peace* (1936), Irene Rathbone attacked banking magnates and propounded the Douglas Social Credit Scheme (initiated by C. H. Douglas as a defence of the individual against the State monopolies and aimed towards 'adequate purchasing power' for everyone), so that human relationships could follow a more natural course.

67. Gilbert Cannan, *Pugs and Peacocks*, 1921, p. 37.

68. Sleath, *Sniper Jackson*, p. 240.

69. Frederick Sleath, *The Seventh Vial*, 1920, pp. 287–8.

70. Naomi Ellington Jacob, *Time Piece*, 1936, pp. 325–7.

71. Ian Hay, *The Willing Horse,* 1921, p. 258. Philip Gibbs's *Young Anarchy* (1926) is not a war novel, yet, as Stuart Laing points out, the discussion of the General Strike is a parallel to the Great War, with references to the 'spirit of the trenches' as a response and an ideal. (Stuart Laing, 'Philip Gibbs and the Newsreel Novel', in Peter Humm, Paul Stigant and Peter Widdowson (eds), *Popular Fictions: Essays in Literature and History,* 1986, pp. 139–140.)

72. John Galsworthy, *The Burning Spear; Being the Experiences of Mr. John Lavender in Time of War,* 1919; Edward Shanks, *The Old Indispensables: A Romance of Whitehall,* 1919; Gerald O'Donovan, *How They Did It,* 1920; F.O. Mann, *Grope Carries On; Being the Further Adventures of Albert Grope During the Great War,* 1932.

73. Edward Shanks, *The Old Indispensables,* 1919, p. 231.

74. John Galsworthy, *The Burning Spear,* p. 3. In *Nurse Benson,* Lord Messiger is President of the 'League of Self-Denial'; his niece calls it the 'League for Popularising Deprivations'. (Justin Huntly McCarthy, *Nurse Benson,* 1919, p. 17.)

75. Gerald O'Donovan, *How They Did It,* 1920, pp. 111, 149.

76. Compton Mackenzie, *Sylvia and Michael: The Later Adventures of Sylvia Scarlett,* 1919, p. 265.

77. Compton Mackenzie, *Fairy Gold,* 1926, p. 279.

78. Berta Ruck, *The Land-Girl's Love Story,* 1919, p. 341.

79. Deane, *The Victors,* pp. 4, 5.

80. 'Say the Germans have 3,000,000 effectives and we can put 6,000,000 into the field altogether, and the casualties on each side on all fronts are roughly 100,000 a month – 70 per cent. of those wounded, allow 30 per cent. of those return...Allow a million and a half to keep the front, let each side drop 1,200,000 a year, of which 800,000 return, put on 300,000 each year for those going up, take off 100,000 for general wastage and that's – no it isn't – anyway, I remember he worked it out to something between four years and five....He explained it all to me – clever chap – fellow on the Staff, you know. They get all this worked out there. Nothing left to chance at G.H.Q.' (Ronald Gurner, *Pass Guard at Ypres,* 1930, pp. 85–6.)

81. Warwick Deeping, *No Hero – This,* 1936, p. 295.

82. Arthur Hamilton Gibbs, *Chances,* 1930, p. 187.

83. Ernest Raymond, *The Jesting Army,* 1930, p. 317.

84. Preface to Harold Begbie, *Mr. Sterling Sticks It Out,* 1919, p. ix.

85. Begbie, *Mr. Sterling Sticks It Out,* p. 143.

86. Jerome Klapka Jerome, *All Roads Lead to Calvary,* 1919, pp. 251, 245–6. Another 1919 novel, Herbert Tremaine's *Two Months,* which portrays life in a small town near London during two months in the war, gives an account of the stodgy, inflexible views of the members of the local War Tribunal.

87. A. S. M. Hutchinson, *He Looked for a City,* 1940. Nine conscientious objectors died in prison during the war. As Rae points out, this figure is not exceptionally high when one takes into consideration that nine out of 1,200 imprisoned COs in three years was a lower percentage than for all the prisoners – and that several of these men, some of whom went on hunger strikes, were in poor health when they arrived. (John Rae, *Conscience and Politics: The British Government and the Conscientious Objector to Military Service,* 1970, pp. 226–7.)

88. Ronald Pertwee, *Pursuit,* 1930, pp. 173–74.

89. Bennet Copplestone, *The Last of the Grenvilles,* 1919, p. 306.

90. Compton Mackenzie, *Heavenly Ladder,* 1924, p. 243.

91. Pulleyne, *This, My Son,* p. 266.

92. Begbie, *Mr. Sterling Sticks it Out,* p. 17.

93. Henrietta Leslie, *Mrs. Fischer's War,* 1930, p. 59.

94. Ethel Boileau, *The Arches of the Years,* 1930, p. 248.

95. Gladys Bronwyn Stern, *Children of No-Man's Land,* 1919; Philip Gibbs, *Back to Life,* 1920; Thomas Henry Hall Caine, *The Woman of Knockaloe; A Parable,* 1923; Douglas Pulleyne, *This, My Son,* 1927; Oliver Madox Hueffer, *"Cousins German",* 1930; Henrietta Leslie, *Mrs. Fischer's War,* 1930; Cecil Edric Mornington Roberts, *Spears Against Us,* 1932; Philip Gibbs, *Blood Relations,* 1935. This last novel traces the story of the marriage between an Englishwoman and a German soldier. She has almost a love/hate relationship with her 'alien' son, and is

heartbroken at witnessing the rise of Nazism.

96. G. B. Stern, *Children of No-Man's Land*, 1919, p. 108 ff.

97. In another genre of fiction, Ford Madox Ford's *No More Parades*, Titjens's wife is the most famous example of such a character.

98. Gilbert Frankau, *Martin-Make-Believe*, 1930, p. 270.

99. Sleath, *Sniper Jackson*, p. 257; Henrietta Leslie, *Mrs. Fischer's War*, 1930, pp. 219–20; J.B. Morton, *The Barber of Putney*, 1919, pp. 198–200.

100. Ida Margaret Poore, *Rachel Fitzpatrick*, 1920, p. 260.

101. Warwick Deeping, *No Hero – This*, 1924, p. 190.

102. Patrick Miller, *The Natural Man*, 1924, pp. 190, 17. The novel won a prize offered by publishers for the first novel of the best literary quality. This unlikely distinction was awarded by the judges Eden Phillpotts, Gerald Cumberland, Osbert Sitwell and Grant Richards.

103. *Times Literary Supplement*, 7 August 1924, p. 488.

104. *London Mercury*, September 1924, p. 539.

105. Shaw, *The Red Horse*, pp. 291–5.

106. Keable, *Simon Called Peter*, p. 69.

107. A. S. M. Hutchinson, *If Winter Comes* (1921), Albert Kinross, *God and Tony Hewitt* (1925), Harold Begbie, *Mr. Sterling Sticks it Out* (1919), Robert Keable, *Simon Called Peter* (1921) and Graham Seton, *Life Without End* (1932).

108. Keable, *Simon Called Peter*, p. 69; Frankau, *Peter Jackson*, p. 650; H. F. P. Battersby, *The Edge of Doom*, 1919, p. 197; Harold Begbie, *Mr. Sterling Sticks It Out*, 1919, pp. 80–81.

109. Harold Begbie, *Mr. Sterling Sticks it Out*, 1919, p. 80.

110. Even such a slight novel as *Marriage While You Wait*, a tale of the difficulties of settling down to a marriage contracted hastily during the war, sought to provide a readjustment strategy which reconciled the different experiences of husband and wife. (J.E.Buckrose (pseudonym of Annie Edith Jamieson), *Marriage While You Wait*, 1919.)

111. Phyllis Bottome, *A Servant of Reality*, 1919, p. 52.

112. See page 35.

113. Hamilton, *Special Providence*, pp. 108–9.

114. There was a direct acknowledgment of women as victims of war in Peter Deane's *Harvest*, a collection of short stories about the common tragedy of war across the nations and the sexes. The cover exhibited the concluding sentence of Philip Gibbs's foreword: 'War would not happen so often in the world if, like Peter Deane, we had pity for the women who do the harvesting.' (Philip Gibbs, cover of Peter Deane's *Harvest*, 1926.)

115. Mrs Victor Rickard, wife of Lieutenant-Colonel V.G.H.Rickard, killed at Rue du Bois in May 1915, wrote an account of her husband's regiment, *The Story of the Munsters at Etreux, Festubert, and Rue de Bois* (1915), a tribute to 'the men who gave their lives for an Ideal' (p. v). Another woman who presented herself as the shadow of her husband was the author of *Rachel Fitzpatrick*. Lady Ida Margaret Poore published *Recollections of an Admiral's Wife, 1903–1916* in 1916 and *An Admiral's Wife in the Making, 1860–1903* in 1917. Having spent her life as a Navy wife, she presented a reassuringly familiar, intimate picture of military life. Her son Roger, Lieutenant in the Field Artillery, was killed in September 1915. In the chapter 'Christmas Thoughts, 1915' she told how she and her husband thought of the parents who did not know how their sons had died, of the parents of prisoners of war: all worse off than they, 'to whom sacrifice was sweetened by the swift glory of the end.' *(Recollections of an Admiral's Wife, 1903–1916*, 1916, p. 338.)

116. Mrs Victor Rickard, *The House of Courage*, 1919, p. 120.

117. The cover also exhibited Philip Gibbs's endorsement: 'This novel has a tragic beauty which is rare in modern fiction'.

118. Pamela Hinkson, *The Ladies' Road*, 1932, p. 71.

119. John Brophy, *The World Went Mad*, 1934, p. 265.

120. The blunt provocativeness of the novel was an expression of the frank discussion of sex in the inter-war years. Apart from Marie Stopes's *Married Love* (1918), Theodore van der Veldis's *Ideal Marriage*, translated from the Dutch in 1930, provided advice on 'sexual fulfilment' and went through 43 impressions; the Christian manual *Threshold of Marriage*

(1932) discussed orgasms for both husband and wife and sold half a million copies. (John Stevenson, *British Society 1914–1945,* Harmondsworth, 1986 (first published 1984), p. 179.)

121. Irene Rathbone, *We That Were Young,* 1932, pp. 464, 465.

122. Peter Deane, 'The Tragedy of the Survivors', *The Nation and Athenaeum,* 18 October 1930, p. 103.

123. Richard Blaker, *Medal Without Bar,* 1930, pp. 637–38. Blaker, with the RFA in France, Egypt and Palestine, had himself fought with big guns. A similarly detailed account, this time of the RAMC, was F. H. Snow's only novel *No Names, No Pack Drill* (1932). This very lengthy work detailed the routine of a sanitary squad from recruitment at Aldershot to service in France.

124. Gordon Stowell, *The History of Button Hill,* 1929, p. 416.

125. Storm Jameson, *Farewell to Youth,* 1928, p. 150. An interesting text of memory of war of the younger, pre-war generation is Sylvia Thompson's *Hounds of Spring* (1926), published when the author was only 24. In it the final romantic choice is part of the wreckage and waste of war, as a woman desperately defies social convention and leaves her husband in order to be reunited with the fiancé she believed killed in the war. The final word is about the hope of the future resting with the next generation, that of Wendy, the very young sister, who has the energy and wisdom of those who have knowledge without having been irreparably wounded by it.

126. Stephen Mckenna, *The Way of the Phoenix,* 1932, p. xi.

127. Irene Rathbone, *They Call It Peace,* 1936, p. 553. (italics in the text)

128. Hugh Walpole, *Vanessa,* 1933, p. 813.

129. Storm Jameson, *That Was Yesterday,* 1932, pp. 111, 270. Storm Jameson's novels were often thinly disguised autobiographies. In *Farewell, Night; Welcome, Day* (1939) she evoked the death of her brother in the RFC, and its effect on her mother, on the eve of the war that would kill her sister and see her son take her brother's place.

4 The Quest for Continuity

...No experience can be too strange and no task too formidable if a man can link it up with what he knows and loves.

John Buchan, *Memory Hold the Door*

Nothing was stable, nothing permanent... And yet how could one endure without something stable, still, perpetual, in time but not of it, nor knowing its touch?

Ernest Raymond, *A Family that Was*

1 Preserving the Past

If popular novels recognize the unprecedented nature and consequences of the war, their reconstructions and interpretations link them in the majority of cases to familiar questions. Their attempt to accomplish a successful synthesis between old and new is one of the most significant functions of these novels, which reassure the readers (and the writers themselves) that in spite of the traumatic changes brought about by the war the basic pattern of society is still visible. They negotiate, as it were, their own Versailles treaty; peace with the new in terms that will not deprive people of the certainties of the past.

In these works of fiction the first source of evidence of their support of traditional values is in the approach to literature. Middlebrow writers condemned the work of the highbrows, whose esoteric writing they considered the worst expression of modernism, because of their detachment from the experience of most readers. They denounced the cryptic, cynical, ironical, abstruse language of highbrow writers as a conscious attempt to defile common conceptions of the beautiful and the familiar. Fictional characters themselves weigh in with their judgment on the literary state of the nation. In *Prelude to Calvary* people like the reader of the *Chimes Literary Suckling* and *The New Quiver* are derided for being fatuous intellectuals who cannot recognize the authenticity of idealism.[1] The novelist-protagonist of *John Cornelius* (1937), expressing his opinion in the year before the publication of the novel, sums up thus the development of English literature in the preceding two decades:

> It seemed, even the best of it, of small importance, and I fancy that from that year to this one – from 1917 to 1936 – English letters have never recovered the quiet happiness and friendliness that they had before 1914. Fretful, restless, irritable, innovating for innovation's sake, so it has been, much of it, since then.[2]

Notes to Chapter 4 can be found on page 142

'Innovating for innovation's sake' mimics the aesthetic slogan of 'art for art's sake', true anathema to these authors, who could not in any case have achieved this despised standard. In *The Further Side of No Man's Land* the protagonist (the author's fictional *alter ego*) is a young intellectual, 'a dilettante, a taster of the chance morsels in art and philosophy'. Malory's war experience as an officer in France and a prisoner of war in Germany precipitates a significant evolution in his artistic perceptions.

> He knew that while he retained much of his old artistic sensitiveness he was impatient of the memory of his old precious and priggish self which wished to keep art and life in compartments apart ...He was inclined rather to make a vertical division of society, cutting through the gradations of artistic sensibility and leaving on one side the combatant, the self-sacrificing, the morally fine, and on the other the combatant by proxy, the luster after self, the morally debased.

When he compares his pre-war drawings to his more recent work, he finds the former 'harsh, angular, defiant, crude' while the latter are 'graceful, symmetrical, smooth.'[3] Life in its totality of expression is the territory of the lessons of war, and art cannot be excluded from the practical application of the moral wisdom learnt in the trenches. The symmetry of Malory's war drawings, contrasted with the jarring quality of his pre-war work, is a powerful emblem of belief in continuity rather than discordance.

In *Lament for Adonis* the two protagonists play a game of cricket on Mount Olivet during the last days of Allenby's campaign. These two men represent 'Youth and Valour and Friendship', 'because the things that are eternal' reveal themselves when the time and the person are worthy of them. They are fighting for a civilization quite different from the contemporary one, 'an affair of noise and lights amid which elaborately dined and wined animals move chattering and smiling.' The author's references to the intellectual fervour of his pre-war youth, inspired by the measure of hope intrinsic to the work of Shaw, Wells, and Galsworthy,[4] indicates a great sense of loss about the new literature, ruled by the despair of the denial of principles.

As Simone Weil has expressed in *The Need for Roots*, '...we possess no other life, no other living sap, than the treasures stored up from the past and digested, assimilated and created afresh by us.'[5] Middlebrow authors sifted their memories to provide a reconstruction of the past which above all aimed to be respectful of the underlying, awesome currents of history, moving in a linear progression of meaning through time. Idealism in this fiction is always at the service of historical continuity.

Harold Begbie's *The Great World*, which traced the political education of the young Duke of Rothbury, posited clearly a relationship between time and meaning in a single paragraph encompassing the whole history of civilization:

Those long centuries in which no life existed on this planet; those long centuries in which nature had fashioned myriad forms of life, building up, building up to men and his soul; those long centuries in which civilisation had moved westward, and ever westward across the world, strewing the earth with the ruin of empires; those long centuries of England's island story, from Alfred to Nelson; the great pageant of English history, the rough and stormy birth of the British Empire, the chaos and clangour of the industrial era – all those long centuries, their toil, their agony, their triumph, and their defeats – surely there was a purpose running through it all from the very dawn of creation to this hour.[6]

The import of this passage finds an exact echo in the title of A.S.M. Hutchinson's novel *One Increasing Purpose*, taken from Tennyson's 'Yet I doubt not through the ages one increasing purpose runs.'[7] The Highlander Duncan the Forester, philosopher of the hills, with three sons at the front, distributes strength and courage through a vision of life seen as eternal, spiritual and not to be measured or weighed by killing metal: 'You would jist do as weel by running your swords into the side of Loch Fell and thinking you put an end to it.'[8] Gilbert Cannan's *Time and Eternity* announces through its very title the setting of the plot against an unchanging scheme of values. Several novels employ a wide time-span, the chronological amplitude providing an adequate vessel of meaning.[9] Philip Gibbs's *Unchanging Quest*, which the blurb called 'a spiritual history of England', covered three decades of history: with the aid of this vast sweep of history it addressed the 'unchanging quest' of solving the mystery of suffering and effort.

No attribution of meaning can be more powerful than one relating to the universal pattern of history. If death is the doorway to this crystallization of meaning, then death is utterly saved from futility. Corporal Henry Bateman, in *In Araby Orion*, waits for death in a pit in East Jordan, where his comrades have been forced to leave him, having failed in their attempts to rescue him. He is 'poor, and lonely, and forsaken; helpless and dying.' His is the ultimate degraded position, yet there is meaning to rescue the situation from modern irony: 'In the pit he was sure that eternity had found him, and that its face was full of compassion....To that Figure he lifted up his hands, and sent his whole life out in a cry of appeal.'[10]

By allowing people to remember as well as to learn afresh, the concept of tradition provided a link between their personal history and the war, helping them to hold on to a historical sense of identity. In *The House of Courage* when a young woman marries in Ireland just before the outbreak of war, she reassures her brother that she will not mind the monotony of life in County Cork, its 'perpetual eternity', where earthquakes never happen.[11] But the war and her husband's experience in it do have the effect of an earthquake with the disruption they bring in real and potential terms. In the end the threat of irretrievable social change is completely exorcised by the innate strength of their threatened world. The depiction of the upheaval caused by war, and the final withstanding of its shock by a resilient society, is the theme of many of these popular novels. *Parson's Nine* ends, after the war, with the same scene with which it started at the beginning of the century, a scene of ritual village life, thus confirming Catherine's judgment that 'it takes more than a European war to change life in country parishes.'[12]

The need not to dispense with the models of the past but to make them the foundations of new work underlines most social judgments of these novels. In *John Brown* the writer insists on the need to modernize the New Army and to turn away from the old militarism, a matter of 'brass bands, pipeclay, and eyewash.' But for all the stress on change, a fine balance is struck between old and new by doing away with the old rhetoric and still relying on the age-old principles of chivalry, honour, and valour. Ginger, a Cambridge officer, talking to his radical friend Nobby insists that one should not smash down to build up. 'You can't do that in war-time! Graft the new on to the old, and *we'll win!*'[13]

Models of continuity provide channels of survival. Talking about the death of comrades in war, Michael Howard has commented that it is 'perhaps easier to endure such ordeals and even to take pride in them if one is conscious that there is nothing new in having to do so, that men of earlier generations have faced and overcome them and gained well-deserved renown as a result.'[14] In *The Barber of Putney* Tim and Curly, after wandering into a cemetery and finding a dead friend's grave, talk about how brave he was. 'In this manner, though in a different speech, warriors in old times might have spoken of a lost comrade....When men talk of a friend in that way, one knows one is face to face with that mystery we call tradition.' This mystery, 'a kind of spiritual presence' which holds together the British line, is not manifested in the same way to all classes.

> We call it tradition, but Tim and Curly only knew they were doing their job, and O'Hanlon, maybe, was still dreaming of burning battlements, the music of blade on blade, and all the old things of minstrelsy.[15]

This passage brings together several strands of war memory we have already noted. The meaning of war is perceived only vaguely by the soldiers, but authorial hindsight attributes an underlying purpose; the spiritual core of tradition serves to define the special nature of the men's experience.

Tradition is a motivation which links all classes in an age-long pattern of meaning. In *Love Lane* (1919) the 41-year-old greengrocer Billy Hollis and his unlikely friend Stanning, a Royal Academy painter, have a talk by the Yser about why they joined up. Stanning explains that he comes of an old

Methodist family, people with a 'Conscience' who throughout his life have come back to worry him with it. Billy, in his turn, talks about *his* ancestry, in particular about his father's uncle, Troop-Sergeant-Major William Hollis, who had fought at Waterloo. When his friend comments that this does not seem reason enough for him to drag his 'old bones' to rot in France, he rejoins that it is: 'When we come up against a big thing, it isn't us that really matters, it's what's at the back of us.'[16]

England is synonymous with tradition, the name and reality on which all meaning converges. The land of England represents a memory of rural landscapes and villages, and a concrete notion of timeless tradition. 'Patriotism in London is such a precocious thing. Here it's like the seed in the earth – long sown and long a-growing, but perfect in its time.'[17] In *No Man's Land* love of the English land is intensified by its setting in a disenchanted narrative. Stevenson remembers when, on his last leave home at Ludworth, he stood looking out at the sea.

> Men fought and died, empires grew and fell, civilizations developed and were forgotten. But this great sweep of bay, these magnificent chalk cliffs, defied change, and remained for ever things of beauty which would bring tears to the eyes of men. This was what one fought for, and if he were to be killed he prayed that he might have the time to remember, before he became nothing, the view from the summit of Binden Hill.[18]

Tradition, in the form of an English view which 'defies change' and of a literary turn of phrase from a great nineteenth-century poet, is the subject of this statement. Tradition and love of England are also indistinguishable in the very patriotic sentiments which the writer Maud Diver imputes to her aristocratic hero. In spite of 'the little breed of men' who play with England's destiny, in spite of the 'cranks and the Stock Exchange', there are still men who will stand for the great traditions of their race: 'and Derek Blount, with the record of a great house behind him, knew very well that tradition...is, in its essence, one of the great spiritual forces of earth.'[19]

When this focus of meaning is threatened everything is in danger of being drained of significance. In Storm Jameson's *The Clash* an Englishwoman whose husband is at the front is tempted to have an affair with the American Jess Cornish. At a time when she feels weak and vulnerable and about to face a decision which challenges in a fundamental way the conventions of her class and her time, Jess openly defies her world. He does not need England, he declares, because Americans need nothing of what it has to offer: 'You have nothing, except your past, and your dying tradition.' Her response is sure: 'The tradition did live', embodied in small rural towns throughout her country. When her great-aunt Miriam warns her of the importance of not losing her honour she speaks in terms which appeal to tradition as the philosophy which underpins and explains all: 'Chastity...is a tradition, but so is honour and so is gentleness. The world itself is a tradition. We do not know that we exist, but we have always believed that we do.'[20] Just as this statement starts from the detail of honour to include a universal appraisal of the function of tradition, so the novel moves from a consideration of the woman's personal dilemma to the issue of the ultimate significance of what is happening to the country. The tragedy of war and the circumscribed problem of a tormented personal involvement mirror each other, incongruously, as they are both ultimately made to refer to the concept of tradition for explanation.

The concentration on individual experience provided microcosms of hope as continuity which would have been difficult to achieve in the examination of change within whole communities. The only novel in which the protagonist is a social group is Gordon Stowell's first work, *The History of Button Hill*, which covered the history of the suburban Button Hill, a Yorkshire manufacturing town near 'Fleece', from 1894 to the late 1920s.[21] It is a saga of change, of the rise and fall of a suburban centre, an intimate depiction of cultural transition through the fate of the town's youth.

Nostalgia for the past is expressed in this novel through the memory of the lost language and attitudes of young men. It contains a lengthy portrayal of the Knut, that forgotten male type soon to be decimated in the war; in its descriptive preciseness[22] it reads like an entry for a dictionary of culture.

> The Knut was an urban and suburban phenomenon of the years 1912 to 1914 inclusive. The word 'Knut' looks foolish enough today, but at one time everyone knew exactly what the word meant. It was one of the commonest words of the period. And that preliminary K was essential....A brilliant musical comedy star of that time, whose career was cut short later in Gallipoli, used to sing: "I'm Gilbert the filbert, the Knut with a K"...Knut-hood was a kind of order or craft, for which every male in the realm between the age of fifteen and twenty-five was eligible. It was a concerted revolt against accepted masculine patterns.

The Knut disappeared, 'in truth, he was blown out with some violence', during the war, leaving behind a legacy of male freedom.[23] Vernon Bartlett referred to this character in his wartime sketches as someone 'now virtually extinct...killed by war', whose affected nonchalance, drawl and eyeglass went together with great bravery.[24]

Most of the young men of Button Hill join the 'Pals' Battalion, which is obliterated at the Somme. The break with the past is epitomized by the shock of one of the survivors of the Battalion returning to his town in the late Twenties and finding that the Big Tree, which has been there for centuries and is the oldest thing in Button Hill, has been felled to make way for real estate development.[25] The novel ends with Eric searching for a direction of meaning in the face of the bankruptcy of his past and of the transformation of his town. The framework of temporal and semantic reference of his reflections could not be vaster. Was change just an 'irrational endeavour', or did man through time slowly move increasingly closer to 'his unknown goal?'

> "Wave following wave departs for ever, but still flows on the eternal river." Button Hill must have been a seventh wave. And the tide would continue to flow. The Life Force...Evolution...God?[26]

Button Hill is a recent, homogeneously middle-class suburb, and the felling of the Big Tree implies the failure of the past to take root there. In several narratives what the tree stands for, tradition, finds a focus of reference and strength from the role of the upper classes.

2 The Old Order

The individual answer to the call of Destiny, even when the mysteriousness of its ways is agonizing, readjusts the assessment of the experience of war towards its insertion within a vast traditional pattern. The upper classes, with their traceable, ancient male lineages and their history of prominent national status, figure largely in these fictional explorations of meaning as symbols of British tradition. In *The Parts Men Play* Baxter highlights the rush of the scions of English families to enlist:

> Not with the cry of 'Liberty!' or 'Freedom!' but merely as heirs to British traditions, they took the field. Of a race that acts more on instinct than on reason, they were true to their vision of Britain, and asking no better fate than to die in her service, they helped to stem the Prussian flood while home after home, in its ivy-covered seclusion, learned that the last son, like his brothers, has 'played the game' to a finish.

This contraposition of instinctive service and awesome national purpose presents tradition in the vague idealistic terms which we noted earlier. But the uncovering of the values guiding the 'invisible hand', particularly that of tradition, reveals that the overt apolitical rhetoric contains a practical, conservative plan for the future: 'Let the men who cry for the remodelling of Britain – and progress must have an unimpeded channel – let them try to bring to their minds the Britain that men saw in August 1914, when catastrophe yawned in their path. That picture holds the secret for the Great Britain of the future.'[27]

In *The Willing Horse* (a play of words on the seven horses of the Apocalypse) Ian Hay argues that the prompt, inarticulate response which has won the war automatically makes all soldiers honorary members of 'the Old Order.'

> I mean the people to whom this country, as such, has always really meant something: I mean every mother's son who felt the ancient spirit of our race wake in him, perhaps for the first time, when the challenge came in Nineteen Fourteen. I don't care who he was – squire's son, parson's son, miner's son, poacher's son – it was all the same. If he was anxious then of that single blind impulse to get up and play the game, just because it was the game; just because it was impossible to do otherwise – without any dialectics about Freedom, or Altruism, or Democracy, or whether his job would be kept open for him or not; simply because the Blood told him to – then he belonged to the Old Order!

Although Hay asserts that in 'the Old Order' are included all who answered the archetypal call of race, it is clear throughout the novel that the leading defenders of tradition are the upper classes. The above passage is followed by the lamentation of the unceasing changing of hands of estates in the three years since the end of the war, as the landed gentry were forced to sell because of death duties and income tax: 'It seems a queer way of rewarding people who have given everything – to sell them up because they have nothing more to give! Still, one has the supreme satisfaction of having played the game. Our record stands.'[28] Charles Masterman, in his study of post-war England, paid a less orotund but equally strong tribute to the effort in the Great War of this class, whose purpose for existence he identified as war: they had deserved to be considered 'representative of "all the dead".'[29]

By the end of 1919 a million acres of land had been sold,[30] and between 1914 and 1927 a quarter of England and Wales was sold by landed proprietors to tenant-farmers.[31] In 1920 *The Times* asserted: 'England is changing hands...The sons are perhaps lying in far away graves...and the old people, knowing there is no son or near relative to keep up the old traditions, or so crippled by necessary taxation that they know the boy will never be able to carry on when they are gone, take the irrevocable step.'[32] At the end of his chapter 'The Passing of Feudalism', Masterman raised the spectre of a world in which scientific progress was unmatched by 'moral progress', leaving the memory 'of a time when men did splendid and noble things, in a community which once believed in God.'[33]

The lifestyle of the rural gentleman embodies the innate values of the land, historical tradition and class stratification. The war undermined the standing of this group, but the image of the gentleman remained as a powerful source of cultural reference. *Cousin Philip*, by Mrs Humphry Ward, proposes the political solution of the individual's social commitment *together with the example of the aristocracy.* The novel begins with Lord Buntingford contemptuously reading a leaflet issued by the 'Middle Class Defence League'[34] which invites new members to join it in order to counteract the threat of mob rule: 'Why should we be snuffed out without a struggle....We are fewer, no doubt, but we are better educated. Our home traditions are infinitely superior. It is on the Middle Classes that the greatness of England depends.'[35] In the novel this message is qualified with the important proviso that the truly 'infinitely superior' tradition is the aristocratic one: what is needed is a supra-political alliance between the aristocracy and the middle class, not associations which mimic those of the working class.

Harold Begbie also believed in the crucial importance of the example of the upper classes. In his populist treatise *The Mirror of Downing Street* he lamented the fact that the aristocracy had ceased providing the country with its moral guidance.[36] But what was a concrete lack in society could be provided as a model in fiction. Roger Bromley has examined the presentation of the figure of the aristocratic gentlemen in two bestsellers of the 1930s, Daphne du Maurier's *Rebecca* (1938) and Geoffrey's Household's *Rogue Male* (1939). In particular he discusses how fiction, through contact and marriage between the middle and upper classes, operated a 'transfusion of ideals and values, and a *style* with an important ideological function, that of the gentleman, signed by a morality of fair play, selflessness, courage, moderation and self-control, independence and responsibility.'[37]

Begbie's *The Great World* (1925) is a vibrantly articulated saga of the social attitudes of the family of the Duke of Rothbury from 1870 to the early 1920s. The members of the family live with the constant tension of confrontation between a changing structure of society and their traditional family and class ideals. The grandfather, a contemporary of the despised Gladstone, whom he hopes to outlive as a final act of spite, is a formidable and respected man who has been prominent in political service to the nation. He dies in the 1870s, darkly prophetic about the consequences of Liberal change, but sure of his role and of that of his class. His grandson lives like the relic of a past age, detached from London life and completely devoted to the running of his estate. He dies fighting in South Africa in 1902, a few days after his son is born. His wife's role is to ensure that her son becomes a great man, and she tensely devotes herself to an aristocratically pure upbringing of the boy in a world of deteriorating values. After the war, when her daughters become involved in war work and turn into shrill, ungovernable young women, she joins the Catholic Church as an act of escapism from an increasingly vulgar, that is democratic, world. Her son, in the meantime, with the implied greater balance of his sex grows up to become a man capable of judging what is authentic and valuable in the confused post-war era. Tradition is safeguarded.

Upper-class protagonists abound; their lifestyles lend glamour to the plainest novel and the values inscribed in the perception of their class sustain grandly all plot developments. In *The Way of Revelation* one protagonist is heir to a baronetcy and the other second in line to a barony. The decline of the landed gentry makes their worth stand out all the more sharply, as the importance of what is in danger of extinction is described and therefore perpetuated as a social model through fictional representation. *Caroline England* (1937), the story of the homonymous member of the gentry from 1870 to 1936, ends with Caroline taking her grandchildren to the coronation of Edward VIII, because she wants them to share in her 'advantage of growing up surrounded by tradition.' Shortly before dying she asks her grandchild, child of the son who died in the war, to plant an oak tree in honour of the King's coronation at the hotel which used to be their manor house.[38] Change and loss of aristocratic advantages can be borne if, as the planting of the tree and its location symbolize, devotion to tradition can survive. The protagonist of *The Breathless Moment*, Sabine, a guest in her friends' country house, is at first puzzled and annoyed by the stream of visitors who never leave empty-handed, but the expression of her misgivings to her hosts results in her 'recoiling from the wall of Tradition'. She learns that the survival of the feudal 'bread and salt' custom binds village people to reverence for the family and the family to a service of advice and practical help. The son of the house explains to her that even though birth does not determine the personal qualities of a man, yet 'refined surroundings' and 'the necessity...to set an example of decency' for generations do tell in the end. He likens the ideal of living up to the family's name to the spirit of the regiment. This correlation between the spirit of the upper class with that of the regiment is stressed by the condemnation of the new class of war profiteers, vulgar, rich, with no breeding and no tradition. It is just this kind of people, the Gulls, who buy the Vallances' country seat in St. Mary (which in the end is bought back). Sabine despises the new owners, and deems the displacement of the old mistress a social calamity: 'By what right did such a woman [Mrs Gull], ignorant and malicious, supplant the old landed gentry? She was not a true democrat. She had no sympathy with those who led humble lives on her estate, no knowledge of country needs and no real charity.'[39] This is another example of literary representation of the experience of war purporting to be apolitical but in effect expressing support of a given social model. Values from the trenches and from home reflect each other: the devotion and responsibility of the officers towards their soldiers and that of the gentry towards their people; the tradition of regiment and the tradition of caste; democracy defined in terms of traditional service, and democracy re-asserted against the values of the war profiteer, the man who more than any other negates the lessons of the spirit of the 'willing horse.'

Ancestral homes, treasures of permanent architecture set in the countryside, are important emblems of tradition. Rockover House has belonged for many centuries to the Mortimers, who have an illustrious military tradition which goes back to the Crusades.[40] Captain Hewitt's family has lived at Deerhurst, 'many-gabled house with the Hewitt crest and arms carved over the entry', for five centuries.[41] A young boy who has spent his childhood in Turkey comes to understand, as guest of a schoolmate at 'The Croft', the patrician order of things in England; he learns that belonging to the country gentry means enjoying a graceful life and a beautiful environment, being loved by the villagers, and speaking of humanity at large as 'the masses.'[42]

Women are often portrayed as the upholders of tradition in the domestic sphere of the ancestral home. The wartime tale of adventure and danger *Pursuit* ends with two young lovers reunited and Joan expressing her dream of being 'absolutely stunned and saturated by peace' through the vision of continuity of an upper-class family nucleus:

> I want you and a home and some sons and p'raps one daughter – if she isn't too big a fool – and very serious talks about education and punctual meals and the kind of house that's called The Larches, and servants who call me 'Yes'm' instead of 'Madam' and roast beef on Sundays, and a tennis court and a prayer book and a library subscription, and oh, such heaps of love.[43]

In *All Roads Lead to Calvary* also, the bride-to-be formulates plans for peace which centre on the ancestral home where they will live when they are married. She counters her fiancé's description of her paternal house as 'an ugly old thing' with a personalistic defence: 'No it isn't...It's simple and big and kind. I always used to think it disapproved of me. I believe it has come to love me, in its solemn and brick way.' Built in 1740 by her great-great-grandfather, it has an aura of solid respectability for which she likes it. Within it she envisions the future of their union as the marriage of old and new values. 'We will teach it the new dreams, too. It will be so shocked, at first.'[44] This is the happy romantic resolution of a novel about the inspired ideals of a very 'modern' young woman, who discovers through the war and her involvement with a conscientious objector that love of God is the answer to all. The happiest ending in these fictions comes when there occurs a resolution of the conflict within the private sphere between modern behaviour and traditional values.

There are two tales of a woman's obsessive mission to rescue the past. The house called 'White Ladies' is the protagonist of the novel to which it lends its name. The narrative centres around a baronet's wife's all-consuming dedication to the restoration of a beautiful Elizabethan home. When her son dies in the war she gives up her too-expensive life's work to make a fresh start in her grandfather's home, so that though tradition in the shape of the rich old order of White Ladies has to be abandoned, it still gives comfort. The dedication of Bella Pomfret, the daughter of a wealthy industrialist, to this jewel of ancient beauty in the Black Country turns her mental processes into those of an aristocrat: 'She was coming round, gradually, to Hugo's [her husband's] way of thinking – to the way in which generations of Pomfrets had thought...'[45] Glen Cavaliero judges the 'smooth prose' of the passage above (in its entirety), which includes a lyrical description of the beauty of the White Ladies grounds in the summer, to be 'a deception', as it ignores the social paradox of the industrial devastation of the Stour Valley. In spite of the literary fluency, he contends, '...there is a lazy sensibility at work here. Ultimately the effect is banal.'[46] The effect is certainly poor, but the author's sensibility, blind to social problems outside his central character's class, is busily at work elsewhere. The passage Cavaliero discusses, and the novel in general, are not concerned merely with an aesthetic nostalgia for the past, but with the ideology of the possibilities inherent in a concept of tradition linked to the land and to the model of the aristocracy.

The Vanity Girl, similarly, is the tale of the realization of a chorus-girl's passionate belief in the role of the aristocracy. Having married an earl, Dorothy devotes herself to the Clarehaven tradition, almost as if to balance historically the Liberal victory of 1906, the year of her marriage. The social metaphor here is the encounter of the old with the new and the revitalizing influence of devotion to what is in danger of extinction. When she finds that she is pregnant she is ecstatic: her son would be 'the saviour of his country...not some political pawnbroker like Disraeli, but an incarnation of the benign genius of aristocracy...'[47] Dorothy's self-indulgent and inconsequential husband, who has lost his estate, is killed in France in 1915 and his son is born the sixth Earl of Clarehaven. Dorothy marries the rich Jew who has bought Clare Court on condition that he make it over to her son.

The above five novels about women's visceral, and in two cases pathological, attachment to tradition were all written by men, and they all rest on an obvious partitioning of roles into male responsibility and female procreation. In these novels mourning the carnage of a male generation and glorifying the lessons learnt by young men at the front, male values are the guarantee of continuity; the women's sense of rootedness is at the service of the stability of the men's world. After the war women must be re-integrated into a pattern of traditional commitment to the family to hold the fabric of society together. Storm Jameson's *Three Kingdoms* received this presentation from its blurb: 'Laurence is the business girl of post-war England and the hectic fool of any generation of Eve's daughters. She is aggressive and forlorn; she works in triumph but weeps in self-contempt; she is delicious and infuriating; she is a spur to a man's desire and an abomination to his common sense.' The cover unveils perfectly the novel's message: a baby in a cot, a businesswoman holding a newspaper sporting the advertisement FRESH!, a man, and a ribbon uniting all three. Laurence Storm begins working for an advertising firm during the war while her husband is in France. She becomes devoted to her career and independence to the point of their determining new expectations of her marriage once the war is over: 'Of course I want him to come safe out of it. But I'm not going to let him - I'm not going to let any man interfere with my life.' After the war, however, she eventually leaves her job to devote herself to her husband, live in the country, and 'cherish' her man as all her ancestors had cherished their husbands.[48]

The innately hereditary nature of male tradition explains the emphasis in so many novels on the birth of a son. Meaning as the binding agent between generations is sometimes reaffirmed through the retrospective understanding by the soldier's infant son of the sacrifice of his father's generation. *The Parts Men Play* ends with the protagonist writing a letter to his still unconceived son, to explain to him both the tragedy and the honour of having participated in the Great War. Even Sherriff, in spite of his complete lack of interest in reproduction, wrote for the *Evening Standard* on Armistice Day 1929 a message for youth in the form of a letter written from a father to his nine-year-old son on the eve of his return to France. Should he not come back the letter was to be opened on his son's 21st birthday. The message is one of positive judgment of his involvement in the war: 'I am glad the soldier has just forestalled the scientist in fighting out this last war, while a vestige of war's romance still survives, and makes us sometimes so proud of fighting for our countries that death no longer matters.'[49]

Examples of the continuity of the male line paralleling continuity of meaning are numerous. In *Love Lane* succession is established for both friends who have lost their lives in France when Bill Hollis's son is named after the dead comrade of his dead father. Patricia Querin (*The Plough*, 1919) gives birth to a son two days before her husband is killed. Although a Liberal who is at odds with her in-laws' stultified Tory values, she decides in the end that her son will go to his father's old school and then to Oxford. In *The Willing Horse* Ray, heir to the Baron of Baronrigg, hears that his wife has borne him a son just before he goes into the attack which will kill his own father. One of the most enduring popular narratives of the inter-war years, *Sorrell and Son*, focuses on the love of an ex-officer for his son, a devotion that motivates him to fight against his degraded social and financial status after the war. One novel, G.B.Stern's *Larry Munro* (1920), has as its theme an extreme and absurd level of reprocreation of the male line. The story spans three generations of Larry Munros, all the object of idolatry from their women. Prue, the divorced wife of Larry Munro I, and Felicity, his fiancée, concentrate all their love on Prue's son, Larry Munro II. Kevin, Felicity's son, grows up with Larry; the jealousy of the little boy is further complicated when Larry, at seventeen, becomes Felicity's lover and fathers a girl and a boy. When Larry II is killed in the war Prue and Felicity concentrate their obsessive love on Larry III.

Reabsorption into the Old Pattern Another means of reaffirmation of familiar values was that of post-war reintegration into one's social background. *Pink Roses* is the only novel of the inter-war years to depict a young man's civilian experience, and it provides an interesting document of an outsider's involvement with the war. Trevor Mathew, the son of a wealthy businessman, finds work in a London law firm once he is told that he cannot join up because of a heart murmur. The two friends with whom he shares a flat enlist; within a few months one is dead, the other crippled for life. Trevor feels that he is now 'the last remnant of their world', a responsibility which he finds increasingly cumbersome as the war assumes horrible proportions to which the patriotic commitment of his lost friends or the hysterical emotional response of people at home seem inadequate responses. His only strong feeling about the war is that it has been caused by the old and he despises the old world which his boss represents. When his fiancée's seventeen-year-old brother enlists he listens to the boy trying to explain what made him go into the Army:

> "Well, it's as if things were rushing away from you at about a million miles an hour, and all the things you'd been told were important turned out to be nothing at all, and as if when you tried to play the game according to the rules it turned crazy because the game was a new game, and the rules were old rules." "Why, that's the war!" said Trevor, beginning to grasp what the boy was driving at.

Trevor for a while embraces as a cause the war's challenge to his familiar reality. Yet as the war ends and he has to make choices about his future he realizes that his father played the old game well and decides to carry on from where his father left off. Sketching out his future existence in his imagination, he thinks of his family country home and the pleasant life he, his wife and his brother-in-law would lead there, and concludes: 'That was the way. To pick up old traditions and make them new.'[50] Given such a resolution, a little bit of revolt is better than none: when the prodigal sons return to the fold, their spirits tested by personal upheaval, they do so with a new sense of balance and loyalty.

The shock of the war is sometimes expressed through social displacement. In *God and Tony Hewitt* (1925) the trauma of the war for Captain Hewitt is exemplified by the way in which it brings out the real nature – slovenliness, laziness, addiction to drinking – of his beautiful wife, who is from a vaguely defined lower class while he is the heir of a prominent country squire. Although the title refers to Tony Hewitt's rather superficial and uninteresting religious conversion in Salonica, the real solution of the novel is the serene happiness which derives from the assurance of the traditional privileges of class. When the unhappy captain reveals his love to Vi Carter, a childhood friend, he sees in this woman 'home, their common past, his own breed, his own tradition, the valour and the honesty that were beyond all prize and all counting; and when he kissed her he kissed these.'[51] The war over and his wife having conveniently run away with a war profiteer, the final chapter finds him at his family home; his father has died, and he is now Sir Antony Hewitt. Vi, now his wife, is about to give birth to the 'latest off-shoot of an ancient family' in the big oak four-poster 'carved with the Hewitt arms.' As he awaits the birth of what turns out to be, of course, a son, Sir Antony reflects on his happiness and attributes it to his not having denied God and all He has to give, unlike his ex-wife and thousands of others. The religious tone of his reflections contrasts strangely with the materialistic nature of what he has been given. His salvation is not spiritual but social. The jolt of the war has restored him to the full dignity of his ancestral heritage after the indignity of marriage to a woman of inferior breeding.

The return of the soldier to an aristocratic or upper-class background lends the reassurance of age-long stability and endurance. The theme of *The Arches of the Years* (1930) and *Life Without End* (1932) is the complete reconciliation of the sons of great families to their homes after war-related personal crises have alienated them from their background. In the first novel the hero is the son of an old Scottish family with a distinguished military history. Brought up by his highly idealistic mother to cherish the nobility of the family's tradition, Jock Chisholm becomes a professional soldier. The war crushes all the illusions of this 'son of tradition',[52] who, after the Armistice, abandons his military career. In the end he finds a new expression for his innate idealism in championing Christ against Marx in extremely dangerous secret service work in the East. Hager and Taylor's comment about this novel is that the romantic plot fails 'to support the serious intentions of the author.'[53] On the contrary, the romantic development sustains perfectly the author's intentions, as Chisholm's involvement with an Eastern European woman both provides him with an heir, a son 'to come after him in the old grey castle of the Northern seas...to carry on the unbroken line',[54] and puts him in touch with a cause which gives purpose to his idealism and allows him to fight the redemptive battle for society which the war did not turn out to be.

The evils of a new, materialistic world appear in *Life Without End* not in the shape of Marxism but of interest in agnostic and relativistic philosophies. As a consequence of his war experience, the young curate Hugh Richmond loses his faith and becomes interested in 'the new scientific psychology' coming from Central Europe, and takes to reading Haldane, Huxley, Joad, and Russell. The sign of divine revelation which he receives through his dead comrades[55] reconciles him with his past and restores his lost belief; he returns to England to take his rightful place, now his father is dead, as the heir of the manor house High Trees. This is a great estate which the family has held throughout the history of Wessex: 'through the ages...Richmonds had continued the biological progression, one generation after another, so it seemed, *life without end.*' Hugh Richmond had defined his religious crisis as the perception that life was not 'one far off divine event to which the whole of creation moves, but just one damn thing after another, *life without end.*'[56] The resolution of the novel shifts the interpretation of these words from meaninglessness to the service of tradition. The words of the title imply a close correlation between the upper class, spiritual understanding and historical continuity.

3 Military Tradition

The most obvious way in which tradition is expressed within the experience of war is through repeated references to military tradition. The regiment, the protagonist of much glorious English history, involves directly even private soldiers in a role which makes them experience tradition as a living force. In *The Barber of Putney*, in the midst of a desperate attack the day is saved by the heroic individual intervention of the officer O'Hanlon, who leads the men by shouting the name of the regiment twice. He is killed, 'not unlike some legendary hero, with a battle-cry on his lips.' The men can point out the place where he was killed and how 'his battle-cry became something of a tradition....Wherever the regiment fights his spirit lives on.'[57]

The changed nature of warfare could not be played down, and only Escott Lynn had sufficient patriotic zest to attempt such sleight of hand with history. His *Tommy of the Tanks* portrayed war in France in 1918 as a matter of glorious charging offensives, exciting hand to hand combat and individual efforts of valour, often carried out by charging against the enemy with bayonet and butt in the face of rifle and machine-gun fire. In his novel about the Tank Corps, the end of the 1918 retreat is incongruously heralded by the charge of the cavalry: '...out of the buckets came the lances, the line moved forward at the trot, the lances were lowered to charge, and with a deep, rolling cheer the horsemen swept down upon the Huns.' But if such descriptions of warfare are exceptional in popular war fiction, the constant historical links which Lynn makes with the military experience of the soldiers' forefathers are not. The 1918 retreat, the author explains, is not ignominious as there are illustrious precedents for its strategic necessity, like Wellington retreating from Brussels to Waterloo, old 'Bobs' retreating 'from Cabul to Kandyer' in order to defeat the Afghans, and the retreat of the Normans at Crecy. In the chapter 'Sergeant Bull Quotes History', Tommy Dacre and his sergeant ride their horse past the enemy, in the midst of heavy German shelling, 'following the historic example of Norman Ramsay in his battle at Fuentes d'Oñoro.'[58]

In these novels the past supports the present through men's military genealogy, historical parallels (like the reflection that on 16 August 1914 the infantrymen were fighting even more fiercely than their ancestors at Crecy on the same day 568 years before)[59] and pride in the record of one's regiment.[60] These correspondences with the past established a kind of intimacy with a dramatically new experience and made sense of the war as part of the fabric of history. As the 'jesters' of Raymond's novel travel from Gallipoli to the Sinai, one of them remarks that they are being marched out of the Iliad into the Bible. It is thrilling to be in the land through which not only the Hebrew patriarchs passed, but also the Syrians, the Assyrians, the Chaldeans, the Greeks, the Romans, and Napoleon: 'It was time the British Empire fought here so as to be in the tradition.'[61] The archetypal call of patriotism receives the most ancient reference in *Peter Jackson*, whose protagonist 'had gone out to fight the two-legged Beasts which threatened his country, very much as his ancestors might have gone out to wage war against the four-legged beasts which threatened their caves.'[62]

For some, war represents an awesome, heroic highpoint in the pattern of history. When the elderly Professor Baltazar reads of British heroism in the battle of the Somme he feels thrilled at the realization that he is 'merged into the unconquerable soul of his race.' This military event proves to him that England can still display the qualities that made 'Cressy, Poitiers, Agincourt, ring in English ears through the centuries: the qualities of the men who followed Drake and Marlborough and Nelson and Raglan.'[63] The war affords an opportunity to live up to the call of tradition and make a striking statement about it. In *The Last of the Grenvilles* 21-year-old Dickie Grenville restores the great military tradition of his family through his heroic wartime performance in the Navy. Before the war the continuity with his family's tradition had been broken, as the awesome legacy was perceived as a burden; his father had directed him towards a career in insurance with Lloyd's rather than in the Navy, because he himself 'found it impossible to live up to the standard of the *Revenge* and Flores in the Azores.'[64] The Great War affords Dickie the opportunity to re-confirm the family's ancient valour in the twentieth century. The cover of the book shows a young naval officer on deck, with the ghost of Richard Grenville behind him, his hand resting on the youngest offshoot of the illustrious and ancient family. Bernard Newman, in *The Cavalry Went Through* (1930), used military history in a different way. He described an imaginary early Allied victory in 1917 brought about by a Napoleon-like British Commander-in-Chief; one important consequence of this exercise in military mythology was that of averting the ultimate 'modern' political crime, the Russian revolution.

Angus Maude and Roy Lewis defined English (middle-class) wisdom in terms of the capacity to encompass the lessons of the past: 'The point is that England makes use of her whole past, not just the memories of two or three generations. When the past is closely scrutinized, some of the newer ideas prove to be less new than they at first appeared, and very much less admirable.' The middle class deservedly occupies the central position in society, a role to which the working class aspires in a dynamic of egalitarianism which is 'levelling up, not down.'

> ...the survival of England, and the success of England's message to the world, depends upon the best of middle-class social attitudes becoming widespread throughout society. And, deeply embedded in middle-class ideals, there lies (however distorted or abused) the ideal of Christian gentility.[65]

Their argument, beginning with the intrinsic middle-class capacity for making use of the past, and moving on to the reference of an English 'message' based on 'Christian gentility' (with the aristocratic connotations of the word), makes tradition, class, religion and Englishness converge into a unitary pattern of significance. Middlebrow novels of the memory of war present the same convergence of meaning towards middle-class 'ideals'; the analysis of this fiction is an important historical aid to understanding the components of this particular, influential brand of ideological reasoning.

Notes to Chapter 4

1. Hugh Kimber, *Prelude to Calvary*, 1933, p. 32
2. Hugh Walpole, *John Cornelius*, 1937, p. 435.
3. V. W. W. S. Purcell, *The Further Side of No Man's Land*, Dent, 1929, pp. 31, 230.
4. Edward John Thompson, *Lament for Adonis*, 1932, pp. 63, 94–5.
5. Simone Weil, *The Need For Roots* (first published in 1952 as *L'Enracinement)*, 1978, p. 49.
6. Harold Begbie, *The Great World*, 1925, pp. 319–20.
7. From 'Locksley Hall' (1842).
8. David Campbell, *From the Hill Tops,* 1919, pp. 54–55. The lofty level of the novel contrasts strongly with the virulently militaristic biography Campbell wrote in 1900 of a Scottish military hero of the Boer War. This work was preceded by a poem by William Armagh which replied to accusations that 'war is hell' and 'the great accursed' with the assertion that 'He who made the earthquake and the storm/ Perchance makes battles too!' (*Major-General Hector A. MacDonald, C.B. D.S.O., L.L.O.,* 1900.)
9. Shaw MacNichol's *Between the Days, Being the Writing of Jean Bruyard: A Story of Franche Conté* (1925), which was dedicated 'To Comrades, British and French, Who Consecrated the Ravaged Fields of France with Lives Renounced for Sake of the Future Generations' and was the only novel to be told entirely from the French viewpoint, set its final hope for no more wars by drawing on the lessons taught by the German invasions of 1870 and 1914.
10. Edward John Thompson, *In Araby Orion,* 1930, p. 80.
11. Mrs Victor Rickard, *The House of Courage* 1919, p. 15.
12. Noel Streatfield, *Parson's Nine,* 1932, p. 368.
13. R. W. Campbell, *John Brown: Confession of a New Army Cadet,* 1919, pp. 249, 135 (italics in the text)
14. Michael Howard, 'Military Experience in Literature', *Essays by Divers Hands: Being the Transactions of the Royal Society of Literature,* (New Series), Vol. 41, 1980, p. 36.
15. J. B. Morton, *The Barber of Putney,* 1919, pp. 140, 291–2.
16. John Collis Snaith, *Love Lane,* 1919, p. 166.
17. Mary Fulton, *The Plough,* 1919, p. 127.
18. Vernon Bartlett, *No Man's Land,* 1930, p. 239.
19. Maud Diver, *Strong Hours,* 1929, p. 71.
20. Storm Jameson, *The Clash,* 1922, pp. 163, 192.
21. Stowell was born in Leeds in 1898.
22. Where the previous Masher, Johnnie, Dude and Bhoy were sartorially impressive, the Knut aimed to be as 'sloppy' as he could. A soft velours hat, the brim low over the eyes, with a few feathers, long hair combed back with no parting, soft collars: all these were signs of 'the great crusade for the emancipation of man from the tyranny of starch.' (Gordon Stowell, *The History of Button Hill,* 1929, pp. 184–185.)
23. *Ibid.,* pp. 183-5.
24. Vernon Bartlett, *Mud and Khaki,* 1917, p. 71.
25. Gordon Stowell, *The History of Button Hill,* 1929, p. 412. This episode is reminiscent of the felling of the tree in *Parade's End,* a powerful symbol of the erosion of tradition, in this case of the landowning class. The title *If the Tree Fall* by Simon Dare (Marjorie Huxtable) is inspired by the biblical 'If the tree fall towards the south, or towards the north, in the place where the tree falleth, there shall it be' *(Ecclesiastes,* XI, iii) and alludes to the quality of individual choice affecting destiny. In this very insubstantial novel by 'Simon Dare' (Marjorie Huxtable) adjustment to change is represented by a returning soldier coming to terms with his fiancée's illegitimacy.
26. *Ibid.,* p. 431.
27. Arthur Beverley Baxter, *The Parts Men Play,* 1920, p. 195. The social stability deriving from such sources of inspiration is praised in the international bestseller *Goodbye, Mr. Chips* (1934), which touches on the war from the secure, permanent oasis of the public school Brookfields. The response to the General Strike moves Mr Chips to feel 'stirred emotionally as he had not been since the War....England had burned her fire in her own grate again.' (James Hilton, Goodbye, Mr. Chips, 1932, pp. 110–11.)

28. Ian Hay, *The Willing Horse*, 1921, p. 262.

29. Charles F. G. Masterman, *England After the War: A Study*, 1922, pp. 27–30.

30. Arthur Marwick, *The Deluge: British Society and the First World War*, 1979 (first published 1965), p. 300.

31. E. J. Hobsbawm, *Industry and Empire; From 1750 to the Present Day*, *(Pelican Economic History of Britain*, Vol. 3), Harmondsworth, 1969, p. 201.

32. Cited in John Stevenson, *British Society, 1914–1945*, Harmondsworth, 1986 (first published 1984), p. 333.

33. Masterman, *England After the War*, pp. 45–6.

34. This was almost certainly a direct reference to the Middle Class Union started in 1918, the only middle-class trade union of the inter-war years to display the sort of class combativeness which characterized its German counterparts. Its chairman told the members: 'If you are properly organized...you can possibly hold up all the workers, you could hold up the capitalists, or you could even hold up the Government. You must see to it that you are not crushed or squeezed.' (Geoffrey Crossick, 'The Emergence of the Lower Middle Class in Britain', in Geoffrey Crossick (ed.), *The Lower Middle Class in Britain 1870–1914*, 1978, p. 41.)

35. Mrs Humphry Ward, *Cousin Philip*, 1919, p. 1.

36. Harold Begbie, *The Mirrors of Downing Street: Some Political Reflections*, 1920, p. 208.

37. Roger Bromley, 'Hegemony and Popular Fiction', in Peter Humm, Paul Stigant and Peter Widdowson (eds), *Popular Fictions: Essays in Literature and History*, 1986, p. 163.

38. Noel Streatfield, *Caroline England*, 1937, pp. 382, 387.

39. Muriel Hine, *The Breathless Moment*, 1920, pp. 50, 188–9, 98.

40. Herbert Asquith, *Young Orland*, 1927, p. 7.

41. Albert Kinross, *God and Tony Hewitt*, 1925, p. 98.

42. Cecil Roberts, *Scissors: A Novel of Youth*, 1923, pp. 65–7.

43. Ronald Pertwee, *Pursuit*, 1930, p. 333.

44. Jerome Klapka Jerome, *All Roads Lead to Calvary*, 1919, p. 79.

45. Francis Brett Young, *White Ladies*, 1935, pp. 474–5.

46. Glen Cavaliero, *Rural Tradition in the English Novel, 1900–1939*, 1977, p. 88.

47. Compton Mackenzie, *The Vanity Girl*, 1920, p. 232.

48. Storm Jameson, *Three Kingdoms*, 1926, pp. 27, 402. An exception was *The Survivors* (1923) by Lucas Malet (Mary St. Leger Harrison), whose heroine Lydia chooses writing over romantic pursuit. Her choice of literature, however, is inspired by so idealistic a motivation as to be akin to a religious vocation. Romantic love, the staple of fiction, is a frozen alternative for the heroine in the post-war world, although there is a hint that, with her excellent heart, things may change.

49. *Evening Standard*, 11 November 1929, p. 7.

50. Gilbert Cannan, *Pink Roses*, 1919, pp. 261, 283.

51. Albert Kinross, *God and Tony Hewitt*, 1925, pp. 266–7.

52. Ethel Boileau, *The Arches of the Years*, 1930, p. 13.

53. Philip E. Hager and Desmond Taylor, *The Novels of World War I: An Annotated Bibliography*, New York, 1981, p. 171.

54. Boileau, *The Arches of the Years*, p. 255.

55. See page 109.

56. Graham Seton, *Life Without End*, 1932, pp. 15, 268. (my italics)

57. J.B.Morton, *The Barber of Putney*, 1919, pp. 293–4.

58. Escott Lynn, *Tommy of the Tanks*, 1919, pp. 115, 126, 168.

59. Gilbert Frankau, *Three Englishmen*, 1935, p. 328.

60. In *Seven Days in the Line* one private justifies to another the harsh discipline they are subjected to by pointing out the requirements of duty of their regiment: 'And they [the officers] think something of the traditions of the Ninth, mate; I often feel proud when they give us a lecture on what is expected.' (Frederick B. Keel, *Seven Days in the Line*, 1930, p. 55.)

61. Ernest Raymond, *The Jesting Army*, 1930, p. 171.

62. Gilbert Frankau, *Peter Jackson, Cigar Merchant: A Romance of Married Life*, 1919, p. 672.

63. William John Locke, *The House of Baltazar*, 1920, p. 114. Professor Baltazar, an eminent

mathematician who had left England because of its commercial and vulgar atmosphere which was interfering with the development of his great ideas, and had immersed himself in the mystical profundity of China, finds the war a terrific opportunity to revive and cultivate the more authentic cultural instincts and aspirations of the English.

64. Bennet Copplestone, *The Last of the Grenvilles,* 1919, pp. 3–4.

65. Roy Lewis and Angus Maude, *The English Middle Classes,* 1950 (first published in 1949), pp. 278–9.

5 The Theatre of War: Journey's End

All Quiet on the Western Front was at the centre of the boom of war novels, memoirs, films and plays of 1929 and 1930. Its impact was exceptional: published at the end of 1928 in Germany, it sold 640,000 copies in three months;[1] in Great Britain, where it was published in March 1929, 25,000 copies were sold in a fortnight.[2] To understand the terms of the English public discussion about the written artifacts which the memory of war generated so abundantly ten years after its end, it is necessary to consider the great success of a play which was staged for the first time just as *All Quiet on the Western Front* made its first appearance in the German bookshops. *Journey's End* was to become the great middlebrow success of the inter-war years on the stage, a bestseller on Gollancz's publishing list, and the most successful war play ever produced in Britain.

An analysis of the successful way in which *Journey's End* evoked the past helps to tease out the peculiarly English strand of the subsequent war novel boom of 1929 and 1930. A complete study of the impact of this play involves the interlacing of four different narratives: the story told by the play, the story of the play's success, the 1916–17 experience of Bob Sherriff, and the latter's literary presentation of his memory of war.

1 The Plot of Journey's End

Journey's End portrays life in an officers' trench dugout in St Quentin during the two and a half days preceding the German attack in the dawn of 21 March 1918. James Raleigh, a schoolboy fresh from his training in England, arrives to join C company. He is happy to have managed to be assigned to the Company of his school hero, Stanhope, who has been in France for three years and is the Company Commander. Captain Stanhope, in sharp contrast to the innocently enthusiastic and idealistic Raleigh, is suffering from severe strain and drinks heavily. Osborne, a wise and kindly middle-aged ex-schoolmaster, tries to prepare Raleigh for the change in his friend. Stanhope is upset and angry to see Raleigh, to whose sister he is romantically attached. He feels that the boy, who used to worship him, will despise his weakness, and he is devastated by the thought that there is such a witness from his past life to his present degradation. In spite of Osborne's advice he shows his resentment of Raleigh's presence by being offensively abrupt with the boy.

On the following day, he demands to read a letter the boy has written home, only to find out to his further shame that James has repeated the high praise of Stanhope as a commander that he has heard from other soldiers.

The other two officers are Trotter, an ex-ranker, big, fond of his food, jovially unbowed by the rigours of the trenches, and Hibbert, slight and pale, a victim of his fear, who complains of neuralgia. Stanhope learns that, in view of the expected German attack, Headquarters want him to organize a raid into the enemy trenches to gather information. For this suicidal raid, against whose tactics he protests, Stanhope chooses Osborne and Raleigh as the two most suitable people; Trotter's physique is too cumbersome and Hibbert is 'just not the man.' Osborne knows what awaits them and tries to hide from the proud and eager boy the hopelessness of their chances. In the meantime there is a tense confrontation between Stanhope and Hibbert when the latter tries to go sick because of his neuralgia. Stanhope will not allow him to do this and threatens him with a gun when the subaltern tries to push past him to report to the doctor. Hibbert waits for the shot and then breaks down. Stanhope praises him for the way he did not flinch in the face of death and then comforts him by revealing his own fear; there is no need to take the excuse of neuralgia, he tells him. Hibbert is grateful and asks him not to tell the others about this; Stanhope in a very humane gesture agrees on condition that Hibbert, for his part, will not tell what a funk *he* is.

The raid yields one German prisoner; Osborne and four other men are killed. The Colonel is jubilant and sure of the Brigadier's approval; Stanhope has lost his best friend. That night Raleigh refuses to take part in a rather elaborate dinner that was already planned, as he thinks it heartless after Osborne's death. Stanhope accuses him of being a prig. The incomprehension stems from the gap between the outward response of the man who has been bitterly tried and hardened by three years in the trenches and that of the boy who has just lived his first tragedy in the frontline.

The next day, at dawn, the German attack begins. Almost immediately, Raleigh is hit and his spine is broken. Stanhope orders that he be brought down to the dugout. He comforts him and their brief conversation recaptures their old relationship. Raleigh dies and Stanhope, after a brief pause, goes up the steps to join his men. The explosion of a shell caves in the dugout, transforming it into Raleigh's tomb.

2 Journey to Success

A dirty, gloomy dugout lit with candles; no furniture beyond a rickety wooden table and a few upturned boxes for seats; no love interest; no plot; and no women in the cast: you could scarcely have done better if you had set out deliberately to make the thing as repulsive to a manager as possible.[3]

Thus Sherriff recapitulated, forty years on, the general prognosis for his war play. *Journey's End* was not his first effort as a playwright. An adjustor of insurance claims for the Sun Insurance Office, where his father also worked and where his grandfather had worked before him, he earned four pounds a week and lived with his parents in Hampton Wick, near Kingston-upon-Thames; he devoted most of his spare time to the Kingston Rowing Club, of which he was captain. The Club in the early Twenties found itself in dire financial straits, and they decided to put on a yearly dramatic production to raise money. Sherriff wrote one play a year and worked as stage hand, stage manager and director. These slight works fulfilled their purpose and enjoyed enough local success to encourage him to send four of them to the agent Curtis Brown, who replied routinely with a polite letter explaining the reasons why he could find no company to produce them.

When Sherriff's time as captain of the rowing club expired in 1927, the sudden ending of his hectic round of duties left him with a gaping void in the evenings. This timidly introspective 31-year-old man, younger than his years in appearance and outlook, found that what he wanted to do was to keep writing plays. What story could he tell? He fell back on the plot of a novel he had begun to sketch a few years earlier. Its theme was that of the hero-worship of Dennis Stanhope by the younger Jimmy Raleigh. After their schooldays their roles were to be reversed as Raleigh became the successful head of a business and Stanhope went from job to job; Raleigh would repay what he considered was his school debt by helping his 'bitter, disillusioned friend.'[4]

But once out of the context of school, with which he was familiar, Sherriff was at a loss how to handle the rest of the story. The idea of setting it during the war originated naturally from the necessity to write about what he knew. He had spent a year on the Western Front as an officer and had kept all the letters he had written to his parents. Once he was again in familiar territory, he wrote quickly.

> Dialogue came easily: I merely had to write down what people said. I didn't have to turn up the dictionary for flowery words and hunt through my books of synonyms. The other characters rolled in without invitation. I had known them all so well in the trenches that the play was an open house for them.[5]

This 'labour of love'[6] took a year. Curtis Brown and his readers liked the play very much and sought to secure a production during the spring and summer of 1928. The 1920s had proved that war plays, especially serious ones, were not successful with the public; *Journey's End* offered few prospects of attracting financial backing. Finally, the Incorporated Stage Society, committed to showing plays of merit regardless of their commercial potential, showed an interest in it. Curtis Brown suggested that Sherriff seek

George Bernard Shaw's opinion. The celebrated playwright sent the manuscript back with a fastidiously precise letter in which he professed himself incapable of deciding what reception it might have. He called it a 'document of war'; on this basis, he wrote, 'let it be produced by all means.' Sherriff extrapolated these last words from the letter in relating the weighty verdict to a member of the Stage Society committee,[7] which decided to put on the play on 9 and 10 December 1928 at the Apollo Theatre. The Stage Society did not have the funds to show the play for longer than two performances; the hope was that a manager might like it enough to give it a further trial.

The initial stage of the play's fantastic road to fame benefitted from the enlistment of two talented young men. The only person they could interest in its direction was James Whale, who had different jobs in the theatre, from actor to stage manager, and made his debut as a West End director with Sherriff's play;[8] the lead – Stanhope's part – went to the still unknown 21 year-old Laurence Olivier.

James Whale took over the play. In a sense he 'made' *Journey's End* literally, with his creation of the model of the dugout. Himself an ex-infantry officer, he reproduced the claustrophobic atmosphere of the underground officers' world in meticulous detail. The bold and precise re-creation on the stage of this earthen cavern, with the timber on the roof giving the impression of great weight pressing from above, provided a presentation of the 'troglodyte' habitat of modern warfare which is a fundamental clue to the play's extraordinary impact, explained by contemporaries principally in terms of its 'reality'. Sherriff, who willingly relinquished the play into Whale's hands, was overwhelmed by the young director's setting: 'Above all it was real. There may never have been a dugout like this one: but any man who had lived in the trenches would say "This is it: this is what it was like".'[9]

They did, in a loud unanimous chorus. *Journey's End*, before it became a popular success, was a success among the critics. No one could have anticipated the response of the critics among the audience in the rather exclusive Sunday night audience. Hannen Swaffer, the *Daily Express* formidable drama, critic led the way with a review entitled 'The Greatest Of All War Plays', praise which was echoed by the *Daily Telegraph*'s W.A. Darlington. James Agate, of the *Sunday Times*, changed the plan for his weekly radio talk the next day by devoting it entirely to *Journey's End*. "I have never been so deeply moved, so enthralled, so exalted", he announced. And in what he later admitted was a deliberate attempt to 'shame' managers into an interest in the play, he concluded by saying that all the managers he had talked to about this remarkable work were 'adamant in their belief that war plays have no audience in the theatre.'[10] The *New Statesman* struck a lonely discordant note amidst this paean of praise by asserting that although the play was 'a very efficient piece of realism', it lacked the imagination of good drama.[11]

For a few days the critics' effort to attract a future for the play seemed indeed to have failed, as no established manager came forward. On the strength of his performance Olivier was signed up for the much sought-after lead in *Beau Geste*. Then a second stroke of luck intervened in the play's progress: again, as in the case of the Stage Society, the rescuer was committedly intellectual.

Maurice Browne was a penniless actor-manager whose dream was to revive classical drama; in the United States he had led the Little Theatre Movement in 1912 with scant success.[12] He was an idealistic promoter of serious theatre who, paradoxically, was destined to achieve fame and wealth through the ultimate middlebrow play. Browne was a close friend of Dorothy and Leonard Elmhirst, millionaire owners of Dartington Hall in Devon, a centre for their cultural patronage. They were keen to finance worthwhile theatrical projects and at the end of 1928 gave Browne the money to set himself up as a theatrical producer in England.[13] Ten days after the financial agreement was drawn up Browne stumbled across *Journey's End* through the enthusiastic praise of a friend who had just seen it. He acted quickly, reading the script on the train on the way to Dartington Hall. He was fascinated by the play, and that night he read it aloud to the Elmhirsts, who advanced him £400 for its production; on 21 January the play opened at the Savoy.[14]

Perhaps because of the expectation of an element of eccentricity in theatrical circles, no contemporary commentator of the rags-to-riches career of Sherriff ever remarked on the strangeness of these two men coming together. The author met in the producer a personality in many ways strikingly antithetical to his own. Browne, thirty-three in 1914, was a pacifist and a conscientious objector who had stayed in America throughout the war years. His pacifism did not prevent him from becoming profoundly involved with two important war plays. In 1928 he acted the main part in *The Unknown Warrior*, the English production of Paul Raynal's *Le Tombeau sous l'Arc de Triomphe* (1924), and he produced *Journey's End* the following year.[15] Forty years on, in his autobiography, Sherriff expressed his incomprehension at Browne's interest in the play.

> What made him fall for the play was a mystery to me then, and has remained a mystery ever since. It was totally unlike anything he had produced before, and the sentiments of the character towards the war were in absolute contrast with his own. They were simple, unquestioning men who fought the war because it seemed the only right and proper thing to do. Somebody had to fight it, and they had accepted the misery and suffering without complaint....One would have thought, in the circumstances, that he would have had a violent revulsion against a war play in which not a word was spoken against the war, in which no word of

condemnation was uttered by any of its characters. Possibly he saw in the play a triumphant justification of his own convictions: that the tragedy and misery of it all would never have happened if every man had stood apart, as he had done, and refused to have anything to do with it.[16]

This is the most complete statement Sherriff ever made on the play's standpoint about the war, and by far the most definite. The uncharacteristically strong and categorical terms – 'totally unlike', 'in absolute contrast', 'not a word...no word' – derive from the ideological and social gulf between Maurice Browne and himself. 'Simple, unquestioning' men: unlike the flamboyantly self-conscious Browne, who 'wore an Old Wykhamist tie and gold earrings'[17] and had questioned the war to the point of refusing to take part in it. Sherriff never probed this question with Browne and their relationship was easy. But it was not a collaboration. Whale and Browne believed so much in the play that they let it speak for itself; Sherriff had no wish to interfere and always behaved as if a little in awe of this play, of whose depths he heard so much and could account for so little. The play captured the imagination of a great number of people, a few of whom dedicated to it their intellectual talents, their money and their energies out of a strong belief in its value as a statement about the war. A telling indication of the breadth of the appeal of *Journey's End* was its highbrow launching platform into success, a theatrical society which supported the sort of work and artists completely extraneous to Sherriff's world. The *Evening News* felt duty bound to exorcise the ghost of the Stage Society by reassuring its readers that 'Any fear that there might be anything highbrow about Maurice Browne's production...should be dispelled' by the announcement that a band would play as incidental music 'Tipperary', 'Pack Up Your Troubles', 'Take Me Back to Dear Old Blighty', and 'other good old war-time tunes.'[18]

Victor Gollancz was so impressed by the play's first Savoy performance that during the interval he approached Sherriff to offer to publish the play, in spite of its meagre commercial chances. This venture also turned to gold, as the book sold in such quantities that it established the name of the young publishing house. Gollancz would refer to it as his 'first publication', although it was about his seventieth.[19]

The first sign of the extraordinary effect of *Journey's End* on the audiences' senses was the great, long silence in the theatre which followed the end of the first performance at the Savoy. Sherriff recalled the 'eerie and unnatural feeling' of a thousand people sitting in silence in the dark theatre; the curtain came up on the line of soldiers 'in steel helmets and mud-spattered uniforms', came down again, and still the audience was quiet. Then, as if waking from a dream, the prolonged cheering and clapping started.[20]

Maurice Browne handled the first signs of success recklessly and brilliantly on the following day. Booking agencies were not particularly impressed by good reviews and, unwilling to gamble on a serious play, only offered to pencil in a few seats to be returned to the box office if they were unable to sell them. By mid-afternoon the demand for tickets was so great that they offered Browne a four-week deal; the producer retaliated with the demand for a twelve-week deal that would have guaranteed the run of the play for that period of time. This represented an impossible financial risk and was rejected. Browne's belief in the success of the play was right and within two days, in response to the public's demand, the deal made with the booking agencies represented a record for a straight play in the West End, with a guarantee of weekly sales averaging more than 1,000 a week for a three-month period.[21]

This was the first of a series of records. The play ran for 593 performances,[22] at that time the most successful run ever in the West End, and sold over 175,000 copies, a record for a new play.[23] The Savoy's seating capacity of about a thousand people, with a full house every night for almost a year,[24] means that a rough estimate of half a million people saw it in this theatre alone. It achieved unprecedented international success. Within a year of its Savoy première it had been shown in twenty-six countries in twenty-five languages. In Germany forty companies produced it,[25] and in New York it ran for 485 performances.[26]

On the night before Armistice Day 1929 a special performance of the play was given for holders of the Victoria Cross. *Journey's End* spanned all the media: on Remembrance Day 1929 it was broadcast on the radio;[27] a film version was made in 1930 in Hollywood with an English producer (George Pearson), James Whale as director and Colin Clive as Stanhope;[28] and on Armistice Day 1937 it was shown on television.[29]

The Response of the Press The leitmotif of the reviews in Britain was praise of its realism. 'Star Reality of "Journey's End"';[30] 'absolute *reality* of it all is compelling';[31] 'The War as it Was.'[32] The *Evening Standard* called the play 'full of English character' and offered the most graphic account of its impression of realism by describing the 'entirely physical' effect it must have had on that part of the audience that had 'experience and memory':

> ...relief, from the soles of their feet upwards, that what they saw was "only a play", relief that their boots were not wet and their clothes muddy, that their heads no longer wore shrapnel helmets, and that it would not be their turn in a few minutes to go up those steps at the back of the stage into the dawn of March 21, 1918, the hiss and slap of machine-gun bullets, and the brutal thuddings of bombs. Relief that actuality had at last become only a memory, that could, after 'ten years' delay, finally find its solution in a work of art.[33]

The reconstruction of the dugout on stage; details like fear before the attack causing the officers to yawn,[34] or the report of thirty-four gum boots in the trench stores not corresponding to seventeen pairs ('Oh, no; twenty-five right leg and nine left leg');[35] the knowledge of Sherriff's war experience: all contributed to the strong impression of realism made by the play in 1929. Also, several members of the cast had been in the front line. 'Realism in a War Play. Actors Re-enact their Past In "Journey's End"', announced the *Star*. George Zucco (who played Osborne) had been wounded in a raid at St Quentin in 1916; Alexander Field (Mason) wore in the play the same puttees he had worn throughout the war; Melville Cooper (Trotter) had served with the Highlanders; David Horne (Captain Hardy) had been a captain in the Guards in France and had been wounded; James Whale had been taken prisoner at St Quentin. Colin Clive (Stanhope), Robert Speaight (Hibbert), Maurice Evans and Geoffrey Wincott had been too young to serve.[36] In the original Stage Society production, Olivier had worn Sherriff's Sam Browne belt.

Even criticism of the play was based on a recognition of its successful realism. The *Times* reviewer commented that even though on seeing the dugout in the theatre all exclaimed 'How like it all is!', the play provoked an emotion generated by memory and not by the imagination which could turn it into a great play and transcend its 'efficient realism' by expressing 'the wonder and the awe felt in the war.'[37] Similarly the *Daily Telegraph*, under the headline 'Stirring New War Play – Trench Life Truly Depicted', observed that the play, perfect within its limits, answered the question 'What was our war like?' without addressing the issue 'What does the war mean?'[38] Still, the play was received by the majority of reviewers as if it had found the perfect pitch at which to portray openly the tragedy of war. Remembering the moment when he saw his brother off on a suicidal mission, J. R. Ackerley, platoon leader in the 8th East Surreys, has described the impossibility 'to speak of the most commonplace word or make the most ordinary gesture without it at once assuming the heavy over-emphasis of melodrama.'[39] The scathing criticism of the *New Statesman*'s reviewer constituted an isolated attack amongst the reviews following the Savoy première. He called *Journey's End* an 'orgy of the public-school spirit and Cockney humour' which failed to denounce the stupidity and cruelty of war and reduced it to a 'slaughter-house for athletes and a school for gentlemen.'[40]

Many reviewers interpreted *Journey's End* as a brilliant indictment of the futility of war: this second judgment followed from the first of realism. The *Daily Mirror* commented that its 'unemotional realism' represented 'a much better argument against war than sentimental propaganda plays like *The*

Enemy.'[41] J.B. Priestley, who would that same year achieve middlebrow stardom with *The Good Companions*, wrote in the *Daily Chronicle*: 'Real talk. Real emotion. Real men....It is the strongest plea for peace I know.'[42] Hugh Walpole, one of the most successful popular authors of his time, who, like Priestley, had also been an officer in the war, praised the play for achieving what all war literature until then had not managed to do: it 'recovered our own memories of Reality', therefore managing to 'hit the hardest blow in its swollen stomach that War has yet had, and this without a word of direct propaganda or rancour against anyone or anything...'[43] The myth of accurate memory of war as a denouncement of war received several such reinforcements.

Most reviewers saw *Journey's End* as a protest against war which conveyed its harsh reality without tarnishing its humanity. There were, however, complaints about its portrayal of drunkenness and cowardice, often linked to criticism of the much coarser realism of *All Quiet On The Western Front*, the strident horror of *Death of a Hero*, and the blunt accusations of General Crozier.[44] Sir Ian Hamilton asked that a committee of inquiry should be set up to establish the truth of such allegations in war literature.[45] H. T. W. Bousfield, in the *English Review*, called for action against the negative values of which *Journey's End* was symptomatic through the setting up of a 'Society for the Prevention of Cruelty to Ideals' and National Gymnasia which would help to rescue people from 'mental barbarism.'[46] He found *Journey's End* 'the worst exhibition of bad taste that this century has ever seen' because, in his opinion, it described the experience of war as degrading. He saw this as having an emasculating effect on the nation that was 'the centre of the greatest empire that the world has ever seen.' He praised Mussolini for banning the play. The Italian dictator was the only one to recognize its real message: 'there is no such thing as heroism.'[47] The following month, in the same journal, R. V. Dawson countered Bousfield's argument by suggesting that heroism was a bankrupt notion: the men had simply done their duty and followed 'a common moral obligation.'[48] The play could not be the sign of a 'demoralized Britain' to the twelve countries where it was showing, because, on the contrary, it demonstrated that 'we can realise our obligations and fulfil them, that we can face our weaknesses and transcend them, that in the light of duty we can go through hell to victory.'[49] The debate was no simple dichotomy between a glorification of war – which Bousfield deplored – and a denial of heroism. Rather, it was a dialectic which failed to agree on the memory and the outward representation of the soldiers' heroism. In Dawson's argument, courage was no longer a function of gallant heroism but a manifestation of the relevant new values of loyalty and endurance.

Another conflict of views was played out in the *Cornhill Magazine*. G. A. Martelli, who described himself as a member of 'the post-war generation', wrote of how convincing he had found the play's representation of 'intense physical discomfort' and of 'nervous strain', and its portrayal of 'the effort of persistence rather than heroism protracted almost beyond endurance.' He defended his right as someone who had been too young to fight to take issue with the reviewers' brand of praise of the play, arguing that if anything he was more qualified to judge artistically a war work because of his detachment. He criticized the claims of 'great', 'noble', 'moving', 'inspiring', 'uplifting' which had been made for it. *Journey's End*, he argued, could not transcend a 'sense of common reality' and occasional moments of sentimentality because it could not rise above its subject matter. Martelli's argument was ironic:

> The subject of Journey's End...is a subject for comedy, for melodrama, even for farce, but not for tragedy. The thing itself – the mud, the lice, the pain – is too big and too present to leave room for the sort of feelings which are necessary to the production of creative art. That fact has been made increasingly clear by all the literature of the War, which has striven to seize something sublime but has only succeeded in recapturing the sense of frustration, physical oppression and confusion, which was the predominating motif at the front. Journey's End only confirms the belief which has been steadily growing that the War, as seen by those who fought in it, was nothing but a gigantic catastrophe of exactly the same quality as a railway accident.[50]

Two months later a reviewer from the 'older generation' replied by stating that it was precisely in the 'persistence protracted almost beyond endurance' that the heroism was located, and that the distance in time allowed Sherriff to confer artistic perspective and a tragic framework on a terrible experience. Could it be, Fowle asked, that under their 'superficial hardness', the present young generation was in fact 'more English than the English', and afraid of emotion?'[51] Again, it is endurance and dedication which emerge as the new values of modern warfare and are invested with the burden of heroism.

2 The Experience of 2nd Lieutenant Sherriff

In his biography of Robert Graves, Martin Seymour-Smith, explaining how readers 'recognized the reality' of *Goodbye to All That*, the quality which made it a bestseller, commented:

> There are two kinds of reality. One is what actually happened – which belongs to the historian, who does what little he can with it; the other is what it was like, what happened to the person who was there – which belongs to the individual. Blunden and Sassoon might even be said to have lessened the immediacy of their accounts by laboriously mixing the one reality with the other.[52]

Journey's End and *Goodbye to All That* are profoundly different reconstructions of the war, yet they both owed their success to the impression of reality they conveyed. To understand Sherriff's presentation of 'what it was like' it is necessary to examine the story of 'what happened to the person who was there.'

One of the best-known details of the the young playwright's biography – and one of the strongest confirmations of the 'realism' of *Journey's End* – was that he had based his play on the letters he had written to his parents during his months as an officer in France. These letters, and other personal papers, present us with a new narrative of experience which reveals the more intangible and traumatic core of *Journey's End's* realism.

The greatest insight that can be gained into Sherriff's elusive personality is through these papers, within the context of the world apart on the Western Front, where he was from September 1916 to July 1917. In the summer of 1914 Sherriff had been working for a year as an insurance clerk. He was profoundly unhappy about the harassed, monotonous routine of the City worker and was glad of the opportunity to escape it which the war afforded him. In his autobiography his father recorded that in July 1914 he went with his son on a cycling tour of 570 miles around England; on the first day of August, a Saturday, Bob went for a river camping trip with his friend Dick Webb, from his own Kingston Grammar School, who was killed in France at the end of November.[53] Sherriff enlisted in November 1915 with the Artists' Rifles and trained in the second battalion at Ranford from January to August 1916. In the manuscript of the incomplete novel written probably in 1918, relating his own experience under the name of Jimmy Lawton, he stated that from the day of his joining up 'the boy started upon a new life – a life of adventure filled with agonies of grief and homesickness also of surprising happiness, and friendship, and fear.'[54] He was commissioned as 2nd Lieutenant with the 9th Battalion of the East Surrey Regiment on 5 September and arrived in France on 28 September. In his novel/ autobiography he remembered that on leaving his training camp for France he 'felt exactly as he did when he left his School behind him – he felt that he had [left] the freedom and carelessness of a soldiers [sic] life for the responsibilities and worries of the officers [sic]...'[55] His first day in the Army, as we shall see later,[56] started with the assessment of his school background, and his first day in France invited a comparison with an emotion learnt on leaving school. After the war, while waiting to be demobilized, he would complain about being removed from his battalion to an Area Gas School in these terms: '...the Battalion – your Regiment – surrounds you like an atmosphere – you see the Badge on every mans [sic] cap – every officer you meet is a personal friend and somehow it is like a big school.'[57]

Sherriff at first felt acutely homesick, lonely and displaced. He sought comfort and balance in almost daily separate letters to his mother and father. His letters are not reticent and they exhibit a curious contrast between the open discussion of his fear and the self-control which he constantly tried to glean from philosophical writings. 'When people are going potty they never talk about it; they keep it to themselves' says Osborne reassuringly to Stanhope.[58] But Osborne was the schoolmaster Sherriff never became and Stanhope had been to the public school Sherriff did not quite make: as we shall see, the form of endurance is depicted as a function of class.

He referred often to maxims by Plato, Marcus Aurelius and Epictetus. *Alice in Wonderland*, 'the finest book written',[59] was another soothing companion, particularly suited to the absurdity of his new environment.

> It has reminded me very often of Alice's Adventures through the Looking Glass when I have stood and looked at the little mound of earth that marks "Fritz's" trenches through a Periscope – it is so near and yet so far – you can see to there and no further – you wonder what is going on behind that little earth mound – and just as it actually [is on a] looking glass – just the same thing is going on behind – Germans sit and write home – they do what we do – they are just a reflection of us at present – he runs away from our Mortar shells and we run away from him – we are always wondering what he is going to do next and he wonders what we are going to do – so taking it all round we just sit and frighten each other.[60]

This is Sherriff at his best, observing his surroundings with childish penetration.

In October Sherriff's letters became urgently self-reassuring. He spoke of war as a 'task' to be performed, a 'necessary job.'[61] He appraised with apparent equanimity his chances of survival and even worked out a formula for them: '...when I hear 6 shells go off together I think there are now only x-6 shells to be fired (to use an algebraical expression) before the war ends, so when x-x shells have been fired war is bound to end – I have not suddenly gone mad – but this is a thing to cheer you up when you hear shell after shell whistle overhead.'[62] Later in the month, while in the front line in the Zouave Valley,[63] in a week in which his battalion was shelled badly and three men were killed in action, he wrote, with punctilious reference to Marcus Aurelius, that he thought of death as 'nature's work', a 'dissolution of body and spirit' which nature employs in its eternal creation of life.[64] The letters to his mother written in this week did not mention philosophy. To her he said more openly that there was in this war 'no glory or heroism...I often wish I lived back in the days of old Greece or Rome when they fought on the open ground and not in muddy ditches like we do now.'[65] Once out of the front line he wrote repeatedly of the wish to be transferred to the Flying Corps:

'...there is something freer about the air service than in this trench warfare in which you feel something like a worm crawling with your head down.'[66]

On 12 November the East Surreys began a week in the front line at Hulluch. For the first time Sherriff experienced heavy shelling and he was shocked by his reaction of fear. On the 13th he jotted down a few notes on a small sheet of paper during a bombardment. The short, sometimes illegible, disjointed words are a raw expression of the fear of this 21-year-old man. '...shell whizzes over...feel sick – breathing comes hard heart beats'; and in underlined, capital letters: <u>NERVES</u>.[67] He did not conceal this overwhelming emotion from his parents: 'I am afraid my nerves have suffered since I have been out here...I suppose this will wear off in time, or at least I hope it will, or it may help me get home with "shell shock".'[68] He provided his mother with a great many details of his fear from the first day out in the line at Hulluch. On the 12th the shells had fallen with a great crash just 200 yards behind their dugout and so frightened him that he could not eat anything although he had just sat down to dinner. 'I am afraid I am more nervous than the average because I certainly feel the shock of these sudden dangers more than the average.'[69] In his epistolary chronicle of fear he recorded that on the 14th 'they shelled the district again this morning and really I am quite ashamed of the way it makes me tremble – when I hear a shell whistle overhead I immediately get that sort of cold feeling all up my spine if you know what I mean, and my tongue feels all dry.'[70] Again, having sat down to lunch he could not eat; yet there were men who went about the trenches apparently unmoved by the shelling. In December he was relieved from duty after the new Commanding Officer, who thought he was trying to get a 'soft job' when he applied for a transfer to the Engineers, found some of his men dirty for the second time. Sherriff, who had difficulty disciplining his men - unlike the more appropriately trained public-school officers - found it humiliating to be judged incapable of looking after the men. He clung to his inspirational books: 'I must get out my Aurelius and comfort myself in that.'[71] He pathetically continued to strive for sources of strength within a predicament which was eroding his nerves. When he heard that his transfer had been refused, he wrote that Marcus Aurelius was always of great comfort in such moments, as were Scott and Epictetus.[72]

'Transfer' was a familiar, acceptable term with which to express the wish to escape. Soon he made recourse to another familiar term: neuralgia. On 25 January 1917 Sherriff wrote to his mother that he was on the sick list with his 'old complaint', neuralgia around the left eye. He would be down for one or two days' rest, and wrote of his relief at this decision, as the neuralgia had brought 'a kind of nervy feeling.'[73] A Field Medical Card, with the stamp of the 17 Field Ambulance, describes his affliction as 'Neuralgia, affecting the eyes' and comments that it could be due to 'defective muscular action of the eyes.'[74] After his mention of shell-shock under the first impact of extreme fear during the Hulluch shelling, Sherriff never again used this term. He talked of his neuralgia and of his 'nervy feeling' as two related but distinct problems, in the desperate effort to believe in the legitimacy of his physical complaint.

A letter to his father – whom he addressed as 'Pips' – contained a specific analysis of his feelings in terms of the terrible demands of endurance made by modern warfare. 'I must say that I cannot conceive of anything that has occurred in history that puts men to a greater test than this...' The battles with 'the dear old cannon ball which you can let fall 5 yards from you without harming you' were over quickly whereas in this war 'it is the awful expectancy which is most trying – it is that tells [sic] on different temperaments – some may not feel it at all, to others it is torture.'[75]

While at the officers' rest station Sherriff wrote that he felt 'very mean' to be in such a place while the other officers were in the trenches; but it would not have been fair on the men to have a nervy officer 'who naturally would not feel very confident.'[76]

The War Diary reveals that on the day Sherriff went sick his battalion carried out the only raid against enemy trenches in which it was involved while Sherriff was in France. Its purpose was: '1) To obtain identifications 2) to inflict losses on the enemy 3) to secure a sample of German ration bread.' Six squads of three officers, fifty Other Ranks and six Sappers went over; of these three privates were killed and four were wounded. The result of the raid was: 'at least' nine killed in the enemy trench; 'approximately' twelve killed or wounded in the dugout; three prisoners, 'and a sample of German ration bread secured; also a gas helmet'; Major General Barrow's congratulations; and the MC for three of the officers.[77] Although it is not clear whether Sherriff's 'C' company, the same name as the company in *Journey's End*, was involved, this episode is a striking parallel with Hibbert's attempt to report sick with neuralgia after the raid has been organized.

At the rest station, Sherriff was tormented by the fear of going back to the line. '...it seems the farther away from it you are the more it preys upon your mind and I feel I simply *cant* [sic] go up again.' He determined to talk to the doctor about his nervous condition if he did not feel better within a week. Once again he found an image from his school past to describe his emotional state. 'I feel extremely like the time when I did not want to go to school and worked up a worried expression and said I felt sick, etc., but now, in a greater sense I feel the same thing – nothing bodily wrong – only a great mental tiredness...'[78] He professed himself ready to do any kind of work at all 'so long as I am only away from the awful crack of explosions which sometimes quite numb me.'[79] At the end of March Sherriff was back in the line. Three photographs of the officers of 'C' company, 9th East Surreys, taken at Bully Grenay in March 1917 show clearly the strain on Sherriff's face.[80] In the last interview he ever gave Sherriff identified three officers in one of these photographs with characters in his play: Lt Douglass (Osborne), 2nd Lt Trenchard (Trotter), and, sitting in the centre, Captain Godfrey Warre-Dymond, 'who bore more than a passing resemblance to Stanhope.'[81]

On 2 April he had another recurrence of neuralgia: 'It is funny that when I get a return of this I always get a return of this awful nervousness again...'[82] He was sent to train recruits for a while, but as he still felt ill when it was time to return he reported to the doctor and was sent behind the lines to rest for a few days with 'the same old nagging neuralgia again.'[83] Between 7 and 14 April and 16 and 19 April the 9th Battalion was first at Calonne and then at the Western outskirts of the Cité St Pierre, where they sustained heavy bombardment with many casualties. On the 7th Sherriff wrote that he was training recruits because of another attack of neuralgia which had caused him to stay in bed for a day.[84] On the 14th he explained to his father that he had 'remained behind with the transport while the others have gone further – I cannot describe the feelings you go through when unfortunate enough to suffer from nerves – I absolutely could not bring myself to face the line again...I am perfectly well bodily – it is only this awful mental torture – the knowledge that you absolutely cannot face a thing...'[85] In a long letter written on the 17th, a day when five men were killed in the front line, he expressed how he felt by repeating what he had said in January; he would need to explain to the doctor how his nerves were also affected: ' I wonder how so many continue to go through it day after day...I cannot get rid of the dread of again going into the line'. Later in the day, he reported what the doctor had told him: the neuralgia was caused by his nervousness and he should rest for a couple of days. But he could not rest: '...all the while I have that dread of going in the line again.' He was torn between appearances and desperate need. He wished to talk to the doctor, although it was such a difficult subject 'as it looks as though you are shirking'; he felt 'almost guilty' going into the line when he was so jumpy and he felt 'mean' staying behind though he was right.[86]

In a third letter on this day, while he awaited the doctor's decision whether he should go back to the line, he gave his father a detailed account of the origin of his fear which reads like a history of his increasing inability to cope with the horrors of shelling. The strain got worse with time, he explained. At first there were not as many shells as one might expect and they did not explode too near. Then one would witness the horror of seeing a man blown up by a 'Minnie', see the scattered pieces of his body on the barbed wire, and the bloodied helmet of a sniper's victim:

As day after day goes by you gradually get a habit of gazing into the air for "Minnie" and your ears become painfully sensitive to picking up the sound of a shell coming —and your heart throbs unnecessarily sometimes – your arm hurling against your coat makes a swishing sound and you stop to listen in suspense, a man starting to whistle makes you jump, hundreds of times you become painfully on the alert for a false alarm and at the others for a real alarm...It is when you get to this state – which may take any length of time according to your state of nerves (and with some men apparently never comes) that the suspense of long hours of duty in the line tell upon you...I think nearly everyone gets to this state soon [sic] or later and it is of course a question of their powers of being able to conceal their fear after that.[87]

After this letter he gave few details about progress, as if in an attempt to normalize his predicament. On 22 April he was with his company, which was resting at Petit-Sains and Lozinghem. The month of May in the Hodge Sector was a relatively quiet one, with no casualties.[88] He reported that he was thinking 'along the right lines' and therefore could cope with 'mental distress'; there were again several literary references in the letters to his father. After his ten-day leave home in July he prepared himself for the imminent return to the line. 'The only thing is to hope one will come through and to fall back on Philosophy to save ones [sic] mind...'[89] On the evening of 1 August the 9th Battalion started its tragic advance at the 'Old French Trench', in the second wave of attack in the battle of Passchendaele. In the Battalion's War Diary entry it was reported that because of the previous heavy rainfall they could not use the communication trench and had to proceed overland. C company was shelled heavily and had twenty casualties, of which six died.[90] 'However, the men were not to be discouraged, and they went on cheerfully', completing the relief by 1.30 am. 'It was today that the Army (Fifth-General Plumer) Commander sent his congratulations to the 24th division on their steady and determined work done during the British Advance on July 21st 1917.' (Plumer would be at the première of *Journey's End* at the Savoy almost twelve years later.) The emphasis of this report is the opposite of Sherriff's 1968 account of this day, told within the context of the generals' guilty blunders. He described the advance to the position gained by the first wave of attack as 'a drawn out nightmare'[91] in a sea of mud with no means of direction or communication.

Sherriff was wounded by the splinters of a pillbox hit by a whizzbang, with fifty-two small pieces in the right side of his face and in his right hand. His later account lengthens his participation in one of the most tragic battles of the war by stating that he was wounded in the afternoon, whereas the letter to his mother written on the day with his left hand said that he had been wounded in the morning. The nightmare was finally over and he was leaving with honour. His letters home showed clearly the relief: 'I am very lucky, I think to get off so lightly, considering what some of my men got...had a good tea and feel most happy and comfortable to be out of it.'[92]

But neuralgia was soon mentioned again after he was told on the 17th, at the officers' quarters at the British Red Cross Hospital in Netley, that as his wounds were quite healed the Medical Board about to meet on his case would grant him three weeks' leave before his return to France. He saw a doctor about his neuralgia, who told him it could be caused by wax in his eardrums or 'failing that' by a small protruding bone in his nose. He asked the doctor many questions and again felt uncomfortable about the version he should present: 'It is not fair to exaggerate because it does not seem fair to deceive them – and they probably are able to tell.'[93] The next day he clung to his neuralgia more urgently when he heard that the Board had in fact granted him three weeks' leave and three weeks' Home Service at Dover before returning to the front. 'I shall not of course hesitate to report any trouble I have with my head for I think 10½ months is quite a sufficient spell out there and that I am due at least a couple of months off in England...'[94]

On 15 September, however, he was in St Thomas's Hospital with 'boils.'[95] He never returned to France and was with the Home Service from November 1917 to January 1919, when he was demobilized with the rank of Captain. After living in a nightmare no man's land between courage and nervous collapse, between the desire to escape and the unwillingness to step with some ignominy out of the exclusive world of fear, all was resolved into an intense experience and an honourable war record, a narrative which he began to re-present in fictional form as soon as he found himself permanently out of the line and out of fear.

3 Sherriff's Literary Reconstruction of his War Experience

Sherriff always intended to use the material of war for literary purposes, so that before and after 1918 fact and fiction mesh inextricably. The incomplete novel and the short stories that Sherriff wrote most probably in 1918 [96] reflected, through the emphasis on the more positive aspects of his memories, his great relief at possessing a soldier's record. In the story 'A Quiet Night', he remarked that of all the events which crammed eleven months but which could fill twelve 'ordinary' years, the ones he thought of most were 'the long winter nights' when both sides were apparently resting; in another there is a long description of a dinner in the trenches, with great companionship, songs and cheer.[97] It was not until *Journey's End* that he addressed, although obliquely, the trauma of fear.

Sherriff and Hibbert The evidence about Sherriff's war experience seems at first to find an obvious bridge in *Journey's End* with the figure of Hibbert, who feigns neuralgia because, like Stanhope, who resorts to drink, he cannot bear feeling afraid. The obvious similarities between Sherriff and Hibbert are the whining tone in which they claim to suffer from the same complaint, and their going sick at the time of a raid. Hibbert is seriously ill with fear and Sherriff tries to explain the genuineness of his plight without exposing his own story.[98]

> Stanhope! I've tried like hell – I swear I have. Ever since I came out here I've hated and loathed it. Every sound up there makes me all – cold and sick. I'm different to – to the others – you don't understand. It's got worse and worse, and now I can't bear it any longer. I'll never go up those steps again – into the line – with the men looking at me – and knowing – I'd rather die here. (He is sitting on STANHOPE's bed, crying without effort to restrain himself.)[99]

Hibbert, however, uses neuralgia more obviously as a way of escape, and his social extraction and temperament are quite different from Sherriff's. He is the only one amongst the officers of *Journey's End* who seems never to have played games. He is rich and decadent. While Raleigh has never had a girlfriend, Osborne is respectably married, and Stanhope is almost engaged to Raleigh's sister, Hibbert is the only one to display a crass attitude towards women. At the dinner after the raid he tells a story about his picking up two 'tarts' in his car and shutting up their complaints by driving dangerously fast. He then shows cards of scantily-dressed women to the other men, inviting their comments. Stanhope shouts him away and says to Trotter that he cannot stand Hibbert's 'repulsive little mind.'[100] Nothing could be further from Sherriff's strait-laced character. Hibbert's wealthy self-indulgence estranges him to some extent from the active obedience to the values which have nurtured the other officers' sense of duty. The *New Statesman* reviewer noted that Hibbert seemed to be the only character who had escaped from the 'public school mentality.'[101]

The *Daily Sketch* described Hibbert as an 'honest weakling';[102] the *Evening News* as a 'cringing malingerer'.[103] The *Daily Mail*, more perceptively, under the heading 'WHO WAS NOT AFRAID', observed that this 'worm trying to wriggle into safety'[104] was revealed as 'a semblance of a man' by Stanhope's own confession of fear.[105] The character was generally viewed negatively and perfunctorily. There is evidence that Sherriff, who never openly commented on this character, thought that the public had not understood Hibbert. Amongst his papers is a five-page timetable of the play's events, the skeleton outline which Vernon Bartlett turned into a novel. There is one single comment to interrupt the laconic listing of the character's actions: 'Tuesday 1–4, Hibbert on duty alone (Would this make a chapter?

Sympathetic description of Hibbert's fears might enlighten many who have misunderstood Hibbert in play.)' In the typed presentation of a screenplay for presumably a second film version of *Journey's End* in 1939, he suggested that, for the sake of the length of the film, the part of Hibbert be cut altogether: 'We lose a dramatic scene, but Hibbert and his troubles are not a vital part of the story.'[106] The only major corrections – indeed almost the only corrections of any kind – Sherriff made on Bartlett's typescript all regard Hibbert, in an effort to render the character more 'sympathetic' without exposing himself through a more open intervention. He crossed out several lines which implied Hibbert's manipulative use of his neuralgia. He crossed out a section set in an estaminet, where Hibbert complains of his neuralgia to the medical officer, who regards him suspiciously. In the scene of Hibbert's flirtation with Angeline he crossed out 'The necessity of going back in the trenches could not be thrust out of his memory.' After Osborne praises Stanhope's courage, and remarks that Stanhope had refused to go to the hospital as the doctor had suggested, Sherriff crossed out the words: 'He seemed to be haunted by a fear that people would think he was shamming if he 'went sick' like anybody else' leaving only: 'for nearly three years he had stuck it.'[107] The cause for Madge's (Raleigh's sister) return from a French hospital, a physical injury while driving a lorry, became a 'breakdown', a change that served to stress further the vulnerability of sensitive people to war. In the final version Madge has never been to France, and Raleigh's father, a doctor, takes care of shell-shocked patients. Sherriff's suggestions were too cautious, and in the novel Hibbert's character is fleshed out in a way which exposes his weaknesses and plays down the similarity of his torment and Stanhope's.

Another important link of interpretation between Sherriff's experience of fear and the play is the word 'imaginative.' '...everyone has a different temperament I know, and I may have got a more imaginative one than suits the necessities of trench life..,'[108] he wrote after going sick for the first time. In his play the function of 'imagination' is unfolded through the portrayal of its absence in the working-class ex-ranker Trotter, a stereotyped figure of a burly, perennially cheerful man constantly preoccupied with food.[109] Sherriff distances himself from this character more than from any other by describing him as unimaginative. This judgment is passed on him explicitly by fellow-officers in the play. When Stanhope sees the sketch Trotter has made – 144 circles for each hour in the front line that week – he says that he is going to draw a picture by the circle corresponding to the dawn of the German attack of Trotter blown up in four pieces. To Osborne's objection, Stanhope replies that 'he's no imagination' and will not understand, thus implying that Trotter is better protected than they from the fear of death; Osborne agrees.[110]

STANHOPE: Funny not to have any imagination. Must be rather nice.
OSBORNE: A bit dull, I should think.
STANHOPE: It must be, rather. I suppose all his life. Trotter feels like you and I do when we're drowsily drunk.
OSBORNE: Poor chap!
STANHOPE: I suppose if Trotter looks at that wall he just sees a brown surface. He doesn't see into the earth beyond – the worms wandering about round the stone and roots of trees.[111]

They argue that 'this life sharpens the imagination';[112] its impact is therefore limited on a man who lacks their sensitivity. There is a single acknowledgement of Trotter's vague feelings. A few hours following the raid, after dinner, Stanhope addresses him affectionately:

STANHOPE: I envy you, Trotter. Nothing upsets you, does it? You're always the same.
TROTTER: Always the same, am I? (He sighs) Little you know –
STANHOPE: You never get sick to death of everything, or so happy you want to sing.
TROTTER: I don't know – I whistle sometimes.
STANHOPE: But you always feel the same.
TROTTER: I feel all blown out now.[113]

The difference between feeling and feeling imaginatively is one of depth of vision: when the landscape is one of horror, then the perception of reality becomes unbearable. In *Kitty* Warwick Deeping described the protagonist's nervous condition in terms similar to those used to convey Stanhope's x-ray-like sensibility. When Alex St George is home on leave from France, spending, after a stay in the country, the last three days at the Astor Hotel, he feels terribly uncomfortable surrounded by people, as he can see them too vividly as 'raw, naked emotions', sitting, eating and talking. 'He had imagination, and that was part of his trouble, and why he was what the doctors called a "martial misfit". He had seen dead men, mangled men. The war gave you horrible moments when you saw things as they might be, a bloody head instead of a champagne bottle on a table, or a woman – a woman like that dark little thing over there – being embraced by a brown corpse.'[114]

Raleigh can withstand pressures more easily as his imagination is not as keen as Stanhope's (this point is brought out more clearly in the novel). But Trotter's lack of imagination is very much akin to illiteracy; he cannot 'read' life. Sherriff at one point posits the dichotomy between himself and the working-class officer in terms of the attitude towards his favourite work of literature. When Osborne reads aloud to him an excerpt from *Alice in Wonderland* Trotter declares that he sees 'no point' in it and that it is just a '*kid's* book.'[115] The correlation between imagination and class, and imagination and writing is unmistakable. Imagination – and therefore writing, and the reconstruction of experience – is the domain of non working-class people. At the end of *The Barber of Putney*, a novel replete with 'affectionate' working-class characterizations, the narrator turns out to be a friend of privates Curly and Tim. In the epilogue these two ex-soldiers offer him suggestions about what he should put in the war book he is going to write. Without a middle-class friend who can write, they would have no voice.[116]

Eric Leed and Elaine Showalter have both commented on the dichotomy of diagnosis of 'shell-shock' between hysteria and neurasthenia. Class was the determining factor, closely paralleling the distinction made in late Victorian times in the identification of such manifestations in women.[117] 'Gross physical symptoms' were deemed to be characteristic of the ranks, while higher social strata displayed their war shock through 'purely behavioral expression.'[118] 'In sum, then, the hysterical soldier was seen as simple, emotional, unthinking, passive, suggestible, dependent, and weak...while the complex and overworked neurasthenic officer was much closer to an acceptable, even heroic male ideal.'[119] Hibbert displays the 'gross physical symptoms' of the working class, while Stanhope is the 'heroic male ideal.' Nowhere does Sherriff reveal more openly his uncertain social status, or come closer, paradoxically, to a widely representative character than in the figure of the officer with the lower-class manifestation of fear.

The Public-School Matrix of 'Journey's End' It was an insurance clerk who had not attended a public school who wrote the most successful and 'realistic' account of public-school officers in the war. Robert Cedric (Bob) Sherriff, born in 1896 in Hampton Wick, Surrey, was from a lower middle-class family. He attended Kingston Grammar School, where he did not distinguish himself as a student but excelled at rowing, cricket, rugger and the long jump – 'I'd been a big shot at school.'[120]

The brief description he offered of his school in 'The English Public Schools' centred around terms of social status. They had no playing fields and had to use the public recreation ground, but they had their 'own little built-in pride.' His father had to scrape to pay the ten-pounds-a-term fee so that 'his son should be a grammar school boy with a good start in life.' By contrast, the boys whose parents were unable or unwilling to meet this expense went to board schools and wore nondescript clothes, 'which made us feel superior'. Kingston Grammar School gave '"class" and that was everything.'[121] Sherriff spent his life strengthening this foothold gained into the respectable middle class. *Journey's End* made him about £75,000, of which £6,500 went to the purchase of a beautiful house, Rosebriars, at Esher, set in 'a little park', one of the homes he used to admire on his walks into the country from his 'old shabby house with the railway embankment at the end of that garden.' He employed three gardeners and a household staff.[122] What the present did not provide could be gleaned from the past. Sherriff descended from the Lawrence Sherriff who founded Rugby School in 1557, according to an uncle who wrote a history of the family.[123]

Sherriff, in a sense, was at school for most of his adult life. For ten years after the war his activities with the Rowing Club absorbed most of his free time; after the success of *Journey's End* he went to New College, Oxford, at the age of thirty-five and accompanied by his mother, to study for a history degree. At first he was not accepted as he had taken no Latin at Kingston Grammar School, but in the end his fame and his newly-acquired connections won him a place. He befriended Gilbert Murray, H.A.L. Fisher and Lord Elton; the dons praised his enthusiasm and dedication, but told him that he had little chance of passing the exams. As with his relative failure as an officer, Sherriff accepted without feeling humiliated the ultimate impossibility of his academic attempt. He distinguished himself at rowing, although an attack of pleurisy deprived him of his greatest dream, a Blue. 'Once achieved ['that dark blue cap'] it was yours for life. You were one of the aristocrats of rowing.'[124] Failure was written within his incomplete social pedigree and it never really caught him by surprise. He left for Hollywood, again accompanied by his mother, to write screenplays, but he eventually returned to Oxford to coach the New College eight. He felt unhappy and out of place in California: 'Oxford seemed so gay after Hollywood', he mused retrospectively.[125]

In the autobiographical story of Jimmy Lawton the young protagonist learns from the enlisting officer that his school, of which he is so proud, is not considered to be up to 'officer standard'.[126] This dialogue is reported again, in a slightly modified form, as Sherriff's own experience in 'The English Public School and the War.' '"School?" inquired the adjutant. I told him, and his face fell...."I'm sorry," he said, "but I'm afraid it isn't a public school."'[127] Being refused a commission because he had not been to a public school was humiliating yet caused no bitterness in Sherriff, who learnt to accept the validity of this apparently arbitrary criterion of selection. He explained that in public school young officers had

> gained self-confidence, the beginnings of responsibility through being prefects over younger boys. Pride in their school would easily translate into pride for a regiment. Above all, without conceit or snobbery, they were conscious of a

personal superiority that placed on their shoulders an obligation towards those less privileged than themselves.[128]

With the generals so alienated from the concerns of the soldiers in the trenches, the public school officers played a vital role in maintaining the morale of the men and leading them with the example 'from their reserves of patience and good humour and endurance'; they shared their privations and understood their 'spiritual loneliness'.[129]

In his study of the public-school ethos in the Great War, Peter Parker argues that the qualities required of a platoon commander were 'very similar to those demanded of a model school prefect.'[130] A training manual encouraged the platoon commander to praise the men in order to gain their confidence, rather than criticize them unendingly; and to give a good example by being 'well turned out, punctual, and cheery, even under adverse circumstance', putting 'his men's comfort before his own and never sparing himself.'[131] Captain Stanhope's responsibility was the company, with approximately 250 men; the 2nd Lieutenant was in charge of a platoon of about 60 men. In these units, and in the platoon particularly, the close contact between officers and men represented a focus of humanity in the great, faceless mass of the army.[132] Men as different as Captain W. P. Nevill, of the 8th East Surreys (who died on the first day at the Somme after kicking off the advance with a football) and Siegfried Sassoon were loved and respected for the courageous leadership they gave their men.[133] Parker points out that in the play *But It Still Goes On* (1930), written at Maurice Browne's request, Graves used the terminology of romantic public-school friendships in describing the relationship between officer and men: 'Do you know how a platoon of men will absolutely worship a good-looking gallant young officer?..He's a being apart.'[134]

Paul Fussell refers to the ending of *Journey's End* as 'a horrific ironic scene which the Great War contributes to the Second.' He links this scene, which he interprets as the depiction of a dying man being reassured by a friend who does not realize the extent of the injury, to Snowden's death in Joseph Heller's *Catch-22*.[135] This is not accurate: Stanhope is aware of Raleigh's fatal wound from the first moment the sergeant major tells him he has been hit.

STANHOPE Badly?
S.-M.: 'Fraid it's broke 'is spine, sir; can't move 'is legs.
STANHOPE: Bring him down here.
S.-M.: Down 'ere, sir?
STANHOPE (shouting): Yes! Down here – quickly![136]

His determination to comfort his friend, to hide from him the nature of his injuries, is another expression of Stanhope's endurance, of his relentless assuming of duties which involve facing enormous fear and suffering. Stanhope's character provides a retrieval of heroism even within the context of the unprecedented horror of modern warfare. But more than this, all characters, even Hibbert, find in endurance the salvation of the self, the binding agent of the companionship to be found in their dehumanizing world. Stanhope's salient characteristic is his capacity to bear the horrors of fear which torture him. Even his recourse to whisky is a manifestation of his courage, as this desperate refuge from cowardice inflicts on him the added pain of self-brutalization. In his personalistic study of courage in war, Charles Moran, a doctor with the 1st Battalion Royal Fusiliers between 1914 and 1917, entitled the first chapter 'Of How Imagination Helps Some Men and Destroys Others.' The brand of Stanhope's courage is clearly recognizable in the following passage.

> The outstanding personal successes in this battalion at any rate have been among imaginative men. They were able to see more fully than others could that there was no decent alternative to sticking it and to see this not in a hot moment of impulse but steadily through many months of monotony and trial. They understood on what terms life was worth while.[137]

One of Sherriff's 1918 stories centres around Captain MacDonald, like Stanhope a company commander. This man, always completely absorbed by the care and love for his men, is spending the quiet hours of his night vigil thinking of his '200 children': '...he looked on each one as his own child – cared for them, worked, fought, and played with them — helped them to build them up when they were wounded and helped to bury them when they were dead.'[138] In *A Ghost on Vimy Ridge* he told of an experience which reads like his own ('I was commissioned from the Artists Rifles to the East Surrey Regiment in the Autumn of 1916 and joined the 9th Battalion...'), though he never mentioned it elsewhere. Fact and fiction are once again married in the inevitable unity of memory. In the story he recalls seeing the captain of his company running towards Headquarters, after shelling, to get help for his company; later he finds out that the captain had been killed.[139]

In spite of his frayed nerves Stanhope is also a father figure to his men. He talks to them, cheers them on, invites the Colonel to talk to the men before the raid. His short temper makes him intolerant of Hibbert and unfair to Raleigh; yet he comforts them both. He confronts Hibbert as he tries to go sick, puts him to the test by threatening him with a gun, and then praises him for 'sticking it.' The ultimate proof of his humane concern is the revelation of his own fear to Hibbert.

> ...I feel the same – exactly the same! Every little noise up there makes me feel – just as you feel. Why didn't you tell me instead of talking about neuralgia? We all feel like you do sometimes, if you only knew. I hate and loathe it all.[140]

This stress on the officer as father figure and as a source of courage finds very close echoes in a presumably true tale written by the Etonian Gilbert Frankau for the *Ypres Times*, 'The Ghosts of Ypres.' It reveals the same strong paternalistic bond between officer and private present in Frankau's political pronouncements and in his *Peter Jackson*. Frankau began his story with the remark that in a hundred years' time historians of the war would write a 'dull book' filled with information which would convey 'cold geography' but not 'the warm humanity of it all'. The sentence with which he prefaced his own true version of the humanity of war was: 'Better dead, better maimed, than own oneself, to oneself, coward.' Frankau suffered from shell-shock, an experience he related in his 1920 novel, in which the essence of the soldier's identity is conveyed, as in *Journey's End*, through the tension between fear and endurance. The episode 'recalled' by Frankau took place at midnight in 'the City of Fear.' He was sitting in his dug-out, wondering if the other men could feel what he did on that eerily quiet night. 'For I am a poet, and these others are only men....Men who work with their hands, drivers and diggers! Brave, yes, but because they have no imagination.'[141] This train of thought was interrupted by the greeting of a private from the Signal Corps; he could not know he was addressing an officer because Frankau had removed his tunic. '"My God, it's weird out there, all by oneself. There's something rummy about old Wipers to-night....I'm not a 'nervy' chap, but it seems to me as there were ghosts about".' Frankau found this a lesson in humility, because the soldier had revealed to him, together with his secret of fear, 'that not only poets have imagination, not only public schoolboys courage.'[142] He divined the man's temptation to invoke shell-shock and leave: but knew that the 'creed' was holding him there.[143] As an upper-class Eton-educated man, Frankau felt more secure in his social role than Sherriff and therefore less threatened by the working class. But his attribution of imagination to the private is a reflection of his own sensibility and literary activity, which make him capable of interpreting the awkward words of the man, and of giving the episode meaning by transcribing it into a story.

Sherriff, with an insecure class and school background, always felt inadequate in his role as officer. In a letter to his mother he told of how he did not like telling the men off and of the uneasiness he felt in his position towards them. '...why *should* I as an officer have better food, better quarters, better work and everything made easier?' He tried to compensate by being 'nice' and 'easy' with them, but as a consequence discipline and respect towards him suffered.[144]

Stanhope has been in the front line for three years; he is still there at the crucial time of the German attack in March 1918, when Sherriff was in Dover. The fictional captain can be seen as an idealized portrait of the author's own experience, with fear managed dramatically, and efficiency and leadership unimpaired. At a reunion dinner of the 'Gallants' (East Surreys) in 1929, Sherriff told a self-deprecating anecdote about his exit from the war. "'I'm afraid I wasn't much good as an officer...'", he started; then asked Lieutenant-Colonel C.A.Clark (Nobby) of the 9th Surreys:

> "I wonder if you remember, sir, what you said to me when I reported to you that I had just been wounded, and that I was to be evacuated?" "Afraid I don't", smiled Nobby. "You said, "Thank God", remarked Sherriff; and sat down to soldierly applause.

This episode was related by Frankau, also a Gallant, who saw *Journey's End* six times, and remarked on the coincidence that a single temporary unit should have produced his own war bestseller and the most famous play.[145]

Sherriff's ideal image of the public school he did not quite make provided the language, the protagonists and the values of the play. In his first unfair outburst against Raleigh, Stanhope reveals his emotional imbalance by denying their Barford complicity: 'Don't "Dennis" me! Stanhope's my name! You're not at school!'[146] When Raleigh first meets Osborne the credentials of the main characters are soon established in terms of their sporting prowess. Osborne tells him that Stanhope, the Company Commander, is 'a splendid chap.' Raleigh replies: '*Isn't* he? He was a skipper of Rugger at Barford, and kept wicket for the eleven. A jolly good bat too.'[147] Raleigh himself plays rugger and cricket, although he is not 'in the same class as Dennis.' As for Osborne, his great worth and modesty – 'Anyhow, don't breeze about it' – is revealed by Raleigh's thrilling discovery that he once played cricket for England.[148] 'Playing the game' is at the heart of the role these men must fulfil as boys at public school and as officers in the trenches.

The play which *Journey's End* succeeded at the Savoy was John Van Druten's very successful *Young Woodley*. First produced in New York in 1925, it was banned in England because of its controversial topic. When the censor lifted the ban it was produced by the Stage Society in 1928; the book of the play was published by Gollancz.[149] This pattern of success (Stage Society, Savoy, Gollancz) foreshadowed that of *Journey's End*. Set in a public school, *Young Woodley* discusses the love between a sensitive pupil and the young wife of an overbearing, narrow-minded headmaster. The latter is a rigidly prosaic man who holds his young wife prisoner of his social conventions and despises the boy for being a poet. Much has been made of the unexpected reception of *Journey's End* at a time when war plays were doomed to failure, yet an important clue to its appeal lies in the similarities to the play whose set at the Savoy had to be quickly dismantled to make room for Sherriff's play two days later. The threatened sensitivity and innocence of Woodley, the loyalty between the friends, the language of the young boys in the Prefects' Room; all these found clear echoes in the world of Sherriff's officers' dugout.[150]

Amongst Sherriff's war papers are seven little notes – entitled 'Captain's Duty' – devising a strategy in which the military and the ludic are inextricably interwoven; it is indeed impossible to tell whether they were written as a lecture on modern warfare or on rowing. The second note states: 'SIMILE: Rowing stands alone like modern warfare <u>Steps in going to War.</u>'

(1) Seizing up your enemies
(2) Reviewing own men
(3) Preparing attack[151]

In his autobiography Sherriff, in characteristic boyish fashion, did not think it irrelevant to end a brief summing up of his war experience with a reference to rowing: 'There had been bad times in France, but all in all it had been a magnificent and memorable experience, and with my wounds gratuity I bought myself a sculling boat.'[152]

Although the war tests severely the training in loyalty, endurance and leadership of the officers in *Journey's End*, it is not submitted to the test of the men's moral judgment. There are only three statements of criticism of the war. In answer to Raleigh's 'The Germans are really quite decent, aren't they? I mean, outside the newspapers?',[153] Osborne, a schoolmaster at home and Raleigh's front line teacher, replies with a moving tale. He remembers when a man out on patrol at 'Wipers' was shot at dawn; he lay there in great pain all day. The next night some of his friends went over the top to rescue him. When they started dragging him back a German officer cried out to them to carry him; they stood up and carried him back while the German officer fired lights to help them.

RALEIGH: How topping!
OSBORNE: Next day we blew each other's trenches toblazes.
RALEIGH: It all seems rather – silly, doesn'tit?[154]

This comment deprives Osborne's tale of the strength of the parable of war which an extrapolated reading might suggest; the whole dialogue emphasizes the relevance of the public school value of fair play in a brutal arena.

The allusion to the suicidal raid mindlessly planned and demanded by Headquarters is the play's only real protest. Stanhope's bitter reaction to the Colonel's enthusiasm about the raid in which Osborne has died is to turn away and say 'in a dead voice': 'How awfully nice – if the Brigadier's pleased.'[155] In an article published in 1968 Sherriff discussed his memory of Passchendaele and of the disastrous lack of communication between generals and officers. Yet even without the constraint of offending powerful contemporaries and at a time when such criticism was not only accepted but part of the conventional wisdom about the First World War, his accusations are not part of a wider indictment of war. His discussion of the war turned untiringly in the old grooves. The title of this article of war reminiscences he contributed to George Panichas's *Promise of Greatness*? 'The English Public Schools in the War.'

The Play's Title The title of the play was not drawn from *Othello*. Sherriff's own account is that one night, reading in bed, he came to the following words at the end of a chapter: 'It was late in the evening when we came at last to our Journey's End.' He decided to use the last two words as the name of the play he had just completed.[156] The idea of a journey towards death needs to be seen in the context of two awesome images of disaster preceding the First World War: R.F. Scott's doomed exploration and the sinking of the Titanic.

Scott's expedition, the Titanic's voyage and the Great War had in common the meeting of tragedy at the end of a journey towards the South Pole, across the Atlantic, and from England to the trenches. They also shared the legacy of exaltation of male heroism and gallantry, and, significantly, a landscape of death which in its fantastic and awesome singularity aroused new and powerful images of catastrophe in the national psyche. George Orwell remembered that the tale of the Titanic being suddenly upended and rapidly sinking struck his boy's mind with greater horror than later reports from the trenches. An American survivor described thus the 21-mile-long spread of ice: 'The floe glistened like a never-ending meadow covered with new fallen snow. Those same white mountains, marvellous in their purity, had made of the just ended night one of the blackest the sea has ever known.'[157] The subtitle of Wade's interesting book about the Titanic, 'End of a Dream' – echoing also 'Journey's End' – is the title of A.M.N. Jenkin's 1919 war novel. Wade discusses this disaster in terms which are often used to describe the break marked by the Great War, that is, as emblematic of the end of an opulent, smugly complacent age.[158] This judgment was first passed by Thomas Hardy who, immediately after the tragedy, wrote 'The Convergence of the Twain', a poem about the punishment by the 'Immanent Will' of pride and vanity.[159] The *Nation* commented thus about the sinking of the Titanic:

> Although we sometimes pride ourselves upon a higher moral enlightenment in the interpretation of human affairs than was possessed by an ancient people, it may well be questioned whether the Greek genius was not more equal than ours to a relevant understanding of those tragedies which 'stagger humanity' by their magnitude and unexpectedness. To them, at least, this fearful catastrophe with all its apparently fortuitous happenings, would have seemed a plain manifestation of Hubris.[160]

Gilbert Frankau's historical saga of an English family from 1912 to 1938, *The Dangerous Years*, begins with a detailed description of the sinking of the Titanic, in which the father dies. Interestingly, what the Head of the sons' school says to the widow about to see her children after the tragedy has the same urging of continuity after disaster which parallels the popular fictional treatment of the shock of war. He speaks of 'social reabsorption', and urges the mother to smooth over the bad feeling there was about the way the rescue had been handled, so as to help the process of consolation.[161]

In the wake of his sudden literary popularity Sherriff was introduced by Scott's widow, Kathleen Hylton, to J.M. Barrie, his favourite playwright. The latter on 3 May 1922 gave the Rectorial Address at St Andrews University, which was published and sold well. Its theme was 'Courage'. In this speech to Youth, delivered to survivors of the war and in the presence of the Chancellor, Lord Haig, Barrie invoked the memory of Scott. He read from a letter his friend had written to him from the South Pole shortly before his death. The desperate discomfort and isolation, as well as the deliberate cheeriness, is reminiscent of similar tableaux of courage from the trenches: 'We are in a desperate state – feet frozen, etc., no fuel, and a long way from food, but it would do your heart good to be in our tent, to hear our songs and our cheery conversation...'[162]

After *Journey's End* Sherriff announced that his next play would be about Scott; in the end the project was abandoned, allegedly because of concern about eventual distress to his relatives. He contributed the chapter on Scott in the book *Post-Victorians* (1933). The spiritual link between the lost heroes in the Antarctic and the soldiers of the First World War is the subject of a 1930 war play. *The Last Enemy*, by Frank Harvey, has two explorers, who have died in the wastes of the Antarctic, reach the 'First Landing', where it is revealed that they are the spiritual parents of children yet unborn. In the next act these children are two officers in the war. One, a pilot, who is drinking too much whisky to help war-strained nerves, makes a rather violent attempt at seduction which is interrupted by the apparition of his spiritual father; the other receives a visit from his protector as he lies wounded in no-man's-land near Festubert. The play was shown at the Fortune from December 1929 to March 1930; Laurence Olivier played Jerry Warrander, the Stanhope-like young officer who resorts to drink to cope with the brutalization of war.

Like Scott, and like Stanhope and Raleigh, Sherriff never left his youth. In his lecture on 'Courage' Barrie talked about a young man who died by falling down a glacier and whose young friends calculated when the body would re-emerge. Years later, as old men, they gathered at the glacier, to see the body of their friend young as the day he had died. 'So Scott and his comrades emerge out of the white immensities always young',[163] was the moral of the tale.

In Sherriff's case it was also as if the war had frozen his youth and made this stage in life his journey's end, even when chronologically he went beyond it. Interviewers remarked often on Sherriff's youthful appearance and on his open and unaffected manner. He was the schoolboy who never grew up. In the novel/autobiography of Jimmy Lawton which he wrote in 1918, he described the farewell with his mother before leaving for France. Because of the extraordinary closeness between Sherriff and his mother there is no note of sarcasm in the mother's sentimental send-off, which becomes an elegy to youth:

> You don't know yet how sad it is to gradually grow old – to gradually see your skin become wrinkled and your hair turn grey – and if it really happened that you had to die, Jack, I can think of nothing more splendid than passing away in the full vigour of manhood – under the open sky – to go the climax of your life – instead of slowly fading out of long weary old age in some sickly bedroom... [164]

He never married, nor, as far as all evidence shows, was he ever involved with a woman.[165] Like the Prince of Wales and T.E. Lawrence, he had the physical appearance and abstruse personality of the everlasting youth. Sherriff retained the kind of innocence which in an increasingly 'sophisticated' world lent him a strongly anachronistic air. The most striking quality of the autobiography he published at the age of seventy-two is the immaturity of thought. From Sherriff's own perspective on his life one can get only an imprecise sense of the time elapsed between the large formal photographs of Sherriff as a schoolboy in the first eleven and rowing crew[166] and the photo taken for the *Sunday Times* in 1972 (with the 76 year-old writer standing in front of a mantelpiece loaded with rowing trophies and beneath a painting of the Thames). In his autobiography Sherriff presented a seamless account of his past, starting with the opening night of *Journey's End* at the Savoy, in a curious equation of his own life story with that of the play.[167] The only comment in his autobiography about a changing England, was, interestingly, about the advent of the Modern Movement in theatre depriving him of an audience.[168] St. John Ervine, the playwright and critic who served with the Dublin Fusiliers and lost a leg, wrote a long article on Sherriff's personality for *Good Housekeeping*. He maintained that Sherriff did not know what a woman was, and, more revealingly, he described him as the 'essential subaltern, not the *pukka* subaltern of pre-war times, but the extemporised subaltern, the lad fresh from a middle-class school, amiable, good-natured, unfussy, fond of cricket and sport and habitually clad, out of business hours, in grey flannels.'[169] In this he likened him to the Prince of Wales, who 'achieved his immense popularity with all classes because he typified in himself the youth that was lost in the War.' Similarly, Sherriff embodied the spirit of the subalterns. 'He is what we mean when we talk of the gallant lads who went out to the War but never came back from it.' This identification of the playwright with a lost generation of young officers underlines the way in which Sherriff and his play represented for many of his contemporaries a real link with the past.[170]

Sherriff depicted the life of the men of the trenches, but his intention was not to draw a world of separation. His statements about the process of creation of the play indicate a blurring between the war and the post-war youth he drew on; his commitment was to the world of young men. Osborne's figure is an understandable exception in the play; as a schoolmaster he is devoted to the education of the young.[171] Once Olivier had left the cast the choice for the role of Stanhope narrowed down to Colin Clive and Colin Keith Johnston. The former had been too young to fight, while Johnston 'had played the part of Stanhope in reality'[172] in France. Still, although Johnston read the part very well, Clive was the unanimous choice.[173] In a short article entitled 'Why I wrote Journey's End' Sherriff asserted that he had drawn all characters in the play from people he had met in his everyday post-war life. 'I got the notion that it would be interesting to imagine the post-war generation in the atmosphere of the trenches.' He mentioned that he could not remember the men he had met in the war. 'The other fellows I did not clearly remember – except Osborne.' All his personal war memorabilia were not enough: 'I'd got all the fellows down there. But I didn't see them any-more. I saw the post-war fellows and drew them.'[174] In an interview with *Era* he said that he had been able to use the traits of 'certain present-day youthful members of the Rowing Club. I see in the present generation of boys exactly the same people who served with me in the War.'[175] Once in Oxford he felt that he blended in perfectly with the much younger students. He refused to see the present young generation as less worthy than their older brothers. In an interview given in 1933, he defended English youth as valiant upholders of the Empire. The 'bright young things', who attracted so much attention and criticism, would soon turn into harmless older men.

> If you would learn the truth, go below this frothy surface, and you will find a youth unequalled in the world for its physical vitality and mental vigour. We do not breed neurotic students who try to assassinate our kings and ministers. Instead, we send out to our Colonies...a stream of youth equipped by instinct to learn the high art of government by character: equal in every degree to the youth that Rome sent out in the years of her greatest pride.[176]

The 'War Consciousness' of 'Journey's End' The 'realism' of *Journey's End* cannot alone explain its success. Henry Williamson had a truly realistic playlet turned down by the BBC about three months before the successful première of *Journey's End*. He wrote to the *Daily Mail* to explain that he had tried to persuade broadcasting officials to present, as their 'Surprise Item', his play about the last quarter of an hour before zero hour, the time of a big attack. He himself was to be 'a Voice beyond Time and Space' moving around and explaining what was happening 'in gun-pit and on tape-line, in first-aid post and aeroplane cockpit, inside a tank, outside a battalion headquarters...' To compound the impression of reality the background of sound would reproduce 'voices, buzzers, drone of stray shells, the crack of a sniper's rifle, the eerie whine of a ricochet. All designed for the climax of Zero: that is to say, it would have been emotionally taut and bearable until the first moments of "the boys going over", when the "purge through pity and tears" would fuse and justify the whole.' The reasons given for its rejection were that the public did not want to hear of the war, and that one had to be careful about the influence of 'the Glory of War' on listening children. The disappointed Williamson insisted to no avail that this would be a realistic account, not a report akin to that of 1914 war correspondents. After the success of *Journey's End* the BBC broadcast one of its scenes as a 'Surprise Item.'[177] It is very unlikely that Williamson's play could have matched the appeal of Sherriff's. Its reality was too stark and unfiltered through the familiar values which inform the dialogue of Sherriff's officers.

In his first conversation with Osborne, Raleigh describes his trip to the dugout, his first view of the landscape of war. He had come by an 'amazing trench', starting up at the village, miles and miles long, with green lights (Very lights) appearing ahead as far as he could see. Raleigh had not expected to see so many and at such a distance.

> OSBORNE: I know. (He puffs at his pipe). There's something rather romantic about it all.
> RALEIGH (eagerly) : Yes. I thought that too.
> OSBORNE: You must always think of it like that if you can. Think of it all - as romantic. It helps.[178]

This is the first piece of advice that Osborne offers Raleigh. The word that most reviewers singled out of this dialogue must have been the direction 'eagerly', as Raleigh was often described as the enthusiastic, idealistic newcomer whose enthusiasm would soon be brutalized by the realities of war. This interpretation is too simplistic and tidy. Osborne knows the reality of trench warfare and yet he offers a romantic framework as a helpful one; a powerful indication of his belief in the relevance of traditional perceptions of war.

This word, 'romantic', constitutes the subject of the draft for an unpublished article whose title contained the word which was the pivot of the critics' praise: 'In defence of Reality.' The notes are an attempt to intervene in the debate about *Journey's End*, but what the author has to say is spectacularly off the centre of public discussion. The date is impossible to determine; there are several false starts and different versions. With typical modesty, Sherriff sidestepped all praise by choosing to start with a friend's criticism. 'It has been said of the Play "Journey's End" that is it too realistic...'; and in another try: 'I met a friend the other day who said "I have a grumble about your Play "Journey's End." It is too starkly realistic. I don't want realism in a Play:...I want fantasy – farce – romance...I'm tired of the things that really happen".' There is one fragment which toes a conventional line – just a few lines explaining that this realism is necessary in order to prevent another war. The rhetoric is stilted: 'Accidents generally occur when we least expect them....We rarely fall downstairs while we still ache from a previous fall.' But this inauspicious attempt is cut short, and on another page Sherriff writes the title of the article again, and two very similar versions, followed by the beginning of a 'good copy' in pen, spelling give, not to sell. But this life goes against Nature, the only reality there is: '...in the modern life...we have to face an artificial code of living which our nature tries to shun.' A paragraph dealing with the play is crossed out. In it he asserts that there is no reality in *Journey's End*: '...it is a slice of life taken from the [most] fantastic unreal nightmare that man has yet achieved. If this is true we can call a nightmare an achievement.' Here the argument about the reality of *Journey's End* is turned on its head as the meaning of the term itself is negated. Out of the jumbled sketches of arguments from which Sherriff could not coherently extricate himself, two basic notions emerge. One is the dichotomy between meaning and the modern world of 'artifice'. The other is that the war was a 'nightmare', but at the same time an experience which brought men nearer to the real stuff of existence. Romance *is* reality: it is in this light that must be understood the incongruous adjective – romantic – with which Osborne and Raleigh sum up the eerily different scenery of war.

An examination of Sherriff's pronouncements and an analysis of *Journey's End* contradict the interpretation of it as an anti-war play. In a short article written for the *Daily Express* in January 1929 Sherriff explained that he had been meaning for twelve years to write about the 'life which sometimes was a living death, and sometimes – for brief moments – the only kind of life which, I have thought since, was worth living': this time had been necessary to sort out the 'jarring impressions' of the young subaltern. He left no room for ambiguity as to his intentions in writing the play:

> Let me make myself clear. I have not written this play as a piece of propaganda. And certainly not as propaganda for peace. Neither have I tried to glorify the life of the soldier, nor to point any kind of moral. It is simply the expression of an ideal. I wanted to perpetuate the memory of some of those men.[180]

Hannen Swaffer, who had helped the play with his enthusiastic first review, showed insight when he remarked, in a second review at the end of January, that Sherriff had not set out to write a play against war – 'In fact, he rather favours war.' In his opinion Sherriff had written in favour of peace only 'unwittingly.'[181]

At a banquet in the Guildhall Sherriff presented the play's manuscript to the League of Nations, to be auctioned off among the guests.[182] This gesture is put in its proper context by a talk he gave about war literature to the Cambridge branch of the League of Nations Unions. The word propaganda (with its disagreeable political overtones) was the label which Sherriff was eager to ward off. He claimed that war books would help to maintain, as the article reported, 'a certain war consciousness' and that their influence towards 'peace propaganda' would be negligible.[183] This comment confirms the observations about the effect of war books on a younger generation by Herbert Read, who maintained that war books 'were unwittingly ministering to this hidden lust' for violence.[184]

Sherriff, however, saw nothing negative in the transmission of 'war consciousness.' The play sought to depict an exclusive world and keep its memory alive; but the memory of war was assumed to be shared by all. He denied that these books could have a devastating effect upon very young people. The young man who was five years old when the war ended, he argued, 'remembered something of the war, and was inoculated with its conditions. Therefore, he could be trusted to take a war play or a war book in the right spirit.'[185] To reassure himself about the influence of the play, he had taken three boys, just out of school, to see it, in a sort of test of its reception; this experiment had convinced him that they would, in fact, be better prepared to face war.[186]

In 1931 a journalist supported Sherriff's opinion by arguing that the young man who was not grown up at the end of the war after seeing *Journey's End* 'in his inmost heart...would rather like an opportunity of trying' the military experience himself. People were attracted by positive ideals and causes – as witnessed by the middle-class mobilization against the General Strike – rather than by the negative, preventive principles of policing the world to avoid war. In the journalist's opinion the General Election of 1929 had proved that a policy of 'Safety First' could not attract young people: '...there is an element in man that likes discomfort and sacrifice and danger and the hope of glory and "a cause on earth for which we might have died".'[187]

Philip Gibbs addressed bluntly the question of the influence of war literature on the young in the article 'War Books: Are They Educating a Nation of Cowards?' He started by recalling how after seeing *Journey's End* he had heard a girl deplore it for the cowardice it portrayed. In her opinion England would lose its Empire and its 'old heritage' if its fibre was weakened by 'funk'. Gibbs refuted the notion that courage was a quality that need be defined and forged in the arena of war, especially since modern war was more conducive to the 'annihilation' of courage than to the 'training' of it. He did admit to signs of weakening in England – the unwillingness to emigrate and carry the 'White Man's Burden', and the tendency to live in cities; on the other hand, the General Strike of 1926 had provided powerful evidence of the strength of the public spirit.[188]

Sherriff did not write *Journey's End* to show the war as it was, nor to denounce its futility through the realism of the play. Yet the very ingenuousness and artistic naivety of his literary enterprise speaks of an authenticity which is evident even to today's audiences in spite of the obsolete language. *Journey's End* was praised for speaking the truth about war when in fact it merely used as its subject matter an experience which bound the majority of people in 1929 in a solidarity of memory of the past and apprehension about the future. In this sense it was not Sherriff's play, just as its theatrical realization was accomplished by others. It made a powerful emotional appeal to contemporary audiences through its references to sorrow, fear and hope, and through its commemoration of the dead. In the novel based on the play Bartlett expressed the bond between the dead and the survivors with an image of stark brutality. 'Corn would grow where trenches had been, would be ground into flour, kneaded into dough, and children would eat bread that had come from the corpses of their fathers.'[189] It was as if the final scene, showing Raleigh's interment in the collapsed dugout, represented the funeral ceremony which so many dead had not had, and which so many bereaved had not been able to attend.

4 Providing a Social Message

The youthful world of 'school' represented the ideological centre of Sherriff's thought and work. His social thinking was uninformed and devoid of any cogent strategy; yet there is no doubt that he was very aware of the social role of his literary occupation. The kind of success Sherriff achieved made him a very public figure and the subject of innumerable articles. His views were probed; he gave talks and expressed his opinion on a variety of subjects.[190] His interventions were no cursory function of his celebrity. Still unable to envisage a full-time literary career for himself, he thought about ways to translate into public service his philosophy of life; his success persuaded him of the desirability of this step.

In an interview given on the eve of his going up to Oxford he explained that he had changed his ideal occupation from schoolmaster to a vague notion of involvement with politics.

> ...I think there has never been a time when it is more necessary for every man to do his utmost to contribute to the well-being of the nation, and I think the only means of equipping oneself to assess the future is to make a very deep study of the past....Our idea of progress...is all wrong. During the next 200 years I think we shall see a steady development towards simplicity, and a respect for things made with man's hands rather than by mass production.[191]

During the war he had often referred to his desire to live in the country, to teach and to cultivate the study of history.[192] He now fancied that his great love of the past might come to fruition through political service, and he toyed with the notion of becoming a public instrument of moral regeneration. In his 1918 sketched novel he explained Jimmy Lawton's naive worship of officers when he first arrived in France in terms of his innately right historical and political instinct.

> ...deep down in his nature he had an intense love for all that helped to carry to the present day that old pomp and chivalry...he hated the idea of Socialism in which all men should be equal because he knew that it would bury for ever all that was grand and powerfully splendid, and so from the very beginning of his soldiering he had learnt to look upon the officers with silent respect.

Sherriff's credentials for politics, however, were limited indeed, apart from his war experience, his interest in the past and his certificate as Special Constable in the General Strike.[193] The project remained an inconsequential chimera and he opted instead for university.

The next move in his life, leaving Oxford to write the script of *The Invisible Man* in Hollywood for Carl Laemmle of Universal, who paid him 24,000 dollars for the job, was again glossed over with the varnish of social intent. When he asked H.A.L. Fisher, who had been a Minister of Education, his opinion as to whether he should interrupt his studies, Fisher recommended he go:

> A writer may influence a mass of people by remote control: he never meets them individually and never sees the results at first hand. A schoolmaster has only a handful of boys, but he sees them every day and can watch the result of his work as it develops before his eyes...[194]

The most complete indication of Sherriff's social perceptions is in the unpublished sequel to *Journey's End* he drafted some time in the 1930s.[195] The protagonists are Stanhope and Trotter, who survive the attack and are made prisoners of war. Once the war is over their ways part at an English seaport, where they hear a stirring speech by the Mayor which haunts Stanhope's imagination. He is taken back to his days of glory. 'He sees himself as a leader again – leading men in peace instead of war: building instead of destroying – making life vigorous instead of killing it – he sees that the agony he has gone through is at last to be justified.'[196] He is determined to find a job – its nature is left as mysteriously unexplained as the 'building' he envisages - which will allow him to make an important contribution to the effort of reconstruction. But the job hunting proves to be humiliating; he is turned down by 'commerce and business' because of his age and lack of training, and in the end he must accept a job as traveller for Ramsay's Custard Powder.[197] Because of his traumatic displacement he develops feelings of profound bitterness against his own class.

producing *Paul amongst the Jews*: 'It was very highbrow: not my cup of tea at all.'[201] Maurice Browne was 'an intellectual dedicated to the production of highbrow plays to uplift the theatre and pay homage to art for art's sake.'[202] It sounds almost like an insult.

'I can't distinguish between good and bad writing', he told Pamela Frankau in 1939. 'I can only judge whether work is sincere or bogus. Sincere to me is good and bogus is bad.'[203] Not surprisingly, amongst his favourite reading was *Diary of a Nobody*, to which he devoted a week every year;[204] all his early plays were based on Barrie's plays, which inspired him with their 'beautiful simplicity.'[205]

In an article written for *Pictorial Weekly*, illustrated with two photographs of charming thatched cottages, Sherriff explained his philosophy of life under the headline 'I BELIEVE IN SIMPLICITY': 'Why not behave before our friends in the manner that we dig our gardens or fall downstairs – naturally?' Two models of people which he often refers to are chosen to illustrate his argument. One is the dreaded pretentious and 'sophisticated' person who forfeits the simple pleasures of life for 'some preposterous form of excitement – lunch in a London sewer or dinner on a Wapping barge'. The other is the example of a friend of 'good birth' forced to sell tea and hiding this fact out of shame.[206] Vernon Bartlett remembered Sherriff for his acute, instinctive understanding of 'the little people', a sense which he found equally keen, although of a different nature, in Hitler, whom he had interviewed three times.[207]

Most of Sherriff's literary efforts centred around the 'simple man.' The first play he wrote after *Journey's End*, the bland *Badger's Green* (1930), discussed the resistance put up by villagers against development plans. Trying to settle down on the right style in the effort to write his first – and only – novel, he realized that it must match his aim 'to write about simple, uncomplicated people doing normal things.'[208] *The Fortnight in September* (1931) portrayed the uneventful yearly summer vacation in Bognor of a lower middle-class family. The novel was published by Gollancz – 'an intellectual and a perfectionist'[209] – who found it 'delightful.'[210] The *Morning Post* heralded the publication of this novel with: 'NOT FOR SNOBS. Mr. Sherriff's Story of Plain People'.[211] Sherriff found in the strong artistic affirmation which he received from people like Browne and Gollancz a powerful confirmation of his literary instincts. It is possible to trace to this day the strength of the appeal of such literary 'ordinariness.' In 1968, on the publication of his autobiography, one reviewer declared it proof 'that sanity and modesty can prevail in the world of the theatre where too often paranoia and arrogance are mistaken for the attributes of genius.'[212]

Recently an American scholar has called *Journey's End* 'reminiscent of against modern art he criticised Expressionism in theatre for its lack of humanity and its blurring of a sense of values and morality. In a familiar easy contrast with the nineteenth century, he complained that 'Dickens leaves his readers in no doubt about the difference between David Copperfield and Uriah Heep, but [Georg] Kaiser and the Expressionists in general perceived no difference between one person and another, nor would they have acknowledged any difference if they had perceived it.'[221] This influence led to the modern 'de-personalised' drama, where people were just 'mass-produced emblems of current doctrines', 'devitalized and emptied of heroic quality.' He could understand Shaw and Conrad but not Auden; could understand Chaucer much better than Eliot.[222]

The truth was that the British theatre of the 1920s and 1930s was free of such subversive innovations. Barrie and Shaw were still extremely popular and two of Barrie's most successful plays, *Peter Pan* and *The Admirable Crichton*, epitomized, as Trussler has pointed out, the conservative, even reactionary content of drama.[223] The war, according to Trussler, was a watershed for American and continental drama, but 'for the British theatre it was little more than a backwater from which, with peace, the sturdy old oarsmen returned...'; Shaw, Galsworthy, Barrie, and now Maugham, respected the conventional expectations of their upper middle-class audiences.[224] Change only occurred with the depression and the threat of fascism; with the formation of The Group Theatre in 1933 politics were finally brought to the theatre with the work of Auden, Isherwood, MacNiece and Spender.[225]

5 Revisited Rather Than Revived

Journey's End has entered the national memory of war as a literary statement straddling an ambiguous line between condemnation of war and representation of bygone values. Recent responses to the play show us the weakening of patriotic ideas with the erosion of the Empire, but also the persistence of cultural models from the past. The most blatant example of the way in which the play can be made to support different ideologies is in a Methuen's Study-Aid book on the play. The catechism of the memory of war for young students is laid out neatly in the concluding section under the heading 'theme': '*Journey's End*, basically depressing, is a message-carrying play designed with a definite purpose in mind: to make people ponder the stupidity and horrors of war. The play succeeds admirably in this purpose and is a striking indictment of the folly of war.' *Journey's End* is grouped with the best-known war books, which all 'gave the lie to the civilian population's notion that there was something noble and heroic about fighting and dying for one's country.'[226] This anti-war message conveyed through a play which does not condemn war is further complicated by the wish that Hibbert might have regained some of his self-esteem by proving himself brave in battle,[227] thus bypassing the real conceptual focus of the play and morally reinforcing the very notion to which war books are supposed to have given the lie.

A 1976 film, 'Aces High', transposed *Journey's End* to the setting of air warfare (an ironic development, given Sherriff's desire to escape the trenches by joining the air force).[228] The themes of hero worship, cowardice, neuralgia, and school spirit are all present. The film, however, is (simplistically) anti-war and anti-establishment, and introduces the most un-Sherriff-like element of sex, with the character corresponding to Raleigh having his first sexual experience in France. A reviewer complained about the overtness of the film's message in terms which profoundly misjudged *Journey's End* and revealed the legacy of anti-war interpretation of the play:

> ...Sherriff left both the horrors and the idiocies of war to emerge without comment from his dialogue; and by the end, flag-waving patriotism and the public school spirit have been buried just as surely as the eager boy who learns in one brief week that glory is nothing but fear and mud and dying.[229]

In the theatre, modern critical perceptions of *Journey's End* reveal a clearer separation between the understanding of the First World War as an unmitigated disaster and the appreciation of the poignancy of the officers' experience. In an interview given during the successful 1972 revival at the Mermaid Theatre, Peter Egan (Stanhope), who like Laurence Olivier in the original production wore Sherriff's Sam Browne belt, decried the relevance of the patriotism of the play: 'I wouldn't go and fight for anyone....it seems ludicrous to run off and start shooting people about issues that are so confused now. We don't have an Empire any more....We're just a small, not very important island now.' Yet he commented wistfully about the contemporary lack of those choices and certainties which could allow Stanhope to say: 'It's the only thing a decent man can do.'[230]

Some of the critics who saw *Journey's End* in 1972 recognized that this was not a play broadcasting an anti-war message. The *Spectator* made the modern assumption that a 'play in which the two most likeable characters are killed in action clearly has a fundamentally pacifistic intent...', but raised the doubt that 'the reticence that may once have seemed a strength does seem...to come dangerously close to glorifying the indefensible, and the moral stature of the work is thereby diminished.'[231] *The Guardian*'s Michael Billington criticized the sentimentality of the play, in which an 'unbridgeable gulf separates pathos from tragedy.'[232] Benedict Nightingale offered by far the most perceptive review of the play written since it was first produced. He noted that to treat the play as an 'exposé' of the Great War was to do so 'without the consent of its author.' He saw the value of the play in its very unselfconsciousness and rootedness in experience. 'The play doesn't show us how a Sassoon, an Owen or a Graves saw life in the trenches. A more representative mind than any of those produced it.' He pointed out the poignancy of the confessional discussion between Stanhope and Hibbert and was the only reviewer since the play was first staged to suspect the weight of personal experience: 'At such points one remembers that Sherriff constructed *Journey's End* out of letters he had written from the front. Once again, you feel you are hearing a man who has it all branded onto his heart.'[233]

Somebody else who also understood the play well, but from a quite different viewpoint, was A. K. Chesterton, G. K. Chesterton's second cousin, supporter of Oswald Mosley and leading fascist 'intellectual' in the 1930s. Chesterton, born in South Africa, had fought in the First World War, in East Africa and in France, earning the MC. At the time of its 1972 production, he wrote in the extremely right-wing magazine *Candour* a long article on *Journey's End* which was preceded by this editorial note: '*Candour's* task is to search for politico-economic realities and to interpret them in relation to policy objectives, which are often esoteric. Our personal motivation, which may perhaps be called our mystique, has not been inflicted on our readers, and we ask their indulgence for the single exception that follows.'[234] *Our mystique*: the emotional core of their ideology is presented in an article on *Journey's End*. In a magazine lamenting the passing of the British Empire and the cultural props which had been swept away with it, it was most apt that such attention should be given to a play whose devotion to unquestioning duty must be related to profoundly conservative political assumptions. Chesterton understood the spirit of the play, except for Hibbert, the 'one unpleasant character.' He knew the exclusiveness of the soldier's world in the trenches – 'This became the world, it *was* the world'; also, he shared Sherriff's perception that the concealment of fear and the fulfilling of duty in that terrible world represented 'heroism, the true splendour of the human spirit.'[235]

The latest revival, in 1988 at the Whitehall Theatre, with Jason Connery in the role of Stanhope, saw a more openly nostalgic approach to the play. The director Justine Greene defined the play as a 'period piece.'[236] In a telling commentary Irving Wardle welcomed the return of *Journey's End* as one of the few plays which were 'revisited rather than revived.'[237] After Brideshead, the Great War is also to be nostalgically consumed.

Martin Shaw, in a recent letter to the *New Statesman and Society*, has pointed out that any debate about citizenship must take into account the fact that 'modern Western concepts of citizenship have evolved...from the association of political (and more recently social) rights with military duty.

The citizen has been a member of the nation-in-arms.'[238] The preceding chapters have explored fictions which attempted to define the concept of national identity, of 'Englishness', and of social change, in terms of military memory. *Journey's End* crystallized on the stage the ambiguity of such perceptions.

Notes to Chapter 5

1. By the end of the year a million copies had been sold altogether in Britain, France and the U.S.A. (Modris Eksteins, '*All Quiet on the Western Front* and the Fate of a War', *Journal of Contemporary History*, Vol. 15, 1980, p. 353.)

2. *Daily Mail*, 30 April 1929. (Press Cuttings, Kingston Upon Thames, Surrey Record Office, in 2332.)

3. R. C. Sherriff, *No Leading Lady: An Autobiography*, 1968, p. 36.

4. *Ibid.*, pp. 33–4.

5. *Ibid.*, p. 35.

6. *Ibid.*, p. 39.

7. *Ibid.*, pp. 45–6.

8. *Ibid.*, pp. 46–7.

9. *Ibid.*, p. 48. One of the first letters about the play which Sherriff received was from Manning-Press, from his own C Company, who praised the play for being so 'actual'. (Letter from Manning-Press to Sherriff, 10 December 1928. R.C. Sherriff's Correspondence 1906–1944 (excluding First World War letters to family), Surrey Record Office, in 2332.)

10. *Ibid.*, p. 64.

11. *New Statesman*, 15 December 1928, p. 325.

12. Maurice Browne, *Too Late to Lament*, 1955, pp. 1.

13. *Ibid.*, p. 305.

14. The money was repaid before a legal agreement was drawn up, as the Elmhirsts and Broane were making a profit of £1,500 a week. (*Ibid.*, pp. 306–7.) Within a year they had made a profit of over £80,000. (*Ibid.*, p. 319.)

15. He also collaborated with Robert Nichols in the writing of the play *Wings Over Europe* (1932). *The Unknown Warrior* ran for 59 performances in London, from 13 February to 14 April 1928. (J. P. Wearing, *The London Stage 1920–1929: A Calendar of Plays and Players*, Vol. 2: 1925–1929, Metuchen, New Jersey, 1984, p. 957.)

16. Sherriff, *No Leading Lady*, pp. 72–3.

17. *Ibid.*, p. 70.

18. *Evening News*, 19 January 1929. (Press Cuttings, Surrey Record Office, in 2332.) The opening music for the 1972 production was Schubert's Trout Quintet. (Drama, Autumn 1972, p. 19.)

19. Sheila Hodges, *Gollancz: The Story of a Publishing House, 1928–1978*, 1978, pp, 47–8.

20. Sherriff, *No Leading Lady*, pp. 85–6.

21. *Ibid.*, pp. 95, 107–09. Ticket-selling libraries made a £16,000 deal over the play starting from February 18th; and a new one of £22,500 at the end of May. (*Daily Mail*, 20 February 1929, Press Cuttings, Surrey Record Office, in 2332.)

22. It showed at the Savoy from 21 January to 1 June, and at the Prince of Wales from 3 June to 7 June 1930. (Wearing, *The London Stage 1920–1929: A Calendar of Plays and Players*, p. 1087.)

23. Sherriff, *No Leading Lady*, p. 192.

24. *Ibid.*, p. 191.

25. Browne, *Too Late to Lament*, p. 319.

26. It was not produced in Italy, where Mussolini had banned war plays.

27. *Morning Post*, 11 November 1929. (Press cuttings, Surrey Record Office, in 2332.)

28. Basil Wright comments that the film was 'almost painfully English' and that its 'strangulated emotions' cannot have conveyed much to audiences outside the Anglo-Saxon world. (Basil Wright, *The Long View: An International History of Cinema,* 1976 (first published 1974), p. 163.) The film did not enjoy much success, but it served to bring Whale and Clive to Hollywood, where they worked together on *The Bride of Frankenstein* (1935).

29. *Sunday Chronicle,* 10 October 1937. (Press cuttings, Surrey Record Office, in 2332.)

30. *Daily Express,* 22 January 1929. (Press cuttings, Surrey Record Office, in 2332.)

31. *Daily Mail,* 22 January 1929. (Press cuttings, Surrey Record Office, in 2332.)

32. *Daily Mirror,* 23 January 1929. (Press cuttings, Surrey Record Office, in 2332.)

33. *Evening Standard,* 22 January 1929. (Press cuttings, Surrey Record Office, in 2332.)

34. R.C. Sherriff, *Journey's End,* 1929, p. 90.

35. *Ibid.,* p. 11.

36. *Star,* 22 January 1929. (Press cuttings, Surrey Record Office, in 2332.) Reginald Smith (the other actor playing Captain Hardy) had also served in the war. Colin Keith Johnston, who headed the cast which took the play to the United States, had enlisted at 18, had been wounded twice, and was awarded the MC for heroism under fire. *(Guardian,* 21 July 1972. Press cuttings, Surrey Record Office, in 2332.)

37. *Times,* 22 January 1929. (Press cuttings, Surrey Record Office, in 2332.)

38. *Daily Telegraph,* 22 January 1929. (Press cuttings, Surrey Record Office, in 2332.)

39. J.R. Ackerley, *My Father and Myself,* New York, 1969, p. 63, cited in Fussell, *The Great War and Modern Memory,* p. 199.

40. *New Statesman,* 2 February 1929, p. 531.

41. *The Daily Mirror,* 23 January 1929. (Press cuttings, Surrey Record Office, in 2332.) Channing Pollock's *The Enemy* (1928) was a sentimentally violent tirade against war, depicting the suffering of Austrian civilians through long improbable anti-war speeches. *(Observer,* 29 July 1928, p. 11.)

42. *Daily Chronicle,* 22 January 1929. (Press cuttings, Surrey Record Office, in 2332.)

43. 'The Theatre and Reality', *Morning Post,* 31 January 1929. (Press cuttings, Surrey Record Office, in 2332.) The Bishop of Winchester, Dr Woods, in the wake of submarine L12 ramming into and sinking submarine H43 in the Irish sea on 9 July 1929, leaving 22 dead, referred to *Journey's End* to support his call for the abolition of submarine warfare: 'It is a play which should go far to cure any appetites for war which still remain. I cannot conceive anyone seeing it without forming a resolution that they will do whatever is in their power to end war.' *(Bulletin* (Glasgow), 13 July 1929. Press cuttings, Surrey Record Office, in 2332.)

44. Frank Percy Crozier, *Brass Hat in No Man's Land,* 1930.

45. *Spectator,* 10 May 1930. (Press cuttings, Surrey Record Office, in 2332.)

46. H.T.W. Bousfield, 'Journey's End: Another Point of View', *English Review,* October 1929, pp. 491, 494–5.

47. *Ibid.,* pp. 491, 496, 492.

48. R.V. Dawson, 'Journey's End: A Supplementary Estimate', *English Review,* November 1929, p. 621.

49. *Ibid.,* p. 623.

50. G.A. Martelli, 'Journey's End'. A War Play and the Younger Generation.', *Cornhill Magazine,* June 1929, pp. 740–2.

51. T.C. Fowle, 'Journey's End: Another View', *Cornhill Magazine,* August 1929, pp. 171–3.

52. Martin Seymour-Smith, *Robert Graves: His Life and Work,* 1982, p. 194.

53. Manuscript autobiography of Herbert Hankin Sherriff. (Surrey Record Office, in 2332.)

54. First World War Papers, 1916-1918, folder k. (Surrey Record Office, in 2332.)

55. *Ibid.*

56. see page 156.

57. Letter to father, 3 February 1919. (Correspondence 1906–1944, Surrey Record Office, in 2332.)

58. Sherriff, *Journey's End,* p. 57.

59. Letter to father, 11 July 1917. (War Correspondence of R.C. Sherriff, 1916–1918, Surrey Record Office, in 2332.)

60. Fragment of letter to father, undated (probably written on arrival in France).

61. Letter to father, 16 October 1916. (War Correspondence of R.C. Sherriff, 1916–1918, Surrey Record Office, in 2332.)

62. Letter to father, 5 October 1916.

63. Although he dutifully gave no indication of his position, the progress of the 9th Battalion can be followed in its Diary. (Allocations of Battalions to Brigades and Division 1914-1918, East Surrey Regiment, 9th Battalion, Richmond, Public Record Office, W.O.95 2215.)

64. Letter to father, 16 October 1916.

65. Letter to mother, 15 October 1916. (War Correspondence of R. C. Sherriff, 1916-1918, Surrey Record Office, in 2332.)

66. Letter to mother, 18 October 1916.

67. First World War Papers, 1916-1918, folder j. (Surrey Record Office, in 2332.)

68. Letter to father, 15 November 1916.

69. Letter to mother, 12 November 1916.

70. Letter to mother, 14 November 1916.

71. Letter to father, 10 December 1916.

72. Letter to father, 20 December 1916.

73. Letter to mother, 25 January 1917.

74. Surrey Record Office, First World War Papers, 1916–1918, folder b, in 2332. The date on the card is illegible.

75. Letter to father, 25 January 1917.

76. Letter to mother, 26 January 1917.

77. Allocations of Battalions to Brigades and Division 1914–1918, East Surrey Regiment, 9th Battalion, Richmond. (Public Record Office, W.O.95 2215.)

78. Letter to mother, 29 January 1917. This feeling was echoed in a fictional, much more overtly explicit statement of fear, A. D. Gristwood's story 'The Coward'. He describes thus how he felt about going back to the line, after a period in the field hospital with a self-inflicted wound in the hand: 'For myself, I was a disconsolate schoolboy at the end of his holiday, and, the spell of routine broken, I came back to the line perhaps stronger in body, but in spirit more than ever unwilling.' (In A.D. Gristwood, *The Somme,* 1927, p. 123.)

79. Letter to mother, 1 February 1917. The exact length of his stay at the camp is not clear; he was still there on 12 February.

80. Memorabilia of R.C. Sherriff from the First World War, 1916-1918. (Surrey Record Office, 2332.)

81. *Sunday Times Magazine,* 16 April, 1972, p. 53. Until then Sherriff had maintained, vaguely and contradictorily, that the protagonists of his play were composite types. In an interview given in 1929 he asserted that the characters were a mixture of 'perhaps half a dozen different men of various types that one saw out there – the ex-ranker, the imaginative man, the schoolboy idealist, the second-in-command.' *(Western Morning News and Mercury,* 23 January 1929. Press cuttings, Surrey Record Office, in 2332.) Warre-Drummond went to France with the East Surreys in January 1915, and was a Captain in C Company of the 9th Battalion when Sherriff arrived in September 1916. He was awarded the MC in October 1918. *(Monthly Army List,* War Office, 1914–1918.)

82. Letter to mother, 2 April 1917.

83. Letter to mother, 17 April 1917.

84. Letter to mother, 7 April 1917.

85. Letter to father, 14 April 1917.

86. Letter to mother, 17 April 1917.

87. Letter to father, 17 April 1917.

88. Allocations of Battalions to Brigades and Division 1914–1918, East Surrey Regiment, 9th Battalion, Richmond. (Public Record Office, W.O.95 2215.)

89. Letter to father, 31 July 1917.

90. Allocations of Battalions to Brigades and Division 1914–1918, East Surrey Regiment, 9th Battalion. (W.O.95 2215.)

91. Sherriff, 'The English Public Schools in the War', p. 147.

92. Letter to mother, 2 August 1917.

93. Letter to mother, 17 August 1917.

94. Letter to father, 18 August 1917.

95. Letter to father, 17 September 1917.

96. In one instance the protagonist's diary entries jump from 4/6/1916 to 4/6/1918, although referring to the same time.

97. First World War Papers, 1916–1918, folder k. Surrey Record Office, in 2332. In May 1921 he went on a tour of the Western Front, and compiled an annotated album of photographs of the places where his company had stayed. On one page there is the photograph of the grave of three officers of the 9th East Surreys, Captain C.S. Pirie, RAMC, Lieutenant C. S. Picton and 2nd Lieutenant P.Y. Bogue, killed in the trenches near Hill 60 on 22 July 1917. Sherriff also had a vast collection of war photographs, many of them from the Imperial War Museum.

98. In a 1937 BBC interview with Arthur Calder-Marshall about the subject of autobiography, Sherriff said he was thinking about writing one, 'But how does one deal with self-revelations?' (Typescript in Surrey Record Office, Miscellaneous Writings, in 2332.) Two years later he used much the same words, exposing an obsessive concern, in an interview with Pamela Frankau: He was thinking of writing an autobiography, '"But how," he asked, spreading out his hands in despair, "does one do self-revelations?" (*Daily Sketch*, 24 April 1939. Press cuttings, Surrey Record Office, in 2332.)

99. Sherriff, *Journey's End*, p. 73.

100. *Ibid.,* p. 108.

101. *New Statesman*, 2 February 1929, p. 531.

102. *Daily Sketch*, 22 January 1929. (Press cuttings, Surrey Record Office, in 2332.)

103. *Evening News,* 22 January 1929. (Press cuttings, Surrey Record Office, in 2332.)

104. This description is derived from Stanhope's first judgment of Hibbert: 'another little worm trying to wriggle home'. Sherriff, *Journey's End*, p. 35.

105. *Daily Mail,* 19 February 1929. (Press cuttings, Surrey Record Office, in 2332.)

106. Miscellaneous Writings, in 2332.

107. Draft of novel based on *Journey's End* (Typescript). (Surrey Record Office, in 2332, pp. 79, 81–2, 95.)

108. Letter to father, 25 January 1917.

109. Besides Trotter the only working-class figure is Mason, the officers' mess servant, the comic character in the play. He tells Trotter after serving him the bacon 'If you look down straight on it from above, sir, you can see the bit o' lean quite clear.' (Sherriff, *Journey's End*, p. 54.) This character was obviously based on Sherriff's own servant in the war, whom he described in a letter home as 'a born comedian'. Contemplating a dinner improvised while in the line, he said: 'Soup – fish – Pork – Beans Corfee – it dont seem to rhyme properly, do it?' (Letter to father, 1 November 1916.)

110. Sherriff, *Journey's End*, pp. 55–6.

111. *Ibid.,* p. 56.

112. *Ibid.,* p. 56.

113. *Ibid.,* pp. 108–09. (The more socially-sensitive Bartlett here inserted 'Trotter was in no mood for confidences'. (R. C. Sherriff and Vernon Bartlett, *Journey's End,* 1930, p. 277.)

114. Warwick Deeping, *Kitty,* 1927, p. 122.

115. Sherriff, *Journey's End,* p. 81.

116. J.B.Morton, *The Barber of Putney,* 1919, pp. 330–333.

117. Elaine Showalter, *The Female Malady: Women, Madness and English Culture, 1830–1980,* 1987 (first published in New York, 1985), p. 174.

118. Leed, *No Man's Land,* pp. 163–4.

119. Showalter, *Female Malady,* p. 175.

120. Sherriff, *No Leading Lady,* p. 316.

121. Sherriff, 'The English Public Schools in the War', p. 136.

122. Sherriff, *No Leading Lady,* pp. 208–11.

123. Letter of Vaughan-Lewis to Sherriff, 21 October 1920. (Surrey Record Office,

Correspondence 1906–1944.)

124. Sherriff, *No Leading Lady*, p. 278.

125. in an interview with Pamela Frankau, *Daily Sketch*, 24 April 1939. (Press cuttings, Surrey Record Office, in 2332.)

126. First World War Papers, 1916–1918, folder k, in 2332.

127. Sherriff, 'The English Public Schools in the War', p. 137.

128. *Ibid.,* p. 139.

129. see p. 152.

130. Peter Parker, *The Old Lie: The Great War and the Public-School Ethos*, 1987, pp. 168–9.

131. Training Manual. War office - Instructions, in Peter Parker, *The Old Lie*, pp. 168–9.

132. *Ibid.,* p. 168.

133. *Ibid.,* pp. 169–71.

134. Robert Graves, *But It Still Goes On*, 1930, cited in Parker, *The Old Lie*, p. 169. The mixture of the serious and the controversial, with two of the protagonists a lesbian and a homosexual, did not represent the sequel to *The Unknown Warrior* and *Journey's End* which Browne was after, and Graves's script was summarily dismissed. (Martin Seymour-Smith, Robert Graves: His Life and Work, 1983, p. 209.)

135. Fussell, *The Great War and Modern Memory*, pp. 33–5.

136. Sherriff, *Journey's End*, p. 122.

137. Charles Moran, *The Anatomy of Courage*, 1945, p. 14. In an earlier study, W.N. Maxwell, a chaplain during the war, defined courage as the resolution between animal impulses and 'self-consciousness': the 'highest level of courage is found in this moral courage'. (W.N. Maxwell, *A Psychological Retrospect of the Great War*, 1923, p. 131.)

138. First World War Papers, 1916–1918, folder k. (Surrey Record Office, in 2332.)

139. *A Ghost on Vimy Ridge* (novel) (19–), R. C. Sherriff. Miscellaneous Writings, in 2332.

140. Sherriff, *Journey's End*, pp. 73–4.

141. Gilbert Frankau, 'The Ghosts of Ypres', *Ypres Times*, January 1922, p. 26.

142. *Ibid.,* p. 28.

143. *Ibid.,* p. 29.

144. Letter to mother, 2 November 1916.

145. Gilbert Frankau, *Self-Portrait: A Novel of His Own Life*, p. 309.

146. Sherriff, *Journey's End*, p. 61.

147. *Ibid.,* p. 19.

148. *Ibid.,* p. 51.

149. Hodges, *Gollancz*, p. 46.

150. The language of *Journey's End* was not easily accessible to those who had received a very different kind of education. In a conversation with M.O'C. Drury in 1936, Wittgenstein mentioned that he had just read *Journey's End*.
WITTGENSTEIN "...I couldn't understand the humour in Journey's End. But I wouldn't want to joke about a situation like that."
DRURY: "It may have been that they had no language in which to express their real feelings."
WITTGENSTEIN: "Oh, I hadn't thought of that. That might well be true: no way of saying what they really felt."' Ludwig Wittgenstein: Personal Recollections,
(edited by Rush Rhees), Oxford, 1981, pp. 144–145.

151. First World War Papers, 1916–1918, folder d. (Surrey Record Office, in 2332.)

152. Sherriff, *No Leading Lady*, p. 316.

153. Sherriff, *Journey's End*, p. 52.

154. *Ibid.,* pp. 52–3.

155. *Ibid.,* p. 99.

156. Sherriff, *No Leading Lady*, p. 39.

157. Cited in W.C. Wade, *The Titanic: End of a Dream*, 1979, p.108.

158. *Ibid.,* p. 296.

159. Thomas Hardy, 'The Convergence of the Twain (Lines on the loss of the 'Titanic')', in James Gibson, *The Complete Poems of Thomas Hardy*, 1979, pp. 306–7.

160. Cited in Wade, *The Titanic*, p. 299.

161. Gilbert Frankau, T*he Dangerous Years,* 1937, pp. 62–3.

162. Cited in J.M. Barrie, *Courage,* London, 1922, p. 31.

163. Barrie, *Courage,* p. 32.

164. First World War Papers, 1916–1918, folder k. (Surrey Record Office, in 2332.)

165. The title of his autobiography, *No Leading Lady,* referred solely to the uniqueness of success of a play with no women, and in no way heralded the explanation of an intimate choice.

166. Surrey Record Office, Photographs, in 1223.

167. *Sunday Times Magazine,* 16 April, 1972, p. 53. In his autobiography he narrated the early stages of *Journey's End's* fortunes in relentless detail: the paper boy, digging in his satchel for a sweet and chatting to the night watchman before delivering the momentous reviews; losing his way while bringing the manuscript to Browne, with a throbbing boil on his buttock. (Sherriff, *No Leading Lady,* pp. 60, 66–7).

168. Sherriff, *No Leading Lady,* pp. 349–350.

169. St John Ervine, *Good Housekeeping,* 1930. (Press cuttings, Surrey Record Office, Surrey Record Office, in 2332.)

170. Stephen Mckenna published his autobiography at the age of 33, in a deliberate attempt to present, while still young, the vision and memory of the youth of his generation: 'I venture to write of this epoch because I hope to present some aspects of it which might elude the historian who ranges over a wider field, pre-eminently the aspect from the standpoint of youth.' (*While I Remember,* p. 11). By youth he meant 'the generation which ended with the peace of Versailles of 1919', destined to be more alienated from what followed that date than any other generation in history because of the profound changes that had occurred and the different motivation behind the same institutions. He wished to depict 'a corner of that old world as it was known to the men who were reared in time to be sacrificed in the later war.' *(Ibid.,* p. 12).

171. In an article he listed as one of his dislikes 'bores over 40'. (*Sunday Dispatch,* Press cuttings, Surrey Record Office, in 2332.)

172. Sherriff, *No Leading Lady,* p. 75.

173. *Ibid.,* p. 75.

174. *Liverpool Express,* 27 February 1929. (Press cuttings, Surrey Record Office, in 2332.)

175. *The Era,* (undated). (Press cuttings, Surrey Record Office, in 2332.)

176. Cited in *Oxford Times,* 10 April 1933. (Press cuttings, Surrey Record Office, in 2332.)

177. *Daily Mail,* 12 June 1929. (Press cuttings, Surrey Record Office, in 2332.)

178. Sherriff, *Journey's End,* p. 24. In the novel, Bartlett removed both this pronouncement and the one about war being 'silly' (p. 61).

179. Miscellaneous Writings, in 2332.

180. *Daily Express,* 23 January 1929. (Press cuttings, Surrey Record Office, in 2332.)

181. *Sunday Express,* 27 January 1929. (Press cuttings, Surrey Record Office, in 2332.)

182. Sherriff, No Leading Lady, pp. 181–2.

183. *Publisher and Bookseller,* 7 November 1930, p. 1067.

184. Herbert Read, 'The Failure of the War Books', *A Coat of Many Colours: Occasional Essays,* 1945, p. 74.

185. *Surrey Advertiser,* (Guildford, Borough Hall), 25 October 1930. (Press cuttings, Surrey Record Office, in 2332.) Sherriff gave the same speech on war literature at different meetings.

186. *New York Herald Tribune,* 27 April 1930. (Press cuttings, Surrey Record Office, in 2332.) One schoolmaster wrote about the successful reception of the play by schoolboys. He stressed the simplicity and Englishness of it, pointed out the restraint of emotions as a note of particular appeal, and compared the play at great length with Shakespeare, establishing several parallels: 'I dare to prophesy that the schools of 1950 will be reading "Journey's End" just as to-day they are reading "Hamlet".' *The A.M.A.* (Journal of the Incorporated Association of Assistant Masters in Secondary Schools), March 1930, pp. 82, 84. (Press cuttings, Surrey Record Office, in 2332.)

187. Kathleen Conyngham Greene, 'The War-Wise Generation', *Daily Mail* (Bombay, India), 17 April 1931. (Press cuttings, Surrey Record Office, in 2332.)

188. *Sunday News,* 4 May 1930, p. 7. (Press cuttings, Surrey Record Office, in 2332.)

189. Sherriff and Bartlett, *Journey's End,* p. 103.

190. Abroad he spoke as an ambassador of his country. In the American *Good Housekeeping* he wrote about the burden of the empire, from which 'we have grown rich in everything but money, and that is to say we are rich beyond the dreams of avarice.' ('The Burden of Empire' reprinted in *Montreal Daily Star,* 16 May 1931. Press cuttings, Surrey Record Office, in 2332.)

191. *Daily Express,* 10 October 1931. (Press cuttings, Surrey Record Office, in 2332.)

192. Letter to father, 29 September 1917.

193. Amongst Sherriff's papers is the certificate acknowledging his work as Special Constable during the General Strike. (Correspondence 1906–1944. Surrey Record Office, in 2332.) Another strike he witnessed at first hand was a riot in Glasgow in February 1919, where he was at the Area Gas School, waiting for demobilization. The description he gave of it to his father reported much violence by the Constables against the strikers, but registered only distaste for the uprising working class. Of course they had 'extraordinarily little common sense', that quintessential middle-class, English virtue: '...they only want a loud mouthed vulgar russian Jew to get up and shout a lot of rot about "Peoples rights – shorter hours – more pay" and shower compliments on to his miserable audience and tell them they are very strong if they only care to show it – and these extraordinary things all gibber with glee and puff their chests out and say "we are indispensable – they must give us everything we want". The 'ordinary Scotsman', he concluded on an optimistic note, 'favours a Lewis gun as the best cure: as long as no disinterested people were hurt – I don't think there would be any loss to the nation excepted a few good bullets.' (Letter to father 3 February 1919, Correspondence 1906–1944, Surrey Record Office, in 2332.)

194. Sherriff, *No Leading Lady,* p. 245. He received an Oscar in 1942 for co-writing the script of *Mrs. Miniver,* a sentimental film about the courage of an English widow in the Second World War.

195. Among Sherriff's papers there is also an incomplete filmscript of the sequel. (Surrey Record Office, in 2332.) Vernon Bartlett's novel began with Raleigh's and Stanhope's childhood, but did not carry the story beyond the collapse of the St Quentin dugout.

196. Draft of novel based on *Journey's End,* p. 5. (Surrey Record Office, in 2332.)

197. *Ibid.,* pp. 6–9.

198. *Ibid.,* pp. 10–12.

199. *Ibid.,* pp. 14–19.

200. *Ibid.,* p. 19.

201. Sherriff, *No Leading Lady,* p. 43.

202. *Ibid.,* pp. 66–7.

203. *Daily Sketch,* 24 April 1939. (Press cuttings, Surrey Record Office, in 2332.)

204. *Morning Post,* 5 March 1930. (Press cuttings, Surrey Record Office, in 2332.)

205. Sherriff, *No Leading Lady,* p. 175.

206. *Pictorial Weekly,* 29 November 1930. (Press cuttings, Surrey Record Office, in 2332.)

207. Vernon Bartlett, *This Is My Life,* 1937, pp. 243–44.

208. Sherriff, *No Leading Lady,* p. 228.

209. *Ibid.,* p. 229.

210. The novel sold 20,000 copies in a month and was published in as many countries in Europe as had produced *Journey's End. (Ibid.,* p. 230.)

211. *Morning Post,* 17 October 1931. (Press cuttings, Surrey Record Office, in 2332.)

212. *Times Literary Supplement,* 19 September 1968, p. 1054.

213. Eldon C. Hill, 'R. C. Sherriff, *Dictionary of Literary Biography,* Vol. 10 (part II): *British Novelists 1890–1929,* Detroit, 1982, p. 150.

214. C.M. Bowen, '"Journey's End" and "Hamlet"', *Drama,* June 1929, p. 132.

215. *Country Life,* 3 May 1930, p. 641. (Press cuttings, Surrey Record Office, in 2332.)

216. *Truth,* 30 April 1930. (Press cuttings, Surrey Record Office, in 2332.)

217. Ivor Brown, 'Underground', *Saturday Review,* 26 January 1929, p. 107.

218. C.O. Douie, 'Two War Plays', *Nineteenth Century,* June 1929, pp. 839, 843.

219. *Ibid.,* p. 844.

220. St. John Ervine, 'The Wars and the Drama', *Fortnightly Review,* July 1940, p. 64.

221. *Ibid.,* p. 66.

222. *Ibid.*, pp. 66–8.

223. Simon Trussler, 'Introduction' to *20th Century Drama*, (Great Writers Student Library), 1983, p. 2.

224. *Ibid.*, p. 4.

225. *Ibid.*, pp. 4–5.

226. *Notes on R.C. Sherriff's Journey's End*, (Study-Aid Series), London, 1976, p. 24. In a similarly random exercise in interpretative reductionism, the *Financial Times*, in a review of Robin Lane Fox's *Play Up and Play the Game*, spoke of 'the anti-war and anti-school brigade of Sassoon and R.C. Sherriff.' (30 August, 1973. Press cuttings, Surrey Record Office, in 2332); and Nicholas de Jongh, reviewing the 1988 production of the play, commented that it was 'still packing a late, hard hook to complacency and jingoism'. ('Playing by the rule', *Guardian*, 21 April 1988, p. 21.)

227. *Ibid.*, p. 23.

228. The film was directed by Jack Gold, and starred Malcolm McDowell, Christopher Plummer, Simon Ward, Peter Firth, and John Gielgud.

229. Tom Milne, review of 'Aces High', *Monthly Film Bulletin*, June 1976, p. 119.

230. 'For King and Country', *Plays and Players*, July 1972, p. 23. (Press cuttings. Surrey Record Office, in 2332.) The quotation is from Stanhope's talk to Hibbert about their fear. (Sherriff, *Journey's End*, p. 75.)

231. Kenneth Hurren, 'War Game', *Spectator*, 27 May 1972. (Press cuttings. Surrey Record Office, in 2332.)

232. *Guardian*, 27 May 1972. (Press cuttings. Surrey Record Office, in 2332.)

233. Benedict Nightingale, 'Jolly Good Show', *New Statesman*, 26 May 1972. (Press cuttings. Surrey Record Office, in 2332.)

234. *Candour*, July 1972, p. 165. (Press cuttings. Surrey Record Office, in 2332.)

235. *Ibid.*, p. 166.

236. 'Schooled for conflict', *Times*, 19 April 1988, p. 18. Greene had gone to Winchester at the age of 13 and had preserved a memory which helped him understand the play: 'What struck me was that 13-year old boys were walking around like cabinet ministers. You can see how that system – or one very similar – would have prepared people for war.' *(Ibid.)*

237. 'Equally anthem and epitaph', *Times*, 21 April 1988, p. 18.

238. *New Statesman and Society*, 17 February 1989, p. 6.

Conclusion

War may be degrading, but it did not degrade.
Graham Seton, *Footslogger*

*A tale of humanity under the horror of war; realistic, but possessing the
perspective and permanent qualities of a book written in tranquillity.*
Advertisement for J.B. Morton's *The Barber of Putney*

1 Summary

The authors of the fiction we have been examining were not artists. There is
not a sign in their writings of aesthetic consideration of how the subject
matter and the literary medium suit each other, and that is why their names
failed the test of literary criticism. They were much less interested in artistic
construction than in vouching personally for every opinion expressed in their
works. The story and the more or less subtle exhortation accompanying it
were the motivating forces behind their writings, and as such their imprint
can still be traced in contemporary middle-class culture. What the literary
critic views with distaste and handles, if at all, with fastidious fingers, the
historian picks up with vivid interest in the quest for patterns of perception,
waving aside aesthetic considerations. Yet there *are* standards that the
historian of popular culture applies when selecting evidence. A weekly gossip
magazine or advertisements will yield material for cultural analysis, but a
novel represents a more sustained and thoughtful project of communication.

The commitment of these middle-class, popular authors to a didactic
literature of social communication was based on the assumption of values
and experience shared with their readers. Their credentials for addressing a
wide audience about topical issues were in many cases impeccable. Of those
who had not seen active service, several had offered their services to the
government or done war work, and a few had reported from the Western
front. After the war many of these authors were not only purveyors of social
solutions and commentators on their times in both non-fictional works and
in the imaginative medium of fiction, but were also public figures. The main
areas of activity in which they were engaged were journalism, publishing,
education and politics; some authors, indeed, worked in more than one of

Notes to the Conclusion can be found on page 205

196

these fields. These occupations were a logical complement to writing fiction for a vast audience, sharing as they did the common denominator of communication and instructive exposition. These writers' social observations, sifted through the historical disaster which they had survived, tell us far more about post-war society than about war itself. They attempted to make their mark in contemporary history with persistent commitment, harnessing their literary skills, their war experience and their knowledge of contemporary issues to a message of reconstruction.

The middlebrow novelists of the inter-war years were engaged not with the sense of an irretrievable world, but with a commitment to avoid the fragmentation of what they saw as 'English' culture. The question of the difference between highbrow accounts of the memory of war, such as those by Graves, Sassoon and Ford, and middlebrow works can best be approached, apart from the obvious issue of literary quality, as that of a different engagement with modernity, and with the cultural and moral role of the author in a changing society. The war experience was remembered by many novelists as a discovery of reality, a brutal awakening to essential issues. More importantly, war had been the ultimate test of confrontation with that modern reality they were trying to 'tame.' In the years of readjustment following the war, popular writers struggled to make 'common sense' (in both meanings of the expression) of the new world, and fulfilled their traditional function as social commentators by providing readers with models through which to absorb the trauma of their experience. This process of communication with the reader was based on disclosing correspondences between the past and the present, a process which Maurice Halbwachs has defined as collective memory.[1]

The word 'meaning' has recurred as a shorthand reference to the efforts of these writers to make sense of an aberration in their history. They fashioned meaning out of change by describing the lessons learned in the ordeal of war, and by highlighting values which would reaffirm the strength and importance of links with the past. Morality, religion, tradition: such words made up a litany of appeals for post-war regeneration.

The emphasis placed in these novels on the realization of individual potential (which corroborates Modris Ekstein's contention that the 'popular activities of the twenties as a whole were, more or less, a bewildered encomium to a by-gone age of individualism')[2] underlines the devaluation of politics which is a constant throughout these texts. Politics was about topical specificity, about conflict and change: continuity had to be based on the overriding influence of permanent values. After the war, when, to follow W. N. Maxwell's terminology and argument, 'self-assertive elements' replaced the 'team spirit',[3] the self sought unity of meaning out of the shattered elements of experience. Retrospectively, the experience of war was overlaid with the vague, gentle, undefined presence of an 'oblique idealism.'

The terrible legacy shared in the exclusive world of the soldiers included the memory of fear as an intimate exploration of the myth of courage in a war against machinery, and the constant closeness to death both in a physical sense and in the communion with the ghosts of dead companions. The use of elevated language and of spiritual images allowed the writers to portray the wounds etched in the memory of the survivors of the trenches while also offering the consolation of directions of meaning, in particular the absolute value of comradeship. These novels posited endurance, in spite of doubt and terror, as the way to renew the older conceptions of courage and heroism: the same resilience in the face of the pressures of change was presented as the secular faith of the post-war years.

The almost otherworldly, non-materialistic daily existence of the soldier served to intensify the contrast with the pettiness of the political world: satires like Edward Shanks's *The Old Indispensables* poured ridicule over Whitehall and echoed the bitter criticism present in other war novels. They exposed those people – the coquettish woman, the profiteer, the hysterical propagandist – who transgressed the English standards which were being purified and set in high relief by the predicament of the soldiers. In the post-war world it was socialism – humourless, city-based, internationalist, intolerant – which represented the strongest threat to Englishness. War novels often probed the question of identity in dichotomous terms: the ordeal of the soldier was set against the obtuseness of the civilian's sensibilities, and the English/British character was defined against German characteristics. At the same time, women's writings and the portrayal of conscientious objectors revealed that contrasting identities could also be incorporated in a process towards a common understanding of the war experience in which they all shared an uncompromising respect for those English ideals that nobody could spell out.

Tradition was both the highest expression of Englishness and the keystone of reconstruction. The words *Life Without End*, the title of Graham Seton's novel about an embittered soldier's retrieval of meaning in his post-war life, encapsulated to great effect the source of solution. It was contained in those values which were taken to be the underlying foundation of the whole of national life: religion, the country, England. The immutability of 'traditional values' was the most powerful myth asserted in these novels. Anything which belonged to it – the history of the regiment, past great battles, country homes, nineteenth-century fiction – was invested with profound meaning; to link one's experience to great manifestations of English tradition was to become part of it.

The unexpected success of *Journey's End*, a play with 'no women in it', as so many reviewers kept pointing out as an index of its greatness, is evidence of the education the public had received by 1929 about the soldiers' experience of war. The play came as a soothing, balancing statement within the controversy about war books in 1929. There was drunkenness, there was fear; but the effort of dealing with them was heroic and ennobling. St. John Ervine concluded an article on what he deemed sensationalistic war literature by asserting that his faith in mankind was confirmed when he remembered 'how many men who might have been expected to collapse under the strain, kept their heads up and did not forget that they had a divine spark in them.'[4] To many it seemed that a divine spark must have moved a lower-middle-class, modest clerk like Sherriff to produce so unexpectedly a play which became the epitome of the English memory of trench warfare. The play showed candidly the effects of the brutal challenge to personal identity in the war. Its popular success lay in the terms in which he described the officers' desperate endurance, and in the presentation of middle-class, public-school values as common English standards of behaviour.

2 The Centre Can Hold

J.B. Priestley never wrote about his experience as an officer in France, but he gave an unequivocal verdict on one consequence of the war: 'One thing is certain, that whatever the First World War might have done or not done, it did literature no good.'[5] Following an allusion to Yeats's poem 'The Second Coming', he remarked that

> It is possible that if there had been no First World War, or if it had been brought to an end...before the worst took over from the best, the centre, not only in politics but in literature, might have held. If it had, then it might have restored to literature a balance between introversion and extroversion, between man's inner world and the outer world of the society in which he lived, between what consciousness discovered groping towards the dark and what it faced in the light, between what a few hypersensitive and perhaps unstable minds wished to reveal and what the mass of men enjoyed reading.[6]

This kind of outraged cultural grieving over the contamination of the best, the wholesome and the stable in society, had no doubts about dating the inception of this pernicious disease from the war years. Middlebrow fiction offered its readers an anchor of meaning within the confusing and contradictory world of the 1920s and 1930s; in its antagonists' opinion, highbrow fiction at best merely delved into the new disruption. 'Get Rid of the Highbrows!' was the title of an article in *Theatre World* in which the need was argued for a new drama which reflected life instead of destabilizing it. 'The War brought chaos, mixed mentalities, muddled thinking, "smartness", pertness, impudence, "sex" and "shockers".' But things now were changing: 'Let the plays be constructive. Let them say something which can be understood. Let us learn through the old way, not deride it. That is the Highbrow way.'[7] This hybrid social/literary argument was lent particular strength by the huge success which *Journey's End* was enjoying at the time.

Most of the great modernists of the 1920s and 1930s – Yeats, Joyce, Lawrence, Huxley, Eliot – did not participate in the war, whereas the middlebrow bestsellers, by far the most widely-known literary figures of those years – Frankau, Hutchinson, Keable, Priestley, Deeping, Walpole, Sherriff – had all served as officers. It is not surprising that the literary pilots of values in post-war England should be men who had lived as protagonists the central experience of their contemporary history. By discussing an experience shared by a whole nation their novels provided a reference of communal understanding. Against the negative explorations of modernism they set the positive assurance of the cohesive power of familiar meaning. The function of these writers was intrinsically pre-modern and pre-ironic. Fictional production in the inter-war years became polarized between the idealism of the traditional canon and the ironic approach of the modern. The shock of transition represented by war/peace, traditional/modern, mimetic/aesthetic ranged morality against relativism, truth against aesthetics. Together with the isolation of the artist in an elitist enclave goes an autonomy which holds the capacity to push back ever further the limits of the inviolable – few people in the west today can have missed a public outcry about art's inroads into decency or sacredness.

Class unrest in 1919, the erosion of free trade, the first Labour government, the General Strike and the abandonment of the gold standard in 1931 (the 'given' economy, the symbol of fixed value in society) were all dramatic symbols of change. In order to counter such severe historical fluctuations middlebrow writers provided their readers with a 'gold standard' of meaning. To ensure the durability of their middle-class world, the encroachment of the working class was warded off by denying the existence of class divisions. The concept of Englishness assumed unity of identity and provided an effective talisman against both the divisive threats of the modern post-war world and the dangers of socialism. Ernest Barker, commentator on all things essentially English, in 1927 wrote *National Character*, and in 1947 developed it into the more complete *The Character of England*, at the end of which he synthesized thus the salient English traits: (1) social homogeneity, (2) love for the amateur role, (3) the figure and the idea of the gentleman, (4) the voluntary habit, (5) eccentricity, and (6) youthfulness.[8] Barker asserted that the quality of social homogeneity had the capacity to rise above class conflict, as proven by the traditional English reluctance to live through social groups and to trust associations (for associations read trade unions).[9]

A tradition of literary rhetoric was ready at hand to bolster such arguments. Tony Davies points out that the nineteenth-century debate on education, whose most famous contributor was Matthew Arnold, followed upon the 'first major economic and ideological crisis in mature industrial capitalism', and presented the concepts of idealism and universality as the linchpins of literary value.[10] This concern with the function of literature in society sought to comprehend the working class in the future development of education and literature. The title of the Victorian landmark of cultural observation, *Culture and Anarchy*, refers to a new relationship between the different social groups. The famous 'sweetness and light' passage from Arnold's work shows the concern with the assimilation of the danger of the mob which is also a vivid preoccupation of the literature of the inter-war years: 'Culture does not try to teach down to the level of the inferior classes... It seeks to do away with classes; to make the best that has been thought and known in the world current everywhere.'[11]

In the aftermath of the Great War, the Arnoldian panacea of literary formation was often invoked by educationalists as a solution to social problems and class conflict.[12] An artificial model of English literary tradition was set up,[13] notably by the Leavises. While I.A. Richards and the Leavises analysed and expounded artistic value and saw in the explosion of popular fiction the inevitable corruption of the great tradition of English literature and a degradation of culture in general, middlebrow writers saw artistic quality as subordinate, and often antithetical, to the need to defend cultural continuity as a principle. Although alarm about the modern was sounded in both fields it was weighted quite differently, and the Leavises identified contemporary 'respectable bestsellers' as a manifestation of those concepts, but from a literary point of view. For all the similarity of wording – the misleading appearance of surface patterns – their concern and their work had dissimilar directions. The middlebrows' brand of crusading for tradition and Englishness used literature as a vehicle, but did not serve it.

Middlebrow social idealism advocated the necessity of a 'classless' culture based not on a realignment of existing social structures but on the denial of the ugly symptoms of class: envy, acrimony, the eruption of demands. Paradoxically, the war years, for all their violence and horror, served as the ultimate example of class fraternity. Much of the meaning extrapolated from the war experience rests on the challenge of translating the companionship of the trenches into an enduring resolution of class hatred. The social cohesion enforced by war, imbued as it was with the collective experience of effort and suffering, was held as a value which transcended politics. A central component of inter-war middle-class attitudes is the way in which the language of war memory was harnessed to the myth of an apolitical sense of communality. This lexicon of high-minded politics forged in the trenches, or rather polished in the literature remembering them, is sometimes still invoked nowadays. George Panichas's collection of war memories, *Promise of Greatness*, was followed in 1982 by his *The Courage of Judgment*, a conservative study of moral attitudes to society which is strongly informed by the notion of a watershed between a sensitive, reflective pre-war society and a crass social morality after 1919. He quotes John Maynard Keynes's comments about the emblematic downfall of Asquith: 'Asquith possessed most of the needed gifts of a great statesman except ruthlessness towards others and insensitiveness for himself', while Lloyd George had 'that flavour of final purposelessness, inner irresponsibility, existence outside of or away from our Saxon good and evil, mixed with cunning, remorselessness, love of power.'[14] Panichas clinches this argument by noting that, 'interestingly', Lenin considered Lloyd George the 'greatest political leader that Britain had produced – a regard symptomatic, surely, of the political mentality of the modern thug.' The next example invoked by Panichas as evidence of a lost moral dimension is none other than *Journey's End* and its qualities of 'loyalty, generosity, patience, honesty, bravery, dignity, and decency.' Thus the spectres of the threat of mass politics and revolution, and the pre-1919 values expressed in a 1928 war play, are invoked to prove the argument that the 'Armistice signalled modern man's retreat into an existential vacuum.'[15]

Recently, Martin Wiener has read into the rural ideal in literature a strong criticism and rejection of industrialism.[16] Middlebrow literature does contain many examples of vilification of industrial landscape, and the most explicit ideal of the soldiers was England remembered as the rural home: '...the English farm, the village green with a cricket match going on, the hedgerows in spring, the woods in autumn, and the hill in all weathers...'[17] But to translate idealized images directly into a pattern of contemporary attitudes is to mistake models for the critique of an economic process. We have seen how often members of the aristocracy appear in middlebrow novels to portray and defend lofty values: but they are there as social and moral prototypes, not to represent a feudalistic rejection of democracy. Like industrialism, democracy is criticized for its occasional excesses or ugliness, but it is an achievement and a reality none of the writers ever wishes to repudiate.

The major institutional positions of power in the inter-war years were occupied by the middle class, as had been the majority of literary places since the nineteenth century, from education and journalism to criticism and fiction. The composition of all parliaments of the period 1918-1938 was predominantly middle class, with a noticeable change towards commercial and industrial representation among the traditionally landowning Conservative members. The same was true of the Cabinets between 1919 and 1937, with 81 Cabinet Ministers out of 158 drawn from the ranks of the middle class.[18] The social judgments of these novels were articulated by and for members of a middle class conscious of its worth, and alert in the face of what were perceived as threats against it. The vigorous stance of outraged middle-class individuals during the General Strike spoke eloquently against the most dreaded peril, socialism. There were less dramatically evident perils to guard against. The degradation of officers who could not find a job and who slid into working-class circumstances – Stanhope's post-war brutalization through demeaning work, Michael's suicide in *The Victors*, Captain Sorrell's humiliation at the hand of the brutish head porter – graphically illustrated the worst possible consequence of the war, failure to regain one's social rank. There were also dangers arising from within the middle class: the cultural onslaught of the modernists or the political machinations of socialist intellectuals who transgressed against their own roots. The balance was forever being redressed by tapping into that experience which Beverley Baxter made Austin Selwin anticipate so accurately in *The Parts Men Play*. Invited before the war to one of Lady Durwent's 'artistic' dinner parties, where everyone puts down England as decadent, Austin expresses his confidence in the national resurgence of moral fibre: 'If I listen to my senses, to my subconscious mind, I feel that a great crisis would reveal that she [England] is still the bed-rock of civilization.'[19] Soon, of course, not only had his 'prediction' come true, but it required him to wear a uniform.

The fictional low-mimetic depiction of the ordeal of the war and of choices and readjustment in the post-war years, the presentation of beliefs, attitudes and social formulas to deal with change and to reaffirm the value of the past, afford us an important insight into middle-class ideology. This book has endeavoured to re-present the host of middlebrow novels of the 1920s and 1930s as important evidence for the history of mentalities, which Michel Vovelle has defined as 'the study of the mediations and dialectical relationship between the objective conditions of the life of men and the way they perceive them.'[20] And befuddle them. The lofty level on which discussion of the English nation was conducted relegated the political and economic functioning of the State – and its central institutions: Westminster, Whitehall, the City, the Church – to the realm of the technically prosaic. A study of inter-war middle-class ideology will help to explain the resilience of conservative government in these years and the choice of a grand aristocrat to guide the nation through a second world war.

The faith of popular writers in British resources of character was confirmed by the marshalling of this strength in World War II. Ironically, the circle of meaning came to a terrible completion. Francis Brett Young in 1944 wrote a letter to St.John Ervine whose rhetoric closely resembles that so frequently heard during the preceding war. The Battle of Britain had been won by the middle-class 'who proved, in that superb hour, that the Elizabethan virtues were not dead, and that we are still a great race...This is the class – our class, my dear St. John – which proletarian jealousy and the whims of the leftist intellectuals...would like to see taxed or ground out of existence.'[21] In the same year Young wrote an epic poem, 'The Island', which was a hymn to the English people from the origins of their history to the Battle of Britain. The poetic vehicle chosen and the content of the patriotic paean could hardly have been less ironic.

The concept of patriotism as the leveller of class distinctions motivated, during the Second World War, George Orwell's pronouncement about the possibility of socialism in Britain in spite of the inevitable resistance from the upper and middle classes:

> ...because patriotism is finally stronger than class hatred, the chances are that the will of the majority will prevail...If it can be made clear that defeating Hitler means wiping out class privilege, the great mass of middling people, the £6 a week and £2,000 a year class, will be on our side.[22]

This is an understandable surrender to the myth of English patriotism, and of the essential national character finding expression in a rallying together of this 'family' with 'a private language and common memories'. Yet patriotism cannot explain the attitudes of the middle class. It is the other way around; the language, memories and values of the 'middling people' in the 'rather stuffy Victorian family'[23] reveal the texture of inter-war patriotic feelings.

Arthur Marwick has addressed briefly the question of why, after eleven million people supported the League of Nations in 1935 through the 'Peace Ballot', 'in 1939 this island paradox of Britain once again entered into a world war against Germany.' He helps to interpret this historical contradiction by pointing out how in the inter-war years real change was neutralized by Conservative entrenchment in power.[24] Orwell would probably not have had this.

> Patriotism has nothing to do with Conservatism. It is actually the opposite of Conservatism, since it is a devotion to something that is always changing and yet is felt to be mystically the same. It is the bridge between the future and the past.[25]

Yet it is exactly this language – relation with the past and engagement with change held together by a 'mystical' constancy of significance – which was used by middlebrow writers.

The conclusions about war reached by middlebrow fiction remained anchored in a mode of idealist/romantic condemnation, whose limited nature is often reflected anew in contemporary critical works. Léon Riegel concludes his study of comparative war literature with the remark that war has been for too long a break between peoples and a retreat of civilization: it should become an object of common meditation, a fund of memories on which nations can base a new spirit of economic collaboration, political fraternity 'et, pourquoi pas, d'amour dans leurs relations d'homme à homme.'[26] This complacent belief in a positive relationship between the consequences of war and the power of individual evaluative reflection mirrors many of the literary hopes analyzed in this book.

To emphasize the ironic element present in selected texts is to make an inspired judgment of what the memory of war *should* have been like. Whereas we can describe war, trace its origins, discuss its consequences, we cannot give it a meaning, or war would be justified. *Tout comprendre c'est tout pardonner.* In this sense, inter-war popular fiction did justify the 1914–20418 war. It recalled the horror of war and sometimes condemned the short-sightedness of the generals and derided the role of Whitehall: but the underlying effort to contribute to reconstruction along traditional lines sought to find significance in the experience of war. Popular war novels attempted to make sense of the contradictions, ambiguities and conflicts of the war experience, and in the process offered a blueprint for a conservatism which still finds echoes in our own day.

Notes to Conclusion

1. See Maurice Halbwachs, *The Collective Memory*, New York, 1980 (first published as *La Mémoire Collective*, 1950).

2. Modris Ekstein, '*All Quiet on the Western Front* and the Fate of a War', *Journal of Contemporary History*, Vol. 15, 1980, p. 358.

3. W.N. Maxwell, *A Psychological Retrospect of the Great War*, 1923, pp. 284-5.

4. St. John Ervine, 'Men, Women and Events', *Time and Tide*, 16 May 1930, p. 632.

5. J.B. Priestley, *Literature and Western Man*, 1960, pp. 375. For another writer who had fought in France, L.P.Hartley, music – in the form of the emergence of jazz, with its 'indifference to sense, and morality, and genuine emotion'– was another sign of the collapse of the centre of things: 'Perhaps the world has been slightly out of tune ever since.' (L.P.Hartley, 'Three Wars', in George Panichas, *Promise of Greatness*, p. 251.)

6. *Ibid.*, pp. 374–5.

7. W.Macqueen-Pope, 'Get Rid of the Highbrows!', *Theatre World*, March 1929, p. 17.

8. Ernest Barker, *The Character of England*, Oxford, 1947, p. 563.

9. *Ibid.*, pp. 29–30, 40–2.

10. Tony Davies, 'Education, Ideology and Literature', in *Red Letters*, no. 7, 1978, pp. 4 ff.

11. Matthew Arnold, *Culture and Anarchy*, cited in *Ibid.*, p. 5.

12. Chris Baldick, *The Social Mission of English Criticism, 1848–1932*, Oxford, 1983, pp. 162–195.

13. Robert Colls and Philip Dodd (eds.), *Englishness: Politics and Culture, 1880–1920*, 1986, p. 118.

14. John Maynard Keynes, *Essays in Biography*, New York, 1951 (first published in 1933), pp. 35–6, 45, cited in George Panichas, *The Courage of Judgment: Essays in Criticism, Culture and Society*, Knoxville, 1982, p. 234.

15. Panichas, *The Courage of Judgment*, pp. 235–7.

16. Martin J. Wiener, *English Culture and the Decline of the Industrial Spirit, 1850-1980*, Cambridge, 1981.

17. Harold Begbie, *Mr. Sterling Sticks it Out*, 1919, p. 188.

18. Roger King, John Raynor, *The Middle Class*, 1981 (previous edition 1969), p. 70.

19. Arthur Beverley Baxter, *The Parts Men Play*, 1920, pp. 61–2.

20. Michel Vovelle, 'Ideologies and Mentalities', in Raphael Samuel and Gareth Stedman Jones (eds.), *Culture, Ideology and Politics: Essays for Eric Hobsbawm*, (History Workshop Series), 1982, p. 11.

21. Cited in Jacques Leclaire, *Un Témoin de l'Avènement de L'Angleterre Contemporaine: Francis Brett Young, L'Homme et L'Oeuvre, 1884–1954*, Rouen, 1970, p. 292.

22. George, Orwell, 'The Lion and the Unicorn: Socialism and the English Genius', vol. 2: *My Country Right or Left, 1940–1943*, in *The Collected Essays, Journalism and Letters of George Orwell*, Harmondsworth, 1970, pp. 117–118.

23. *Ibid.*, p. 88.

24. Arthur Marwick, *The Deluge: British Society and the First World War*, 1979 (first published in 1965), pp. 310–313.

25. Orwell, 'The Lion and the Unicorn', p. 127.

26. Léon Riegel, *Guerre et Littérature: Le bouleversement des consciences dans la littérature romanesque inspirée par la Grande Guerre (littératures française, anglo-saxonne et allemande) 1910–1930*, Paris, 1978, p. 552.

Index